# Psychology-Based Activities for Supporting Anxious Language Learners

## BLOOMSBURY GUIDEBOOKS FOR LANGUAGE TEACHERS

This series brings together books that enhance language educators' teaching practice. The books provide practical advice and applications, suitable for use in a range of contexts and for different learning styles, which are evidence-based and research-informed. The series appeals to practitioners looking to develop their skills and practice and is also suitable for use on a variety of language teacher education courses. The books feature a range of topics and themes, from critical pedagogy, to using drama, poetry or literature in the language classroom, to supporting language learners who have anxiety.

### Forthcoming in the series:

*Using Theories for Second Language Teaching and Learning,* Dale T. Griffee and Greta Gorsuch

*Teaching Beginner Level English Language Learners,* Lesley Painter-Farrell and Gabriel Díaz-Maggioli

*Critical Pedagogies for Modern Languages Education,* edited by Derek Hird

# Psychology-Based Activities for Supporting Anxious Language Learners

## Creating Calm and Confident Foreign Language Speakers

EDITED BY NEIL CURRY
AND KATE MAHER

BLOOMSBURY ACADEMIC
LONDON • NEW YORK • OXFORD • NEW DELHI • SYDNEY

BLOOMSBURY ACADEMIC
Bloomsbury Publishing Plc
50 Bedford Square, London, WC1B 3DP, UK
1385 Broadway, New York, NY 10018, USA
29 Earlsfort Terrace, Dublin 2, Ireland

BLOOMSBURY, BLOOMSBURY ACADEMIC and the Diana logo
are trademarks of Bloomsbury Publishing Plc

First published in Great Britain 2024

Copyright © Neil Curry, Kate Maher and Contributors, 2024

Neil Curry, Kate Maher and Contributors have asserted their right under the Copyright, Designs and Patents Act, 1988, to be identified as editors of this work.

For legal purposes the Acknowledgements on p. xvi constitute
an extension of this copyright page.

Series design: Grace Ridge
Cover image © Kondo-Maher Design

All rights reserved. No part of this publication may be reproduced or transmitted in any form or by any means, electronic or mechanical, including photocopying, recording, or any information storage or retrieval system, without prior permission in writing from the publishers.

Bloomsbury Publishing Plc does not have any control over, or responsibility for, any third-party websites referred to or in this book. All internet addresses given in this book were correct at the time of going to press. The author and publisher regret any inconvenience caused if addresses have changed or sites have ceased to exist, but can accept no responsibility for any such changes.

A catalogue record for this book is available from the British Library.

A catalog record for this book is available from the Library of Congress.

ISBN:  HB:     978-1-3503-5280-3
       PB:     978-1-3503-5279-7
       ePDF:   978-1-3503-5282-7
       eBook:  978-1-3503-5281-0

Series: Bloomsbury Guidebooks for Language Teachers

Typeset by Integra Software Services Pvt. Ltd.

To find out more about our authors and books visit www.bloomsbury.com
and sign up for our newsletters.

Online sources Online resources to accompany this book are available at https://www.bloomsburyonlineresources.com/psychology-based-activities-for-supporting-anxious-language-learners. If you experience any problems, please contact Bloomsbury at: onlineresources@bloomsbury.com

# CONTENTS

*List of Figures* viii
*List of Tables* ix
*List of Contributors* x
*Foreword* xiv
*Acknowledgements* xvi

1  Introduction 1
   *Kate Maher and Neil Curry*

**PART ONE** Assessing FLA: Identifying FLA and Causes in Your Context

2  How are you coping? A tool for identifying situations that cause FLA 13
   *Neil Curry and Kate Maher*
3  You are not alone: Shining light on FLA perspectives through classroom data collection 21
   *Jonathan Shachter*

**PART TWO** The Classroom Environment: Creating a Positive Learning Space

4  'I am worthy and special; I am not afraid to speak.': Creating a sense of belonging to increase students' self-confidence 35
   *Shatha Talib Al-Ahmadi*

5   Creating enjoyable learning environments: Student-centred socially motivating classrooms  43
    *Wendy Davis*
6   Flowing classrooms: Incorporating principles of flow in classroom activities to reduce FLA  51
    *Fernando D. Rubio-Alcalá*
7   Making speaking tasks emotionally engaging: Incorporating flow principles in task design  61
    *Haydab Almukhaild*

**PART THREE** Cognitive Techniques: Thinking through Anxiety

8   Stoic sayings for alleviating anxiety: Epictetus, Stoic philosophy and the art of cognitive distancing  73
    *Ian Gibson*
9   Boosting your students' confidence in second language learning: The confidence-building diary  83
    *Jo Mynard and Scott J. Shelton-Strong*
10  Facing worries head on: Discussions for raising awareness and tackling communicative anxiety  97
    *Amelia Yarwood*
11  Positive attributions: Using attributional retraining techniques to reduce students' speaking anxiety  109
    *David McLoughlin*
12  Looking for evidence: Using CBT-based activities for FLA  119
    *Neil Curry*
13  What makes you nervous?: A cognitive behavioural theory-based approach to identifying FLA triggers  129
    *Kate Maher*

**PART FOUR** Visualization Techniques: Imagining Confidence

14 Imagine how I will face up to speaking anxiety: An imagery-focused mindfulness approach to preparing for speaking situations 145
*Sarah Ng*

15 Rewrite your inner script: Make friends with oral presentation 155
*Zsuzsa Tóth*

16 Focusing attention outwardly: A coping strategy for speaking tasks based on task concentration training 165
*Jonathan Rickard*

**PART FIVE** Well-Being Techniques: Creating Mindful Foreign Language Speakers

17 'I see you, I hear you, I cheer for you!': How to overcome speaking-related anxiety through dialogue skits with positive communication in mind 177
*Dorota Záborská*

18 Three good things about their English: A positive psychology-inspired evaluation, building confidence and encouraging learners to speak 187
*Katarzyna Budzińska*

19 Being positive in the present moment: Mindfulness meditation for reducing anxiety in foreign language classes 197
*Nihan Erdemir and Sabahattin Yeşilçinar*

*Index* 206

# FIGURES

- **2.1** Scenario 2  16
- **3.1** The nervousness metric  23
- **6.1** Checklist with clear task goals to provide progress feedback  55
- **6.2** Table for self-assessment  56
- **10.1** Activity timeline  101
- **10.2** Example prompts used in a Japanese English university classroom  103
- **13.1** CBT cycle  134
- **13.2** Example CBT cycle  135
- **13.3** Identifying triggers  137
- **17.1** Model of positive communication  179
- **17.2** Students engaged in PC dialogue skits  184

# TABLES

**1.1** Summary guide 4
**3.1** Questionnaire 1 26
**3.2** Questionnaire 2 27
**3.3** Questionnaire 3 28
**3.4** Mock data set for Questionnaire 1 31
**5.1** Top 16 responses from students to the IC questionnaire 46
**11.1** Attribution handout 114
**12.1** Common answers 126
**16.1** Task table 171
**18.1** Three Good Things chart (optional) 191
**18.2** Example responses of Three Good Things chart 191

# CONTRIBUTORS

**Shatha Talib Al-Ahmadi** is Assistant Professor in Applied Linguistics and Teaching English as a Second Language at Umm Al-Quraa University, Saudi Arabia. Her research interests are in the psychological aspects of foreign language education. She has published on the multilevel aspects of L2 learner's silence with a focus on female learners of English in the Saudi context. Her most recent article is 'Silence Behind the Veil: An Exploratory Investigation into the Reticence of Female Saudi Arabian Learners of English' (2022).

**Haydab Almukhaild** is Assistant Professor in the Department of English at King Saud bin Abdulaziz University for Health Sciences, Saudi Arabia. She has a PhD in Applied Linguistics from the University of Leicester, UK. Her research interests include speaking-related anxiety, language learner engagement and task-based language teaching.

**Katarzyna Budzińska** is Lecturer of English in the Language Centre at the Lodz University of Technology. Her research interests focus on psychological aspects of foreign language teaching and learning. She has been studying emotions accompanying foreign and second language acquisition, mainly language anxiety. Katarzyna is also interested in positive psychology. She is a pioneer investigating the third positive psychology pillar – positive institutions. She is the author of several papers in this field as well as a co-editor of a recently published volume *Positive Psychology in Second and Foreign Language Education* (2021).

**Neil Curry** has been a learning advisor in the Self-Access Learning Center at Kanda University of International Studies in Japan for the last ten years. As well as being responsible for the department's curriculum development, his primary interests include learner autonomy, self-directed learning, foreign language anxiety and reflection on learning.

**Wendy Davis** is a teacher of English Conversation at Kyoritsu Girls' Junior and Senior High School and a member of the International Exchange Program Department. A 2019 graduate of Temple University, Japan, with an MS-Ed in TESOL, Wendy has been living and teaching in Japan since 2001. As a proponent of positive learning environments and reducing learner anxiety, she has been using the Ideal Classmates activity since learning about its effectiveness in 2017. She was the first to use the Ideal Classmates activity in Japan at the junior high school level and continues to see positive results from it.

**Nihan Erdemir** is Assistant Professor at the Department of English Language Teaching at Süleyman Demirel University. She trains EFL teachers and offers graduate courses. She holds an MA from the University of Vienna, Austria, and a doctoral degree from Gazi University, Türkiye. Her research interests are in the areas of academic writing, technology and positive psychology in language teaching and teacher education.

**Ian Gibson** is Professor at Kyoto University of Foreign Studies in the Department of British and American Studies. His research interests focus on the theory and practice of peace education and conflict resolution.

**Kate Maher** works in the learning support department of Shoreham College and has a PhD in Applied Linguistics from the University of Leicester, UK. Having worked in Japan teaching English for over sixteen years and completing her MA in English Education there, her main research interests are student silence, speaking-related language anxiety in the classroom and affective elements of language learning. Her most recent paper is 'Language Anxiety and Learner Silence from a Cognitive-Behavioural Perspective' (co-authored with Jim King, 2023).

**David McLoughlin** is Associate Professor in the School of Global Japanese Studies at Meiji University in Tokyo, Japan. He holds an EdD in TEFL from the University of Exeter, UK, and an MPhil in Applied Linguistics from Trinity College, University of Dublin, Ireland. He has taught EFL since 1993. His main area of research is motivation in second language learning, covering topics such as the role of interest in sustaining self-regulated motivation and learning, and the attribution theory of achievement motivation and emotion. Other research interests include language learner autonomy and the role of affect in self-regulated learning.

**Jo Mynard** is Professor, Director of the Self-Access Learning Center and Director of the Research Institute for Learner Autonomy Education at Kanda University of International Studies in Japan. She completed her Doctorate in Education (TEFL) at the University of Exeter, UK, in 2003 and her MPhil in Applied Linguistics at Trinity College, Dublin, in 1997. She has co-edited or co-authored over 100 scholarly works, including several books on learner autonomy, advising, reflective dialogue and social learning spaces. She has been the editor of *SiSAL* (*Studies in Self-Access Learning*) *Journal* since 2010.

**Sarah Ng** is Founder and Director of Epicloud, UK, which specializes in mindfulness training and research with a focus on use of language and imagery in mindfulness. She has received academic and professional training across human-focused subjects, namely neuroscience, linguistics, psychology and education. The research she conducted as a university academic over more than fifteen years was geared towards understanding mind-body connection and its role in emotion regulation. Her latest research focuses on how language learners regulate their anxiety through cognitive change and expressive suppression.

**Jonathan Rickard** teaches academic English at Hong Kong Baptist University and professional English communication at Hong Kong Polytechnic University. His research interests include language learning motivation, goal theories and English-medium instruction, and he is working on a PhD project combining these three areas. He has worked with students dealing with foreign language anxiety in a range of situations, including speaking in class, speaking online, speaking exams, presentations and interviews.

**Fernando D. Rubio-Alcalá** is Professor at the University of Huelva, Spain. His area of expertise is language learning, and his research focuses on two areas: affective language learning and multilingualism. He has published the book *Self-Esteem and Foreign Language Learning* (2007) and has written many other papers in the area of affectivity. His most recent study is 'Construction and Validation of Self-Esteem in the Foreign Language Classroom Scale' (*SEFLS*) (2022). ORCID: 0000-0002-1478-2168.

**Jonathan Shachter** is Lecturer at Kyushu Sangyo University in Fukuoka, Japan. He earned a BA in Trumpet Performance from Virginia Tech, an MEd in Education from the American College of Education, and a Masters in Psychology from Macquarie University. He is currently a PhD Candidate in the Faculty of Education at Monash University. He is a firm believer that the skills developed in studying the language of music can be applied to language acquisition. His current research interests are affect, performance and educational psychology. He is the co-founder of the academic podcast 'Lost in Citations'.

**Scott J. Shelton-Strong** is Senior Learning Advisor and Lecturer at Kanda University of International Studies, Japan. His research interests include advising in language learning, self-determination theory, positive psychology, emotions in language learning and developing an understanding of the connections that interlink these to learner well-being and engagement both within and beyond the classroom. Recent publications include the co-edited volume *Autonomy Support beyond the Language Learning Classroom: A Self-Determination Theory Perspective* (with Jo Mynard, 2022) and a journal article, 'Sustaining Language Learner Well-being and Flourishing: A

Mixed-methods Study Exploring Advising in Language Learning and Basic Psychological Need Support' (2022).

**Zsuzsa Tóth** is Associate Professor at Pázmány Péter Catholic University (Hungary) in the Department of English Language Pedagogy and Translation Studies. She is an EFL instructor and teacher trainer. Her professional interests include individual differences in L2 learning, teacher education issues and EFL teaching methodology. Her main research area is the study of foreign language anxiety. She has authored the book *Foreign Language Anxiety and the Advanced Language Learner* (2010).

**Amelia Yarwood** is a doctoral student at Kansai University's Graduate School of Foreign Language Education and Research, Japan. In her capacity as Visiting Lecturer for the Research Institute for Learner Autonomy Education (RILAE), she continues to practice spoken and written advising with students, and mentors the next generation of Learning Advisors. Her research interests include curriculum development and learner autonomy, emotions and identity through a narrative lens.

**Sabahattin Yeşilçınar** is Assistant Professor in the Department of English Language Teaching, Muş Alparslan University. He holds an MA in English language literature from Van Yüzüncü Yıl University and a PhD in English language teaching from Gazi University, Türkiye. His research interests include teacher education, teacher assessment, technology and positive emotions in language teaching and learning.

**Dorota Zaborska** is Assistant Professor at Osaka University, Japan. She has been teaching English at the primary, secondary and tertiary levels since 2002. Her main research theme is the psychology of language learning, motivation and learning foreign languages in the third age. Through the lens of positive psychology, she explores the concept of savouring, the capacities to consciously attend to positive experiences in one's life. As a pedagogue, she explores tailored CLIL approaches in language classes, and developing critical thinking, speaking and writing encouraged through and enhanced by extensive reading from graded readers to authentic texts.

# FOREWORD

The fields of applied linguistics and psychology have become increasingly intertwined in recent years with an outpouring of research involving a psychological component into how languages are taught and learnt. It is now widely acknowledged that psychological ideas can help improve learning processes and lead to better academic outcomes as teachers employ methods that take into account the social, emotional and cognitive processes of their students. At its heart, psychology helps us to better understand human behaviour, and it therefore holds important clues about why learners act in the way that they do. My own experiences as a language educator, and later as a researcher, bear this out. When I arrived in Japan over twenty years ago to take up a new job teaching English at one of the country's national universities, I was at first puzzled and then frustrated by the lack of oral participation my students showed in class. Initially, I was persuaded that their silence must have been down purely to Japanese sociocultural factors (e.g. as a way of showing respect in the presence of someone senior – how wrong I was about that!). It was only later when I decided to investigate the phenomenon in depth for a large-scale study involving nearly a thousand learners (King, 2013) that I realized that a fair proportion of the reticence I was encountering was actually linked to students' socially situated feelings of anxiety. Leafing through a manual of mental disorders (American Psychiatric Association, 1994) one day in my university's library, I was struck by how perfectly my study's data, based on classroom observations and interviews with silent learners, mapped onto the manual's description of social anxiety disorder. This lightbulb moment led me to adapt Clark and Well's (1995) cognitive model of anxiety for subsequent publications (e.g. King, 2014) to explain how an anxious language learner's shaky sense of self combines with increased watchfulness, negative thought processes and avoidance behaviours to support his or her avoidance of classroom talk.

I ought to make it clear at this point that it would be a mistake to consider all anxious language learners to be in some way mentally ill and in need of treatment. Feeling apprehensive when confronted with certain foreign language tasks in the public forum of the classroom is perfectly natural, and experiencing negative emotions is all part of the human experience. However, high levels of anxiety can potentially wreak havoc with a student's in-class performance and ultimately impact their academic achievement, particularly where communicating in the target language is concerned.

Therefore, while it would be unrealistic and an overreaction to expect language teachers to be also trained counsellors skilled at psychological medical interventions (after all, they have enough on their plate with often difficult working conditions and a lack of support; see Sulis et al., 2022), arming them with some easy-to-use practical techniques to combat anxiety and some hands-on psychology-based ideas to support anxious learners is highly advisable. This book achieves this aim with aplomb. The editors, Neil Curry and Kate Maher, have brought together an impressive team of contributors hailing from various parts of the world and working in a variety of different educational contexts. Some are just dynamically starting their research careers, while others are already well established and respected for their psychology-based language education work. What they all share is a desire to provide readers of this volume with straightforward, practical activities based on sound psychological concepts that will motivate teachers to improve the affective aspects of their pedagogy. The book is positively bulging with helpful hints and advice accompanying chapters on such issues as language anxiety causes, cognitive techniques, visualization and imagination, positive learning environments, learner well-being and so on. I am certain this well-informed and accessible collection will become a 'must read' text for anyone interested in how psychological theory and educational realities meet within the sphere of language learning.

*Jim King*
University of Leicester, UK

## References

American Psychiatric Association. (1994), *Diagnostic and Statistical Manual of Mental Disorders*, 4th edn. Washington, DC: American Psychiatric Association.

King, J. (2013), *Silence in The Second Language Classroom*, Hampshire: Palgrave Macmillan.

King, J. (2014). 'Fear of The True Self: Social Anxiety and The Silent Behaviour of Japanese Learners of English', in K. Csizér and M. Magid (eds), *The Impact of Self-Concept on Language Learning*, 232–49, Bristol: Multilingual Matters.

Sulis, G., S. Babic, A. Mairitsch, S. Mercer, J. Jin and J. King, (2022), 'Retention and Attrition in Early-Career Foreign Language Teachers in Austria and The United Kingdom', *The Modern Language Journal,* 106 (1): 155–71.

# ACKNOWLEDGEMENTS

We want to express our sincerest appreciation to everyone involved in this project. This edited volume would not have been possible without their collaboration and enduring support. The idea for this book was born during numerous conversations with each other, colleagues and fellow conference attendees, all of whom were keen to get new ideas for activities and strategies to support anxious learners. Although a plethora of intervention research is available, unfortunately, there is not always space to publish details of the interventions themselves. So, quite often, teachers depend on people who are generous enough to take the time to share their activities through other means. We are extremely grateful to all the generous contributors in this book who have taken much time and effort to share their helpful ideas and valuable experience, joining us on this publishing journey. It has been our privilege to collaborate and learn from you all.

We are indebted to Laura Gallon at Bloomsbury, who has been incredibly supportive and understanding throughout this project.

We must also say a big thank you to Jo Mynard, who has been a constant source of support from the start, helping out with countless queries and providing invaluable advice. Also, a massive thank you to Jim King for providing such a thoughtful foreword and helpful advice, as well as introducing us to one another and forging our research friendship!

We also want to thank Shigeo Kondo for the wonderful book design that perfectly encapsulated the calming image we wanted to pass on to readers and students through the activities.

Lastly, we hope this book is a fixed feature on the readers' desks, with tatty corners, tea stains and other signs of being a well-used constant companion when planning lessons.

# CHAPTER ONE

# Introduction

## Kate Maher and Neil Curry

For some foreign language learners, moments of success in their language learning journeys can feel far and few between despite hard work and commitment to studying the target language. Anxiety related to language learning has been defined as 'the worry and negative emotional reaction when learning and using' the target language (Gregersen and MacIntyre, 2014: 3). Foreign language anxiety (FLA) can distort how some learners perceive their abilities (Gregersen and Horwitz, 2002; Horwitz, Horwitz and Cope, 1986), and the resulting negative emotions may mean they cannot take advantage of communicative opportunities (Bao, 2014; King, 2014). Most language teachers will likely work with students who experience these inhibitive effects of FLA, which is one reason why FLA arguably remains one of the most significant research interests within second language acquisition (SLA) and a major affective factor in language learning (Daubney, Dewaele and Gkonou, 2017).

Over the past four decades of FLA research, a substantial focus has been placed on developing classroom interventions to support anxious language learners. Young's (1991) seminal text demonstrated the importance of creating a positive classroom atmosphere. In recent years, approaches aimed at increasing learners' positive emotions and making them feel more at ease when using the language have been adapted from positive psychology (Oxford, 2017; Williams, Puchta and Mercer, 2021). Toyama and Yamazaki's (2021) comprehensive systematic review of FLA classroom interventions highlights the vast range of approaches, including meditation, affirmations and relaxation techniques. This volume builds on this existing body of work by creating a practical guide on using psychology-based approaches to support learners who experience FLA.

The motivation for putting together this edited volume was to make the theories accessible and encourage the practical application of these theories by sharing interventions and strategies as a collection of classroom activities. Moreover, we hope this collection of activities contributes to the discussion that Horwitz, Horwitz and Cope (1986) initiated with their 'pioneering' (Horwitz, 2017: 31) conceptualization of FLA and diagnostic instrument, the Foreign Language Class Anxiety Scale (FLCAS). Identifying FLA in the classroom is just the first step in getting the discussion started with learners and supporting them in managing this negative emotion (Horwitz, 2017). We hope this book contributes to the discussion by providing teachers with techniques and strategies they can use with their learners.

## Focus of this book

The activities in this book can be adapted to support learners with general FLA and skill-specific FLA (listening, reading, speaking and writing). However, most of the activities are directed towards speaking-related FLA. In the foreign language classroom context, anxiety has been identified as having significant potential to affect oral performance (King, 2014; Woodrow, 2006). Also, previous studies show that speaking tends to be the most anxiety-inducing of all the skill-specific anxieties in language learning, which suggests that learners who do not experience general FLA can become anxious when faced with speaking situations (Gregersen and Horwitz, 2002; Horwitz, 2010). So, this book builds on the growing body of research looking at interventions to encourage more oral participation in the classroom (Curry, 2014; King et al., 2020). Furthermore, as teachers who have worked with motivated and proficient language learners who became despondent at not being able to perform as well as they hoped due to their FLA, we felt compelled to create activities that might help give them, and others like them, a confidence boost.

Building language learners' confidence is also at the heart of this volume. Although there are arguments that FLA can be facilitative and 'motivate' learners (Ohata, 2005), we take the side of Horwitz, Horwitz and Cope (1986) and other researchers (Oxford, 2017; Toyama and Yamazaki, 2019; Young, 1991) who believe in the importance of supporting learners to overcome the debilitative effects of FLA and whose interventions are aimed at foreign language anxiety reduction (FLAR). As Horwitz (2017: 40) so persuasively argues, learners can often mask their anxiety with behaviours that make them appear unmotivated. In that case, it would be better to focus on increasing their motivation rather than risk not recognizing their FLA or using anxiety to engage them. The classroom is often the main opportunity where learners can develop their language skills, so teachers must create a supportive environment where their speaking confidence can develop too.

So, as well as usually being the primary learning space for content and skills, we believe that the language classroom should also function as a place for acquiring tools to manage FLA and other affective factors that influence language learning. Studies have demonstrated that affective strategies have the potential to reduce FLA and, therefore, should be taught alongside linguistic knowledge and skills (Oxford, 2017; MacIntyre, Gregersen and Mercer, 2019; Toyama and Yamazaki, 2021). Moreover, some students are unaware of affective influences or dismiss them, focusing on acquiring linguistic knowledge and skills. However, a consequence of this can be that they negatively attribute low proficiency or a nervous performance to having a lack of ability. In our experience, when talking with nervous learners about how to improve, common responses have been, 'I will learn 200 words a week, so I know more vocabulary', or 'I will study grammar more so that I make fewer mistakes'. Of course, these types of goals can be effective in helping learners gain speaking confidence. However, these are not always appropriate strategies as the learner could be overlooking other, more powerful, underlying factors related to affective influences (Maher, 2021).

In raising awareness of the importance of the affective factors that influence language learning, we also hope that this book contributes to the ongoing development of the psychology of language learning (PLL). This rapidly growing field applies theory and practical approaches from psychology to language learning and teaching (Gregersen and Mercer, 2022). The interdisciplinary nature of PLL suggests numerous inspiring and insightful opportunities for the context of language learning, broadening the possibilities for gaining knowledge and the development of interventions in the language classroom. The diverse range of perspectives is a characteristic that we have tried to emanate in this volume, incorporating approaches from engagement and flow theory, cognitive-behavioural theory, visualization and positive psychology.

## The target audience

We hope this book will interest foreign language instructors – from trainees to experienced teachers – working in secondary schools, universities and adult education. The book's activities are grounded in existing theories within the field of the psychology of language learning and are presented in a way so that readers who may not be overly familiar with these theories will find them accessible. The contributors in this volume work in various educational contexts and come from different national, linguistic and cultural backgrounds. Each person has included elements of personal experience in their chapter. By describing the reasons and events which gave rise to the development of the activities, we hope that readers will be able to recognize their own experiences when reading the entries and realize how they can put the activities into practice in their contexts.

# How to use this book

The book is organized into five parts, each with a different psychology-based approach. The parts contain chapters that introduce theoretical background in an accessible way and practical, easy-to-follow classroom activities to reduce FLA and increase learners' confidence when using the language. Each author has also provided some background explanation on why they use their chosen approach to give context so you can picture how it might be a good fit for your teaching context and students.

We recommend that you start by using the instruments in Part One to assess what levels of FLA are present in your class and what the possible causes are in your context. Starting here would be especially beneficial if you are at the beginning of a course with new students, have concerns about your class or individual student, or if this is your first step in investigating the FLA of your students. Once you have established an initial understanding of your students' FLA, choose a section from Parts Two to Five with an approach depending on your context, interests and the needs of your students. Ideally, your students' responses to the questionnaires in Part One will help inform which approach and activity to choose first. Table 1.1 is intended to act as a quick guide to help you navigate the book. We hope this volume will be a helpful resource to have next to you when planning lessons.

TABLE 1.1 Summary guide

**Part One. Assessing FLA: Identifying FLA and causes in your context**
Two instruments for assessing FLA and identifying potential underlying factors causing it. These instruments are also intended to prompt discussions with students about their experiences of FLA and to inform which activities from Parts two to five to use. Both can be easily adapted for different contexts.

| Chapter title (shortened) | Key points of chapter |
| --- | --- |
| 2. Identifying emotions and thoughts | • Questionnaire instrument<br>• Identify which situations make students anxious and why<br>• Assess what coping strategies students use in these situations<br>• Encourages students to reflect in detail |
| 3. You are not alone | • Questionnaire instrument<br>• Includes a speaking activity<br>• Raises students' awareness of FLA and that they are not the only ones to feel nervous<br>• Quick and simple to use |

## Part Two. The classroom environment: Creating a positive learning space

These activities aim to create a positive and engaging learning atmosphere. The classroom context is an important factor in FLA, and some class groups need support to develop better interpersonal relationships and rapport to facilitate effective language learning practice tasks.

| | |
|---|---|
| 4. Creating a sense of belonging | • Useful as an ice-breaker activity to help create rapport<br>• Boosts self-esteem by talking about themselves<br>• Speaking activity that most teachers will find familiar and simple to set up<br>• Appropriate in contexts where students are not familiar with communicative activities |
| 5. Student-centred socially motivating classrooms | • Builds rapport and trust among classmates<br>• Student-centred activity to create class rules for how to support one another<br>• Class discussion can be made into a speaking practice activity<br>• Adaptable for different contexts and ages |
| 6. Flowing classrooms | • Uses elements of 'flow' theory to make the classroom a space where students can more easily become engaged<br>• Practical steps on how to incorporate 'flow' into language learning tasks<br>• Simple tweaks that can easily be applied to existing lesson plans and other activities |
| 7. Making speaking tasks emotionally engaging | • Creates a more relaxing classroom atmosphere to build rapport<br>• Aims to increase students' emotional engagement in their language learning<br>• Useful in contexts where students are not familiar with communicative tasks or group work<br>• Ideas on how to apply 'flow' to language practice tasks |

## Part Three. Cognitive techniques: Thinking through anxiety

How an individual interprets their environment determines how they feel about it and what action they take. Cognitive-based approaches emphasize the importance of how students think about using a foreign language and show them how their thoughts can be managed to reduce their anxiety.

| | |
|---|---|
| 8. The art of cognitive distancing | • Teaches affirmations as a coping strategy that students can use independently when needed<br>• Useful for lecture-style or content classes where it may be hard to incorporate support activities or other interventions<br>• Short and simple, with minimal preparation<br>• Can be used as a base for discussion activities with higher-level learners in the L2 |
| 9. The confidence-building diary | • Boosts learner autonomy as can be used independently by students<br>• Can be used with a class or individual students<br>• Adaptable to different contexts and individual needs of students<br>• Useful for classes where there are anxious and more confident students as benefits both |

| | |
|---|---|
| 10. Facing worries head on | • Facilitates sharing and creation of co-constructed ideas to build a bank of coping strategies<br>• Encourages students to test and evaluate coping strategies through reflection<br>• Collaborative discussions can be used as speaking practice activities |
| 11. Attributional retraining techniques | • Encourages students to develop positive-growth mindsets rather than focusing on blaming themselves<br>• Provides students with positive ways to perceive themselves and their performance<br>• Structured approach to objective thinking that can be used independently |
| 12. Adopting a rational approach to building confidence | • Facilitates rapport among classmates as they become aware they are not the only ones who are nervous when speaking<br>• Develops balanced thinking and awareness of the influence of negative thoughts<br>• Can be used with classes or individual students, adapted to situations that worry them |
| 13. Identifying FLA triggers | • Cognitive-behavioural theory-based technique for identifying what factors influence individual students' FLA<br>• Creates an individualized plan to make an informed decision when choosing coping strategies<br>• Students become more aware of their individual needs, making coping strategies and learning goals more effective |

**Part Four. Visualization techniques: Imagining confidence**
Guided by teachers, students are introduced to visualization techniques that prompt them to imagine and focus on positive experiences of using a foreign language, helping to reduce their FLA.

| | |
|---|---|
| 14. An imagery-focused mindfulness approach | • Students are guided to focus on positive physical experiences and imagery to improve their performance<br>• Can be used independently as a coping strategy once students have learnt the technique<br>• Can be used for a variety of scenarios/activities, and situations, depending on students' needs<br>• Can be used in larger classes |
| 15. Rewrite your inner script | • Positive visualization technique for reducing public speaking anxiety, helping to boost confidence in tasks such as presentations<br>• Promotes group bonding by sharing ideas for coping strategies<br>• Students reflect on the technique and personalize it for independent use<br>• Can be used as a regular feature in class for various speaking tasks |

| | |
|---|---|
| 16. Focusing attention outwardly | • Reduces negative self-focus through task concentration training<br>• Helpful for students who are overly concerned and distracted by what impression they make when speaking<br>• Can be used independently by students<br>• Simple activity to prepare |

**Part Five. Well-being techniques: Creating mindful foreign language speakers**
Mindfulness and positive psychology approaches to help promote positive emotions leading to positive experiences of using the language. Techniques to create calm and reduce anxiety.

| | |
|---|---|
| 17. Dialogue skits with positive communication in mind | • Models positive communication and elements of effective communication<br>• Encourages students to be creative and playful<br>• Helps create and perform dialogue skits, which tend to be familiar speaking activities for students<br>• Can be applied by students in speaking situations outside the classroom |
| 18. Three good things about their English | • Positive evaluation approach for giving peer feedback that focuses on students' strengths<br>• Can be used as a regular class feature in any type of speaking activity or evaluated task<br>• Helps create rapport in the classroom by having students praise one another |
| 19. Mindfulness meditation | • Uses elements of mindfulness meditation and positive psychology to promote mindful attitudes and positive beliefs about students' own abilities<br>• Promotes class bonding through group discussions for sharing experiences and ideas<br>• Encourages reflection through journal writing<br>• Can be done as a regular class feature |

# References

Bao, D. (2014), *Understanding Silence and Reticence: Ways of Participating in Second Language Acquisition*, London: Bloomsbury.
Curry, N. (2014), 'Using CBT with Anxious Language Learners: The Potential Role of the Learning Advisor', *Studies in Self-Access Learning Journal*, 5 (1): 29–41.
Daubney, M., J. M. Dewaele and C. Gkonou, (2017), 'Preliminary Thoughts on Language Anxiety and The Focus of This Anthology', in C. Gkonou, M. Daubney and J. M. Dewaele (eds), *New Insights into Language Anxiety: Theory, Research and Educational Implications*, 1–7, Bristol: Multilingual Matters.

Gregersen, T. and E. K. Horwitz (2002), 'Language Learning and Perfectionism: Anxious and Non-anxious Language Learners' Reactions to Their Own Oral Performance', *The Modern Language Journal*, 86 (4): 562–70.

Gregersen, T. and P. D. MacIntyre (2014), *Capitalising on Language Learners' Individuality: From Premise to Practice*, Bristol: Multilingual Matters.

Gregersen, T. and S. Mercer (2022), 'Introduction', in T. Gregersen and S. Mercer (eds), *The Routledge Handbook of the Psychology of Language Learning*, 1–4, Oxon: Routledge.

Horwitz, E. K. (2010), 'Foreign and Second Language Anxiety', *Language Teaching*, 43 (2): 154–67.

Horwitz, E. K. (2017), 'On the Misreading of Horwitz, Horwitz and Cope (1986) and the Need to Balance Anxiety Research and the Experiences of Anxious Language Learners', in C. Gkonou, M. Daubney and J. M. Dewaele (eds), *New Insights into Language Anxiety: Theory, Research and Educational Implications*, 31–48, Bristol: Multilingual Matters.

Horwitz, E. K., M. B. Horwitz and J. Cope, (1986), 'Foreign Language Classroom Anxiety', *The Modern Language Journal*, 70 (2): 125–32.

King, J. (2014), 'Fear of The True Self: Social Anxiety and the Silent Behaviour of Japanese Learners of English', in K. Csizér and M. Magid (eds), *The Impact of Self-Concept on Language Learning*, 232–49, Bristol: Multilingual Matters.

King, J., T. Yashima, S. Humphries, S. Aubrey and M. Ikeda, (2020), 'Silence and Anxiety in the English-Medium Classroom of Japanese Universities: A Longitudinal Intervention Study', in J. King and S. Harumi (eds), *East Asian Perspectives on Silence in English Language Education*, 60–79, Bristol: Multilingual Matters.

MacIntyre, P. D., T. Gregersen and S. Mercer, (2019), 'Setting an Agenda for Positive Psychology in SLA: Theory, Practice, and Research', *The Modern Language Journal*, 103: 262–74.

Maher, K. (2021) 'Reframing Silence: Insights into Language Learners' Thoughts about Silence and Speaking-Related Anxiety', *Journal of Silence Studies in Education*, 1 (1): 32–47.

Ohata, K. (2005), 'Language Anxiety from The Teacher's Perspective: Interviews with Seven Experienced ESL/ EFL Teachers', *Journal of Language and Learning*, 3 (1): 133–55.

Oxford, R. L. (2017), 'Anxious Language Learners Can Change Their Minds: Ideas and Strategies from Traditional Psychology and Positive Psychology', in C. Gkonou, M. Daubney and J. M. Dewaele (eds), *New Insights into Language Anxiety: Theory, Research and Educational Implications*, 177–98, Bristol: Multilingual Matters.

Toyama, M. and Y. Yamazaki (2019), 'Anxiety Reduction Sessions in Foreign Language Classrooms', *The Language Learning Journal*, 49 (3): 1–13.

Toyama, M. and Y. Yamazaki (2021), 'Classroom Interventions and Foreign Language Anxiety: A Systematic Review with Narrative Approach', *Frontiers in Psychology*, 12.

Williams, M., H. Puchta and S. Mercer, (2021), *Psychology in Practice: A Wealth of Practical Ideas to Put Students in the Best Frame of Mind of Learning*, Salzburg: Helbling Languages.

Woodrow, L. (2006), 'Anxiety and Speaking English as a Second Language', *RELC Journal*, 37 (3): 308–28.

Young, D. J. (1991), 'Creating a Low-Anxiety Classroom Environment: What Does Language Anxiety Research Suggest?' *The Modern Language Journal*, 75 (4): 426–37.

PART ONE

# Assessing FLA: Identifying FLA and Causes in Your Context

# CHAPTER TWO

# How are you coping? A tool for identifying situations that cause FLA

*Neil Curry and Kate Maher*

In this chapter we describe the tool we have developed for collecting data on foreign language anxiety (FLA), which is based on Gkonou and Oxford's (2016) Managing Your Emotions (MYE) for language learning. The tool is used to find out what emotions students report in four (originally five) scenarios when they have to use their foreign language (FL), and whether they utilize any coping strategies. As our study which utilized the tool found (Curry, Maher and Peeters, 2020), students often describe similar feelings and reasoning when discussing FLA. When they are able to acknowledge and share these feelings it can be a great way for them to bond with their peers and begin to develop a different, more positive perspective regarding the communicative situations that make them anxious. The tool can easily be adapted for any context, in class or out of class, simply by introducing scenarios where students may be experiencing FLA. After describing the tool, we include a description of an activity that incorporates the tool to help students reflect over a semester regarding their feelings towards engaging in speaking activities, which encourages them to develop a different outlook.

## Background to the approach

Our interest in this scenario-based approach stems from calls for diversification in researching emotions and their influence on classroom performance. Sampson (2018) believes that a lot of attention has been placed on the role of negative emotions in the language classroom, and a growing band of research has also examined the effect of positive feelings (MacIntyre and Dewaele, 2014; Boudreau, MacIntyre and Dewaele, 2018). Therefore we wanted to make sure that we were not operating from a starting point of assuming that almost all speaking situations will generate FLA. Hence in the scenarios, we provide students with examples of language for expressing both positive and negative emotions. This allows us to learn from more confident students; both the reasons for their confidence and whether they have effective strategies for managing their emotions that can be shared with other students.

A scenario-based tool such as this differs from Horwitz, Horwitz and Cope's (1986) FLCAS and its adaptations, from the premise that we are not attempting to identify students who experience FLA in our classes or quantify how many students have it – we already know it's there. We approach this from the standpoint that learning to manage your emotions is a key skill for learning a new language, which is just as important as learning new vocabulary and grammar, and students often need instruction on how to do this. Using scenarios allows us to not only find out how widespread FLA might be in the class but to also confirm what kind of situations might lead to FLA, how the students experience it (or not) emotionally, how intensely they feel the emotions described and whether they have any strategies for coping with it. It also helps students to reflect on the reasons for their anxiety in these situations.

The intention of finding out what emotions students are describing is influenced by our cognitive behaviour therapy (CBT)-based approaches to help students with FLA, and our desire to not only design a tool for data collection but to see if it also could have application as part of a class activity for raising confidence and reducing FLA. Described in Chapters Twelve and Thirteen in more detail, CBT attempts to re-orient a client's beliefs, which are contributing to their anxiety, from negative to more objective, and allow them to have a more pragmatic viewpoint on the situation which is causing distress. In CBT, the premise is that beliefs contribute to feelings, which then affect actions, so therefore negative beliefs about one's own language abilities will lead to negative emotions, and the likelihood of behaviour which may be detrimental to improving language skills.

The questionnaire we adapted and developed is six pages long and is conducted in the students' L1 in order to get the most honest and accurate descriptions from students. The first page explains the purpose of the questionnaire and how to complete it. We prefer that students complete all four scenarios, but they are given the choice to focus on the one which they can complete in the most detail. This option is in order to avoid questionnaire fatigue; in some higher learning contexts we find frequent requests for students to help in research, which can be frustrating for them. Additionally, it makes the questionnaire more relevant in that they can avoid aspects of it which they feel don't apply. We provide a list of adjectives describing feelings which they can take from to complete their answers if they choose; this is to lessen any anxiety they might feel in choosing the 'wrong' answer. The scenarios are as follows:

1. *You want to say something in English in class but you don't.*

   Here we wanted to find out what emotions students were feeling at these times, and why. This scenario was demonstrated by our research to be rated more negatively than the others, and students lacked coping strategies for dealing with it. Here it typically appears that a student wants to join in a conversation but cannot, often because they fear making a mistake or being misunderstood, which they believe will result in them being negatively perceived by their peers.

2. *There is another student in your class who you think is a better speaker than you. You have to do a speaking activity together.*

   This scenario stems from some students' beliefs that their peers' speaking skills are superior, which leads to feelings of inferiority and an unwillingness to speak.

3. *You make a mistake during a classroom speaking activity and receive or perceive criticism from another student.*

4. *You make a mistake during a classroom speaking activity and receive or perceive criticism from the teacher.*
   For both of these scenarios, we wanted to see how much perceived criticism led to anxiety and how students responded to it. We also wanted to determine if criticism from peers and teachers was received in a similar way, or if one caused more anxiety than the other. We found that our students were more sensitive to peer feedback as they are closer in age and experience. They regard teachers as experts and thus feedback is to be expected.

These scenarios were chosen as they were often described to us by students as being times when they felt nervous and were unable to speak. When initially conducting our study, we wanted some confirmation that these situations were indeed anxiety inducing, instead of just relying on anecdotal accounts. Therefore we wanted to find out how they described their own feelings at these times and whether they had some means of overcoming any negative emotions. The scenarios can be adapted and changed to test other potentially anxiety-inducing situations as the teacher sees fit. There are two ways in which this data can be used. Firstly, it will show

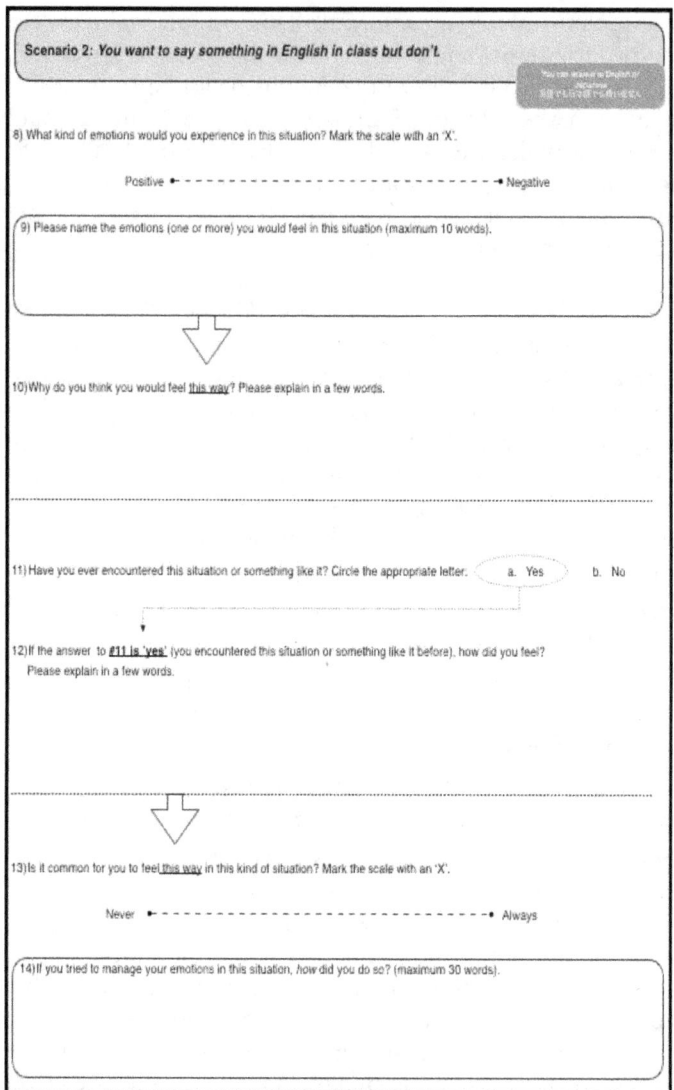

FIGURE 2.1  *Scenario 2.*

the instructor whether the students need help to address any FLA if there are a number of negative feelings recorded, and also informs the teacher what scenarios students feel anxious about in class. Secondly, it serves as a record of the students feelings at that time, which through intervention and instruction they can change if necessary. The scenarios are all constructed in the same way, as per the example of Scenario 2 in Figure 2.1 above (the questionnaire is now conducted online using Google Forms, and the scales used in Questions 8 and 13 are now numbered 0 to 10):

The first questions are to determine whether the student finds the situation to generate largely positive or negative emotions, what those emotions are and why they occur. The scale allows us to collect more comparable data which we can use to determine the overall trend of how students perceive the situation. With the description of feelings and the reasons for them, we are able to see what may be the basis of any negative emotions, and this also gives the student an opportunity to start thinking about why they feel the way they do. If they subsequently can experience some activities which can help them to change their perspective, this serves as a point from which they can refer back to, to see how they have changed. The fourth and fifth questions in each scenario (questions 11 and 12 in Figure 2.1) allow us to determine whether the anxiety might be the result of an actual experience or if it could just be a fear of what *might* occur. This can be the advantage of using a scenario-based tool; students can respond to how they might feel in a hypothetical situation, even if they have not experienced it directly. Additionally, we found that a scenario was evaluated more negatively depending on how much it was experienced.

## Activity

### Aims

As well as for collecting data, Neil has been using the tool as a means for students to confront and monitor FLA in his course on self-directed learning. Compared to the other activities in this volume, this approach takes much longer, but allows students to easily see how their confidence has grown. Additionally, the fact that the tool allows us to identify confident students and potentially effective coping strategies allows for the opportunity for students to share and learn from each other. If they are willing, you can encourage confident students to act as peer role models and share their experiences through classroom discussions. Murphey's research on near-peer role models (1998) shows how effective this can be. Students in his seminar made recordings of other students talking on topics, including making mistakes, and that Japanese speakers can become proficient in English; students who watched these recordings 'changed their beliefs significantly through merely watching these Japanese students talking about taking risks and enjoying English' (1998: 202).

- **Level:** Intermediate and above
- **Materials:** Scenario tool (see online materials), some means to record reflections
- **Time:** See activity in Chapter Twelve.

1. Give the class the scenario tool near the beginning of the semester – I usually choose the second week of my fifteen-week semester, once everyone has settled in. You can look at their responses and get an idea of how they are feeling, but it's not necessary to address them at this point.

2. During Week 4, I introduce the activity described in Chapter Twelve, but another similar one would be suitable. Students are encouraged to reassess any negative thought in the light of evidence which shows that they have communicative abilities and that perhaps the maladaptive strategy of remaining silent for fear of mistakes or embarrassment doesn't need to be followed any more.

3. Subsequently, about a week later, they are asked to reflect on how confident they feel about speaking English in class and why that is. With these reflections and the statements of their feelings from the questionnaire, we are then able to have a basis from which students are able to work towards changing their perspectives and re-evaluating their beliefs. The following is an example of a student's reflection: *Last Friday, we learnt about confidence on class. Thanks to it, I could change my mind. When I made mistakes, no one laugh at me. Mistakes are natural. I can't tell anything and improve skills without good and bad experiences. I remembered that it is the most important to move before thinking. I don't want to forget it anymore. I became a KUIS* (Kanda University of International Studies) *student to study English. I will do a best from now on.*

4. This is followed in Week eight by a reflection question asking students to refer back to the questionnaire scenario for which they felt the least confident and record whether their feelings for that scenario have subsequently changed. This is from the same student:

*However, I have changed my mind absolutely. I can declared it. In these days, I feel lucky girl when I have a chance to speak those who I may be able to learn new vocabulary and expressions from them. And also, they teach me correct English. I was afraid of mistakes in front of them, but they don't mind my mistakes. They gently accept them and help me improve English. Needless to say, they are not terrible, but so kind! Thanks to them, my English skills improve step by step.*

Although it may be difficult in your teaching context to incorporate these types of reflections, we would strongly recommend you attempt it. Reflecting on learning processes enables students to gain more knowledge of how they learn and who they are as learners, and subsequently achieve more autonomy. By responding to their reflections, if possible, you can engage them in a reflective dialogue (Kato and Mynard, 2016) through which they can critically examine their thoughts about their learning and the choices they make accordingly. This will help them to question their beliefs and assumptions regarding issues such as the difficulty of learning new languages, or how others feel about mistakes, and perhaps develop strategies to deal with these issues. This is an example from a different student who described in her learning journal that she had 'declined' to speak during a group conversation:

> Neil: *Why did you decline?*
> Student: *I didn't have confidence. Sometimes when I started to speak, the other member did it at the same time. I gave a turn to her because of lack of confidence.*
> Neil: *How do you feel about this?*
> Student: *I felt a little gloomy. I also regretted.*
> Neil: *I'm sure you don't like feeling that way. Is there something you can do to change it?*
> Student: *Of course! I decided to speak short words like 'oh' before feeling nervous. And it is to make others notice that I want to speak.*

Despite lacking confidence the student has developed a practical strategy for the next time this situation occurs. This allowed me to encourage her to share it with others, and we could revisit this incident at a later date to check if her confidence had improved. Checking in with individual students and setting reflection questions for group discussions are good ways to follow up with students' progress.

## Recommended reading

Kato, S. and J. Mynard (2016), *Reflective Dialogue: Advising in Language Learning.* New York: Routledge.
Written by two very experienced learning advisors, this is a comprehensive guide to how to engage a language learner in a reflective dialogue. It shows how a learner can be aided in achieving a deeper understanding of their own learning processes through advising strategies and tools; examining their beliefs related to learning, how they understand their strengths and weaknesses, what kind of personality they have as a learner and how they can reach their goals and achieve the best results for themselves. It acts as a practical guide with its use of sample dialogues, so it is accessible to educators, whatever their level of experience with encouraging reflection.

Hope, D. A., R. G. Heimberg and C. L. Turk (2010), *Managing Social Anxiety: A Cognitive-Behavioural Therapy Approach,* 2nd edn, Oxford: Oxford University Press.
Comparisons have been made between FLA and social anxiety, especially in regard to the powerful influence of negative thoughts concerned with fears of a negative evaluation when speaking in the FL. This workbook provides

activities for understanding anxiety and skill-building exercises to develop a range of coping strategies, which can easily be adapted for FL classroom use. These activities emphasize the importance of being able to name what emotions a person feels in anxiety-inducing situations, and being aware of what thoughts come to mind and their influence over the person's actions. Moreover, the book also contains activities that encourage the person to plan for success – that is, after understanding their anxiety better, knowing how to take the next steps with coping strategies and maintaining the effort to keep using them, which is a key aim of this chapter's activity.

# References

Boudreau, C., P. D. MacIntyre and J. M. Dewaele, (2018), 'Enjoyment and Anxiety in Second Language Communication: An Idiodynamic Approach', *Studies in Second Language Learning and Teaching*, 8 (1): 149–70.

Curry, N., K. Maher and W. Peeters, (2020), 'Identifying Emotions and Thoughts Related to Speaking Anxiety: Laying the Groundwork for Designing CBT-Based Support Materials for Anxious Learners', *Journal for the Psychology of Language Learning*, 2 (1): 57–89.

Gkonou, C. and R. L. Oxford (2016), *Questionnaire: Managing Your Emotions for Language Learning*, Colchester, UK: University of Essex.

Horwitz, E. K., M. B. Horwitz and J. Cope, (1986), 'Foreign Language Classroom Anxiety', *The Modern Language Journal*, 70 (2): 125–32.

Kato, S. and J. Mynard (2016), *Reflective Dialogue: Advising in Language Learning*, New York: Routledge.

MacIntyre, P. D. and J. M. Dewaele (2014), 'The Two Faces of Janus? Anxiety and Enjoyment in the Foreign Language Classroom', *Studies in Second Language Learning and Teaching*, 4 (2): 237–74.

Murphey, T. (1998), Motivating with Near Peer Role Models. In *On JALT '97: Trends and Transitions* 201–6.

Sampson, R. J. (2018), 'The Feeling Classroom: Diversity of Feelings in Instructed L2 Learning', *Innovation in Language Learning and Teaching*, 14 (3): 203–17.

# CHAPTER THREE

# You are not alone:

# Shining light on FLA perspectives through classroom data collection

*Jonathan Shachter*

Like air travel, anxieties associated with learning a foreign language are quite common because individuals are placed in situations outside their comfort zone. Acknowledging that you have a fear, and others do, too, is a healthy way to start dealing with uncomfortable situations. One way to overcome the fear of flying, for example, is to talk to a pilot and learn the physics of aerodynamics. Another way, of course, is to do some statistical research. In this chapter, I will describe how language teachers can use a 'Nervousness Metric' (NM) to gather key foreign language anxiety (FLA) 'data' about their students. The NM is a brief self-report measurement, which can be used to quickly collect state (i.e. *how you are feeling right now*) reports of FLA. In addition to the NM, I've added a pre-survey, which focuses on previous foreign language experiences. This can help establish why some students are affected by FLA more than others. After data collection, the teacher presents the findings to the class. Through this process, everyone will be more knowledgeable about the existence and degree of FLA in their classroom. Also, as you know, it is important to create a warm, low-stress environment at the beginning of a school year or term. The recommended activities in this chapter can help you do this.

Even though the activities outlined in this chapter are quite simple, there are multiple benefits for you and your students. Firstly, teachers can consider student responses as a means to inform future teaching practices. For example, you could try utilizing the NM before a series of classes where you test different pedagogical approaches, room designs and so on. If students respond with high levels of FLA to a particular task or room design, you may want to adjust or avoid these in the future. Another benefit is that language students who experience debilitating levels of FLA may be too shy or lack the linguistic ability to communicate this directly to you. The NM can help bridge this gap. In a study in 2018, I found that the NM facilitated a non-verbal empathetic relationship between language teachers and students. Later in the chapter, I will also highlight how the measuring tool itself may serve as an anxiety-reducing intervention.

## Background to the approach

A number of students will emote positive emotions in the foreign language classroom (e.g. smiles, energetic body language), while others show the opposite. Maher and King (2020: 118) highlight how anxious learners will display non-verbal cues like 'limited facial expressions in the brow area and the mouth'. However, physical displays of discomfort can vary between cultures, and as a result, incidences of FLA can be less obvious and more difficult for teachers to recognize, depending on the context (Matsumoto, 1991; Matsumoto et al., 2002). This was especially true for me when I gave level tests to incoming students at language schools. Some silent students did not outwardly display that they were anxious, and therefore, I assumed that their language ability was low.

At one particular language school, for example, I was required to give a twenty-minute assessment followed by a twenty-minute mock lesson (which catered to that student's particular level). After asking a basic question at the beginning of the assessment (e.g. *What's your favourite food?*), some students would remain silent, and I would then become unsure of how to proceed. When I first started in this position, I would become frustrated with the time requirement for assessing beginners. Surely, it does not take twenty minutes to determine whether a student is a beginner? What I found after conducting numerous level checks, however, was that I started to see behavioural changes occurring after ten to fifteen minutes of silence.

So this was very interesting – some students would remain silent for upwards of fifteen minutes but then suddenly begin to speak. I wondered if there was a way that I could help these learners move out of the silence faster. During one of these long periods of silence with a particular student, I suddenly remembered pain-intensity assessments I had as a child (e.g. *On a scale of one to ten, how much pain are you feeling right now?*). When faced with prolonged silence, I would start asking students, 'On a scale of one to ten, how *nervous* are you right now?' I would draw a line with the Likert scale and ask them to circle the number. Many students would circle or say 'Ten'. This was a breakthrough!

Not only was the response immediate but I also observed that the level of tension was reduced. I hypothesized that this brief survey served two purposes. Firstly, the student could easily 'communicate' their level of FLA, and secondly, the teacher (or, in this case, the assessor) could convey to the student: *Yes, I am aware of FLA, and I know that it could negatively affect your performance in this assessment.* The latter informed my hypothesis that using the nervousness assessment actually calmed the students down. After a few minutes, I would produce the Likert again, and inevitably, the FLA number had decreased (moving from ten to seven, for example). I would ask again after another few minutes had passed, and the FLA number would inevitably decrease again. It was then that I realized that I shouldn't assess aptitude until a degree of FLA was established.

Using my experiences as a launching point for research, I used the NM as a data collection tool at a public university in Japan in 2017. Over twelve weeks, two other teachers and I distributed this one-item, ten-point Likert scale (1 – totally relaxed, 10 – extremely nervous) at the beginning of class and before a performance activity (e.g. class observed dialogue, individual presentation, group presentation). The NM (Figure 3.1) was initially designed as a fast and efficient way to collect state assessments of nervousness in a university language classroom (see Shachter, 2018), but as highlighted, I also observed that the measuring tool may also serve as an anxiety-reducing intervention.

In my study (Shachter, 2018), I concluded that some language students might be shy, silent or anxious due to lack of language ability. For these students, the NM afforded them a way to communicate with the teacher without having to speak out in front of their classmates or approach the teacher individually. Moreover, anxious language learners may not be aware that there are other students in class who feel the same way and, therefore, may be less likely to raise the issue.

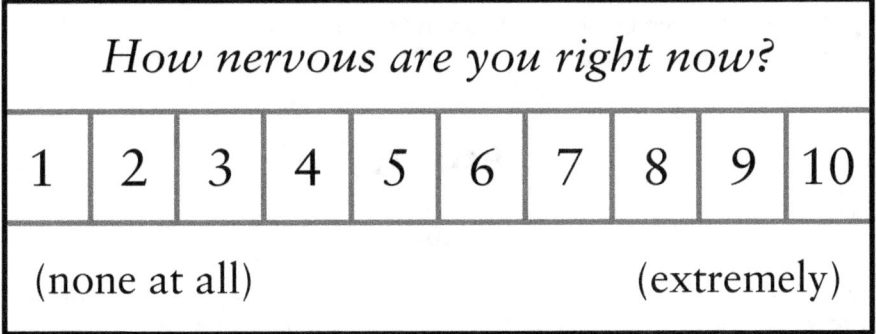

FIGURE 3.1 *The nervousness metric (Shachter, 2018, reproduced with permission of JALT Publications).*

With a short comment section, the NM is also useful in gathering qualitative information. For instance, when I first used the scale in 2018, I was made well aware that some students were hungry or tired. To be honest, I wasn't expecting this kind of response to an FLA survey, but now I understand how some students may feel before or after lunch! Another recurring theme in the comment section was that students felt relieved that their teacher was aware of the existence of anxiety but did not single out students or make a big deal out of it.

Throughout the course of the data collection, quantitative results from the NM indicated that FLA steadily decreased over time *without intervention*. However, psychologists may argue that the NM in itself acted as an intervention (Kassam and Mendes, 2013; Stieger et al., 2021). These psychologists support my hypothesis that the NM actually helped calm students. To learn more about self-reports acting as an intervention, please read the two previously cited studies and check out the recommended reading at the end of this chapter. In short, if you can quantify an internal feeling, you have removed yourself from that feeling enough to objectively rate it. This process activates the amygdala and calms the body.

As teachers, it is important to be cognizant of the fact that student levels of FLA may fluctuate over time and patterns of change may be caused by events or interactions both inside and outside of the language classroom (Şimşek and Dörnyei, 2017). Moreover, certain students may react differently to *you* personally (e.g. your age, sex, nationality, personality). In isolation, FLA is a complicated affective factor, which can be compounded by incidences of miscommunication (e.g. confusion over pronunciation or word choice). Incidences of miscommunication can be followed by a period of silence when both individuals in a conversation are unsure how to proceed. This, of course, could happen outside of a school (e.g. when overseas, my heart races in a foreign bank or post office). It is also important to remember that both technical aspects of the language learning process and cultural disconnects between individuals can also lead to FLA (MacIntyre, 2017). When viewed through these lenses, it is clear how FLA can instigate or result in a vicious cycle (i.e. miscommunications cause anxiety or vice versa). When considering all these factors, remember that this simple activity is a great way to check in with your students and see how they are doing on a particular day.

# Activity

## *Aims*

The main aim of this activity is to help teachers connect with anxious students and foster an environment that lowers FLA while building key language skills. In regard to language development, students will have an opportunity to learn about data collection, presentation skills and practice speaking about a topic that is ever-present in the language-learning classroom.

- **Level:** The activity described in this chapter can be effective for any language class but may be more suited to low intermediate and above. For low-level students, you may need to translate some key terms, spend more time pre-teaching vocabulary and/or cut some sections that require more linguistic flexibility (e.g. presentation, discussion).
- **Materials:** Questionnaires 1–3 (provided); pre-teaching vocabulary aides (optional); basic software to produce the results of the surveys (Word or Excel is fine).
- **Time:** Ideally, you should allocate at least ninety minutes (spread over two classes) to do this activity. I would recommend using this activity at the beginning of a school year or term when you are first meeting your students. When I used the NM at a university, I started in the second class of the term. So over classes 2 and 3 (of the first term), for example, you and your students would get a better understanding of perspectives regarding FLA and previous experiences that may shape current feelings. By using this activity at the beginning of the term, you will also help foster a warm, open, low-stress environment. This is especially important at the beginning of the term when FLA levels may be the highest. Beyond reading this chapter, printing out materials and preparing the data, preparation time for advanced learners is minimal. As I mentioned, though, for low-level learners, you may need more time to pre-teach vocabulary from the questionnaires and possibly add translations as scaffolding.

## Class 1

1. Pre-teach key vocabulary from the questionnaires. It is your option to pre-teach vocabulary before each questionnaire is distributed or pre-teach all words at the beginning of class.
2. Divide the class into pairs (or with one group of three if you have an odd number of students).
3. Distribute Questionnaire 1 (Table 3.1) (<u>**one questionnaire per person**</u>). It is important not to pass out Questionnaire 2 (Table 3.2) until you've collected Questionnaire 1. This will help keep students on task and not become overwhelmed, and it is also easier for you to keep track of the responses. Questionnaire 1 is designed to gather useful background information on foreign language learners. This questionnaire only needs to be distributed once. Questionnaire 2 is designed to assess state feelings of FLA over a range of scenarios – as such, this could be distributed over a series of classes.

As noted, I recommend using it over classes 2 and 3 of the term. The following is a procedural guide over these two classes.

4  When distributed, instruct students to write their names at the top of each questionnaire and then trade with their partner.

5  Partners will ask the questions and fill in the appropriate response, then switch. This is a good way to collect data while incorporating a speaking activity.

6  After both partners have gone through Questionnaire 1, collect and then distribute Questionnaire 2. Again, partners will ask the questions and fill in the appropriate response.

### TABLE 3.1 Questionnaire 1

| Item no. | Questions (Yes/No, brief explanation) |
|---|---|
| 1 | a) Have you ever travelled to a foreign country?<br>b) Do you plan on travelling in the future?<br>c) Where do you want to travel? |
| 2 | a) Have you ever had an English-speaking friend or acquaintance?<br>b) Where did you meet them (e.g. classmate, part-time job, club)? |
| 3 | a) Have you ever met a fluent English speaker?<br>b) Where were you?<br>c) What did you talk about? |
| 4 | a) Did you study English in elementary school?<br>b) Did you like your teacher?<br>c) Why/Why not? |
| 5 | a) Did you study English in junior high school?<br>b) Did you like your teacher?<br>c) Why/Why not? |
| 6 | a) Did you study English in high school?<br>b) Did you like your teacher?<br>c) Why/Why not? |
| 7 | Do you like speaking in English? |
| 8 | a) Do you like studying English?<br>b) Which skill (e.g. reading, writing, vocabulary)? |
| 9 | a) Do you watch content in English (e.g. Netflix, Amazon Prime)?<br>b) What do you watch? |
| 10 | What is more important: nice classmates or a nice teacher? |

## TABLE 3.2 Questionnaire 2

All items on a scale of 1 (none at all) to 10 (extremely).

| 1 | 2 | 3 | 4 | 5 | 6 | 7 | 8 | 9 | 10 |
|---|---|---|---|---|---|---|---|---|----|

(none at all)                     (extremely)

| Item no. | Questions |
|---|---|
| 1 | Today, before class, how nervous were you? |
| 2 | At the beginning of this class, how nervous were you? |
| 3 | How nervous are you right now? |
| 4 | When the teacher asks you to answer a question in front of the class (alone), how nervous are you? |
| 5 | In pair work, how nervous are you? |
| 6 | In group work, how nervous are you? |
| 7 | During a presentation, how nervous are you? |
| 8 | Before a language test, how nervous are you? |
| 9 | If you speak English outside of class, how nervous are you? |
| 10 | How nervous are you right now? |

- Personally, I would end the activity here and announce that you will present the class findings of the two questionnaires at the beginning of the following class.

As you may have noticed, the third question (How nervous are you right now?) was presented twice. The theory behind this is that students' nervousness may, in fact, decrease during the course of this exercise!

## Class 2

1 Before class, organize your data. Data for Questionnaire 2 can be calculated fairly quickly, and you can simply prepare the mean scores. The either/or questions for Questionnaire 1 can also be done quickly. Regarding the short responses for Questionnaire 1, group similar answers first and then order them from highest to lowest. You could also provide columns with percentages.

2 Present the data from both questionnaires. In general, try to present the data in a simple way so the students clearly understand (i.e. there is no need to describe your methodology or run a complicated statistical analysis). Make sure the students have a copy of the

**TABLE 3.3** Questionnaire 3

| Item no. | Questions |
|---|---|
| 1 | Why do you think people get nervous in English class? |
| 2 | What can students do to help nervous students? |
| 3 | What can the teacher do to help nervous students? |
| 4 | What can nervous students do to help themselves? |
| 5 | *Compose and answer your own question* |

original questionnaires. There is a mock data set (i.e. made-up results) for a class of twenty students in Appendix.

3   Guide students through a pair-work discussion activity. After you present your findings, again split the class into pairs and distribute Questionnaire 3 (Table 3.3) (**1 per pair**). In this case (unlike Questionnaires 1 and 2), I have found that only distributing one questionnaire per pair increases engagement between students for this activity.

4   Instruct the pairs to discuss the questions and nominate one person to be the scribe. As pairs are going through this speaking activity, walk around the class, monitoring and supporting.

5   As pairs finish, instruct the scribes to write their answers on the board in columns. This is an efficient and fun way for the class to review answers together.

6   After each pair has written their answers on the board, lead the class in a discussion going over each question. At this stage, you could ask each pair to provide the question they composed and the corresponding answer. Avoid this if you think some students are experiencing high levels of FLA.

7   To finish class 2, assign a reflective writing assignment (at least 100 words). Here is a suggestion, but feel free to use your own:

Write about what you learned about nervousness and English class. What was interesting or the most surprising? Do you think this is an important topic? Why/why not?

## Follow-up tasks and suggestions

- If you find the activity useful, you may want to revisit it at the end of the term to see if student perspectives have shifted. Moreover, if you wanted to replicate or expand on my previous study in 2018 (i.e. collecting state self-reports of nervousness over twelve weeks), feel free! In that case, make sure you allow one class towards the end of the term to go over the data sets and lead the class in reflection and discussion activities.

- I haven't provided explicit instructions on pre-teaching vocabulary – just use whichever method you and your students are most comfortable with. I don't think it is necessary to pre-teach 'foreign language anxiety' nor spend a lot of time talking about the background or why you are doing it. I would recommend jumping right in by saying something like: *Do any of you get nervous when you speak (\*insert foreign language)? Well, today, we will be doing an activity where we learn more about it.* Remember that anxious students in your class may not respond to this prompt, and that's OK. The question simply sets the context for the lesson.

- After going through the data, you may identify a student or group of students who reported high levels of FLA. It is better not to approach these students during class or when they are around fellow students. I have found that it is always better to approach an anxious student casually before or after class with a brief positive comment. Something like, '*I noticed your speaking is getting better*', or '*Good job yesterday with your pair work dialogue*'. I learnt this tip from John Wiltshier on the 'Lost in Citations' podcast (Episode 21).

- From my data collection in 2018, I noticed that self-reports of FLA gradually decreased over the course of the term. You may also find this to be true. For extreme cases of FLA, try to avoid individual presentations in front of the class. An alternative is an individual presentation in front of a group of three to four students. Also, try to pair shy students with gregarious students. I have found that classes that have high student-student rapport help students with FLA. So, over the course of the term, keep working to build a supportive, friendly atmosphere between students. This is as much your job as teaching linguistic skills.

## Recommended reading

Shachter, J. (2018), 'Tracking and quantifying Japanese English language learner speaking anxiety', *The Language Teacher*, 42: 3–7.
This article describes how the NM was employed over three language classes ($n = 75$) at a public Japanese university. Self-reports of FLA decreased 'without intervention' over the period of data collection (twelve weeks). The largest decrease occurred between the first and second weeks. At the end of this paper,

I argue that the NM itself may have acted as an intervention. I hope to test this hypothesis in a future research project.

**Voss, C. and T. Raz (2016),** *Never Split the Difference: Negotiating as if Your Life Depended on It.* **US: Random House.**
Although not labelled as such, this is a really interesting book on psychology. Using his experience as an F.B.I. hostage negotiator, Chris Voss now runs a corporate consulting company named The Black Swan Group. In the book, you can learn about what goes on behind the scenes in high and low-stakes negotiations. Trained negotiators leverage psychological tactics to produce positive outcomes. You might be asking how this relates to FLA. In short, the use of self-reports as an intervention is tangentially related to tactics described in this book.

## References

Harlan, B. and M. Khurana (2022), '6 Tips to Help You Overcome Your Fear of Flying', NPR, 13 June. Available online: https://www.npr.org/2022/06/09/1103923813/get-over-a-fear-of-flying-exposure-therapy (Accessed 1 August 2022).

Harumi, S. (2011), 'Classroom Silence: Voices from Japanese EFL Learners', *ELT Journal*, 65 (3): 260–9.

Kassam, K. S. and W. B. Mendes (2013), 'The Effects of Measuring Emotion: Physiological Reactions to Emotional Situations Depend on Whether Someone Is Asking', *PloS One*, 8 (6): e64959.

Lebra, T. S. (1987), 'The Cultural Significance of Silence in Japanese Communication', *Multilingua*, 6 (4): 343–57.

MacIntyre, P. D. (2017), 'An Overview of Language Anxiety Research and Trends in Its Development', in C. Gkonou, M. Daubney and J. M. Dewaele (eds), *New Insights into Language Anxiety*, 11–30, Bristol: Multilingual Matters.

Maher, K. and J. King (2020), 'Observing Anxiety in the Foreign Language Classroom: Student Silence and Nonverbal Cues', *Journal for the Psychology of Language Learning*, 2 (1): 116–41.

Matsumoto, D. (1991), 'Cultural Influences on Facial Expressions of Emotion', *The Southern Communication Journal*, 56 (2): 128–37.

Matsumoto, D., T. Consolacion, H. Yamada, R. Suzuki, B. Franklin, B., S. Paul … and H. Uchida (2002), 'American-Japanese Cultural Differences in Judgements of Emotional Expressions of Different Intensities', *Cognition and Emotion*, 16 (6): 721–47.

Shachter, J. (2018), 'Tracking and Quantifying Japanese English Language Learner Speaking Anxiety', *The Language Teacher*, (42): 3–7.

Şimşek, E. and Z. Dörnyei (2017), 'Anxiety and L2 Self-Images: The Anxious Self', in C. Gkonou, M. Daubney and J.M. Dewaele (eds), *New Insights into Language Anxiety*, 51–69, Bristol: Multilingual Matters.

Stieger, M., C. Flückiger, D. Rüegger, T. Kowatsch, B. W. Roberts and M. Allemand (2021) 'Changing Personality Traits with the Help of a Digital Personality Change Intervention', *Proceedings of the National Academy of Sciences*, 118 (8): e2017548118.

Voss, C. and T. Raz (2016), *Never Split the Difference: Negotiating as if Your Life Depended on It*, US: Random House.

# Appendix

**TABLE 3.4** Mock data set for Questionnaire 1

| | | | |
|---|---|---|---|
| 1a)<br>yes – 8, no – 12 | 1b)<br>yes – 12, no – 8 | 1c)<br>USA – 5<br>Korea – 4<br>France – 3 | |
| 2a)<br>yes – 5, no – 15 | 2b)<br>high school – 3<br>part-time job – 2 | | |
| 3a)<br>yes – 7, no 13 | 3b)<br>high school – 3<br>part-time job – 2<br>train station (giving directions) – 2 | 3c)<br>movies<br>music<br>food<br>Japan<br>America<br>Directions | |
| 4a)<br>yes – 10, no – 10 | 4b)<br>yes – 15, no – 5 | 4c)<br>yes<br>kind (10)<br>funny (5) | no<br>no smile (5) |
| 5a)<br>yes – 20 | 5b)<br>yes – 8, no – 12 | 5c)<br>yes<br>friendly (4)<br>motivating (4) | no<br>strict (5)<br>tests (4)<br>difficult (3) |
| 6a)<br>yes – 20 | 6b)<br>yes – 12, no – 8 | 6c)<br>yes<br>funny (5)<br>good story teller (4)<br>talked to me (3) | boring (4)<br>tests (4) |
| 7<br>yes – 4, no – 16 | | | |
| 8a)<br>yes – 10, no – 10 | 8b)<br>Reading – 5<br>listening – 5 | | |
| 9a)<br>yes – 20 | 9b)<br>Marvel<br>Fast and the furious<br>Black Mirror | | |
| 10<br>nice classmates – 10, nice teacher – 10 | | | |

**PART TWO**

# The Classroom Environment: Creating a Positive Learning Space

# CHAPTER FOUR

# 'I am worthy and special; I am not afraid to speak.':

# Creating a sense of belonging to increase students' self-confidence

### Shatha Talib Al-Ahmadi

As a teacher of English as a second or foreign language, at some point in your career, you have definitely encountered learner silence. Each of us has faced students' one-word answers, silent responses, or avoidance and lack of oral participation in classroom activities. These reactions are a concern for many teachers. While under the pressure of the curriculum or institutional requirements, some educators might not mind having a quiet audience, for language teachers who believe that oral interaction plays a decisive role in learners' language development (see Izumi, 2003; Swain, 2005), learners' silence represents a serious concern. Likewise, for passionate teachers who invest much effort into activity preparation and lesson planning, receiving silent responses or lack of participation from the students may hurt the teachers' self-esteem, lead to self-blame or result in a loss of interest in teaching (Smith and King, 2018).

To encourage students to break their silence, some teachers might constantly remind them that their unresponsiveness would result in a possible deduction of marks. Others would appeal to quiet students saying that it is okay to make mistakes: 'just try and speak'. However, from my own experiences of being a silent learner who struggled with anxiety, as well as from my teaching practice and my doctoral fieldwork that focuses on uncovering the reasons for learner silence, I know that anxiety and fear were one of the main reasons behind silent displays. We are talking about a complex phenomenon that cannot be attributed to a single factor. Thus, the central question to be answered in this chapter is: how can we, as teachers, help students to manage their anxiety? How can we encourage them to try and speak, thus taking advantage of the many valuable learning opportunities that may not be available outside the foreign or second language classroom? To answer this question, we should first understand the factors that lead to learner silence. Indeed, recent research on L2 learners' silence uncovered many factors that contribute to learners' unresponsiveness, including psychological attributes and social environment (Al-Ahmadi and King, 2022). Based on this theoretical foundation, in this chapter, I propose an activity that can encourage learners' language production and increase their classroom interactions.

## Background to the approach

Before discussing the practical aspects of the proposed activity, I would like to present two central concepts that are essential for understanding second language learners' silence and anxiety, namely, personal identity and self-esteem. Here, personal identity refers to the sense of who we are: 'I am … ', 'I know … ', 'I can … ', 'I belong to … ', 'I believe in … ', 'This is my role … ', 'This is what I do … ', 'This is my community … ' and 'This is what I am like' (Noonan 2019). Furthermore, self-esteem refers to the deep sense of confidence in the value of one's identity (Noonan 2019). Stated differently, self-esteem is a sense of one's personal identity needed in order to live well and function properly under the complexities of the infinite amount of information and number of tasks one might encounter in daily life.

Research on personal identity among L2 learners revealed the great potential of the concept of identity in terms of its positive impact on learners' motivation to participate in the language classroom. Bonny Norton, a pioneering scholar in the field of L2 learner identity, proposed an understanding of the concept of learner identity as 'how a person understands his or her relationships to the world, how the relationships are constructed through time and space, and how the person understands possibilities for the future' (Norton, 2000: 5). As language learning is not a linear process, but rather a dynamic process involving the interaction of many individuals and contextual factors, L2 learner identity cannot be understood as a static construct. A more realistic view of learner identity would be to see it as multiple and capable of change, as well as a site of struggle in the process of transitioning from the L1 to the L2 identity (Norton, 2000; Nematzadeh and Narafshan, 2020).

If we consider language learners as individuals with a complex social history, as well as a rich background that involves hobbies, skills, interests and infinite potential, we will examine their classroom behaviour in a way that captures learners' complex relationships with the target language and their possible multiple desires and motivations. A central issue to understand in the analysis of L2 learners' behaviour is their learning context. Indeed, the relationship between language learners and their learning environment can have an influence on how learners react to various events during the lesson, as well as determine the level of their participation in classroom activities. This process is called 'situated learning' (Wenger, 1998). Since internal relationships are shaped within the classroom community, it is essential to build a secure and safe environment for interaction and bonding among class members.

How can we use this theory to reduce learners' anxiety about speaking and help them feel more at ease in the classroom community? According to Wenger (1998), one of the most important aspects contributing to the level of individual participation in a classroom community is the sense of belonging to that community. This sense of belonging to a classroom community refers to how each student is perceived by his or her classmates and, more importantly, how learners perceive themselves within that community. In this context, an important role is played by learners' self-esteem, which is seen as an outcome of the self-verification process within a group (Rubio, 2021). Said differently, self-esteem is the confirmation of one's personal perceived characteristics and features, or the feeling of 'this is who I am, and this is what I do', that I discussed previously. This meaning comes from a 'role' that a learner finds herself or himself playing in the classroom. In some cases, the choice of this role can be entirely out of students' own control as it can be imposed upon them by teachers or classmates. As a result, learners might feel that they do not like the role they are given or find themselves trapped within such roles.

To give you an example from my teaching experience, I once had a student named Fatimah (pseudonym), who avoided participation in every kind of classroom activity that required speaking, including even small group and pair activities I designed to encourage quiet students to speak in class. These activities never engaged Fatimah. She consistently remained silent and avoided any oral participation. Yet, one thing I noticed about Fatimah was that she was very popular in her class and had vibrant conversations, in a loud voice, with her classmates once the lesson was over. I interpreted this to mean that all anxiety and silence Fatimah showed during my classes were directly related to elements of our L2 lessons. Indeed, there was a stark contrast between Fatimah showing signs of anxiety and discomfort in the English classroom and Fatimah starting to speak and laugh after the lessons. It was as if she was two different people, or a language learner with two different identities. My subsequent conversation with Fatimah revealed an extremely negative perception that she had of her L2 performance. She told me that she refused to speak in class because she was afraid that the teacher and her classmates would mock her English. Other than in English classes, she described herself as a very strong and motivated student. In English, it was not the case, so the identity role Fatimah found herself playing did not match what she desired for herself and did not resemble the way she really was. If a young woman like Fatimah defines herself only by one dimension of her personality – in this case, her low proficiency in English – this may have a negative impact on how she interacts within the target language community, depriving her of developing her skills in using the language. At this point, we have to answer the question: how can we, as teachers, help our students develop positive L2 identities and make them feel good about themselves in the EFL classroom?

I recommend that one way of doing this is through the process of verification of role identity, which increases individual self-esteem. When an L2 learner's self-esteem is built up by self-verification, it buffers negative emotions elicited by problematic self-verification and results in more interactional communication within the group. Since internal relationships within the group are vital in this context, it is important to increase students' sense of belonging to the group by building up positive images of themselves. These positive images will increase learners' confidence and boost their self-esteem. In other words, self-esteem produced through self-verification can help to maintain and stabilize a group of learners and motivate them to form and maintain relationships (Cast and Burke, 2002).

Feeling accepted by the group and having a feeling of worthiness that brings value to that group result in higher self-esteem. In turn, high self-esteem provides language learners with a strong sense of security which encourages them to take risks and challenges in the language classroom. By promoting our students' positive sense of multiple identities, we, as teachers, honour the uniqueness of their personalities. Indeed, group dynamics proved to be a vital element that directly impacts language learners' speaking (Dörnyei and Murphey, 2003). Anxious learners tend to refrain from speaking because they have negative concepts about themselves and their roles in the group of peers. Therefore, the activity I propose and describe in this chapter is specially designed to help increase learners' sense of positivity and belonging to the group. Needless to say, when I introduced this activity in Fatimah's class, it worked well and helped her to speak more during our English classes. The transition in her interaction pattern in the classroom, and her self-confidence, was remarkable.

# Activity

## *Aims*

The purpose of this activity is to promote learners' self-esteem by developing a sense of belonging to the group they are in, as well as to create and promote a sense of bonding within the class. The activity starts by asking students to share a piece of knowledge they own or believe they know exclusively. This information can concern both the learners themselves and the wider context. In this way, learners get the feeling that their ownership of a piece of knowledge or information is unique, in the sense that other group members don't have this knowledge. When learners pick this 'unique' information they want to share, they will feel encouraged to participate and share it, which gives them a sense of confidence and helps reduce their level of anxiety. In fact, learners pick information on their own, based on their own beliefs, and this is what makes this information so special. Therefore, for this activity, it is essential that the teacher does not set rules that specify the kind of information that the students should share. For this activity to be effective, it is crucial that students have full authority over what to say and what to share. This activity aims to encourage anxious students who normally tend to remain silent and avoid participating in oral activities to eventually take a risk and speak. Importantly, the goal is not to produce a linguistically perfect utterance. In my experience of using this activity in class, I did not object to students' usage of their L1 during the discussion of this activity. Again, the most important goal here is to boost anxious and silent students' self-confidence. This activity is very useful at the beginning of the term and can be used as an ice-breaker to establish a warmer atmosphere among students and between the students and the teacher. This task helps to bring the class community closer together and helps anxious L2 learners to build up a positive self-image.

- **Level:** Any.
- **Materials:** Pen and paper if students want to make notes.
- **Time:** The activity takes around thirty to forty-five minutes, depending on the number of students and the level. I would recommend assigning a whole class period for this activity if possible. While I used this activity with EFL university students, with very positive results, it can also be offered to young learners, possibly with the introduction of fun elements, such as a softball to nominate speakers.

1. First, divide the class into groups of five to six students. Organize all groups to be seated in circles. Then, start the discussion by clarifying the nature and the steps of the activity. Specify that each person will share with peers a piece of information they believe only they know or tell the group a positive characteristic about themselves. To encourage students to start, you may brainstorm some positive characteristics individual students could have. For instance, you might start by saying, 'I am good at listening to others and helping them feel better', and provide a brief example. This should not take more than two minutes. Then, in groups, ask the students to spend five to

seven minutes thinking about a positive feature of their personalities or a piece of information they have.

2. Next, it is time for students to start sharing their ideas within their groups. There are two versions of this step: (i) students can either share their ideas with their groups only, so only group members will hear individual contributions or (ii) the whole class will listen as each student shares her or his information. It is up to the teacher to decide which works best. In my experience, I prefer the first option, as it gives more privacy to anxious students, and they are more likely to share. After all groups exchange their ideas (fifteen to twenty minutes), ask if anyone would like to share their contribution with the class. This should be left entirely to the students' preference. In my experience, students tend to share personal information about their conditions, homes, pets or practical knowledge that they have learned while travelling or working part-time. It is interesting to observe which side of their personality each student decides to show to the class. Students will also have the choice to speak in their L1 and then ask the teacher or peers to help with translation. To reiterate, the goal here is to help students to build up a positive self-image in the classroom community.

3. Ask the students to name a weakness they believe they have and their feared emotions related to it. Again, your demonstration with a personal example is helpful in this context. For instance, you might say, 'I am afraid to mispronounce a word when I speak; I fear that everyone might laugh at me.' This demonstration will encourage students to speak openly about their most feared prediction. Give the students time to think about what they would like to share. This part of the activity should take about five to seven minutes.

4. Before students start sharing their weaknesses with their groups, you will clarify that all students other than the speaker are encouraged to raise their hands and propose solutions to their classmates' feelings. This solution should start with the sentence, 'If I were you, I would …..' As I observed in practice, many students get truly empathetic and emotional during this stage. This part is very useful to boost students' confidence in both roles – the one who shares his or her weakness and the one who gives advice. For Fatimah, she reported that this was her favourite part of the activity. She enjoyed giving advice to her peers when they shared their weaknesses. She found her voice; her confidence really came through during that part of the activity. In a way, the activity provided a space for her to bring a dimension of her personal identity into the classroom, which helped empower her and make her feel more confident.

## Suggestions

This activity has greatly helped me to increase the level of students' participation, involvement and interaction in my classes and led to noticeable results and changes in students' attitudes towards themselves and their peers. However, not all students welcomed the idea of sharing personal information or ideas, even in small groups. This might happen, and it is okay. I would not recommend insisting that such students participate. Most of them only need more time to listen and test the atmosphere, and then they will eventually participate in the proposed activity. It can be helpful in this case also to offer an option for the reluctant ones to write their contributions down as a dialogue until they are encouraged to read and share out loud. This step could give especially anxious students the needed time and privacy prior to speaking.

## Recommended reading

Rubio, F. (2021), *Self-Esteem and Foreign Language Learning*. Cambridge: Cambridge Scholars Publishing.
This book is one of the very few sources that focuses specifically on the aspect of self-esteem in FL learning. It is written from a practical pedagogical perspective with a strong focus on classroom application. The book also includes practical strategies that are helpful to EFL educators.

Wright, A. (2021), 'Implementation and Classroom Application: Stories: Who We Are and Are We OK?', In F. Rubio (ed), *Self-Esteem and Foreign Language Learning*, 144–59, Cambridge: Cambridge Scholars Publishing.
This particular chapter sheds light on the cultural differences in perceptions of the meaning of personal identity and self-esteem. It gives language teachers who are dealing with students from different backgrounds a deeper understanding of the potential cultural meanings of an individual's sense of personal identity and self-esteem.

## References

Al-Ahmadi, S.T. and J. King (2022), 'Silence behind the Veil: An Exploratory Investigation into the Reticence of Female Saudi Arabian Learners of English', *TESOL Quarterly*.

Cast, A. D. and P. J. Burke (2002), 'A Theory of Self-Esteem', *Social Forces*, 80 (3): 1041–68.

Dörnyei, Z. and T. Murphey (2003), *Group Dynamics in the Language Classroom*, Cambridge: Cambridge University Press.

Izumi, S. (2003), 'Comprehension and Production Processes in Second Language Learning: In Search of the Psycholinguistic Rationale of the Output Hypothesis', *Applied Linguistics*, 24 (2): 168–96.

Julian, C. and E. R. Diaz (2021), 'Practical Activities to Promote Teenagers' Self-Esteem in the EFL Classroom', in F. Rubio (ed), *Self-Esteem and Foreign Language Learning*, 153–91, Cambridge: Cambridge Scholars Publishing.

Nematzadeh, A. and M. Haddad Narafshan (2020), 'Construction and Re-construction of Identities: A Study of Learners' Personal and L2 Identity', *Cogent Psychology*, 7 (1): 1823635.

Noonan, H. (2019), *Personal Identity*. London: Routledge.

Norton, B. (2000), *Identity and Language Learning: Gender, Ethnicity and Educational Change*, Harlow, UK: Pearson Education/ Longman.

Rubio, F. (2021), 'Self-Esteem and Foreign Language Learning: An Introduction', in F. Rubio (ed), *Self-Esteem and Foreign Language Learning*, 2–12, Cambridge: Cambridge Scholars Publishing.

Smith, L. and J. King (2018), 'Silence in the Foreign Language Classroom: The Emotional Challenges for L2 Teachers', in J. D. Martinez Agudo (ed), *Emotions in Second Language Teaching*, 323–40, Cham, Switzerland: Springer.

Swain, M. (2005), 'The Output Hypothesis: Theory and Research', in E. Hinkel (ed), *Handbook of Research in Second Language Teaching and Learning* (Vol. 2), 471–83, New York: Routledge.

Wenger, E. (1998), *Communities of Practice: Learning, Meaning, and Identity*, Cambridge: Cambridge University Press.

Wright, A. (2021), 'Implementation and Classroom Application: Stories: Who We Are and Are We OK?', in F. Rubio (ed), *Self-Esteem and Foreign Language Learning*, 144–59, Cambridge: Cambridge Scholars Publishing.

# CHAPTER FIVE

# Creating enjoyable learning environments:

# Student-centred socially motivating classrooms

*Wendy Davis*

Anyone who has stepped into a classroom as a student or as a participant in a seminar knows that anxiety can rarely be checked at the door. *How should I act? What do people expect of me? What if I say the wrong thing?* In the foreign language classroom, the added pressure of communicating in the new language can amplify such anxiety. *What if I make a mistake? Will my classmates laugh at me? Should I stay quiet to avoid embarrassment?*

Put yourself back in the shoes of a student. What is the best learning environment for you? Do you feel anxious walking into a classroom of strangers? What makes learning with others enjoyable for you? What if you were able to share how you could best enjoy and improve your learning with fellow classmates and vice versa? Imagine you and your classmates being able to adjust your behaviour in ways that would help you, and reciprocally support each other's learning. In this chapter, you will learn how to foster this type of student-generated, socially motivating classroom through the use of Ideal Classmates (IC).

After using the IC activity, my students told me they found learning more enjoyable. They thought about others more, they cooperated and taught each other, and students started mirroring the positive behaviours of their peers. This short twenty-minute activity could help foster a positive learning space for your own students to feel less anxious and more comfortable actively participating in class.

Suitable for both young or older students, foreign and second language classrooms, and small and large groups; the IC activity can be used in any type of group learning environment. While some adjustments may need to be made to adapt it for young learners or in an ESL classroom, the activity itself can be administered easily. It can consist of a simple reflection and discussion among students or can be expanded into other activities as desired. This chapter will explain the IC activity and discuss some ways in which teachers can utilize IC as a seed for other activities.

## Background to the approach

IC developed out of the possible selves theory (Markus and Nurius, 1986) and the L2 motivational self system (Dörnyei, 2009). While these theories are concerned with ideal images of ourselves, Ideal Classmates is focused towards one's peers or ideal others. Reciprocal idealizing (Murphey, Falout, Fukuda and Fukada, 2014: 242–53) is the notion that if students know how their classmates want them to act, they will adjust their behaviour in order to meet those expectations. At the university level, Murphey et al. found 'a resonating group-framed motivational effect in which students tended to become more helpful and resourceful for each other' (2014: 242). Likewise, in the first study applying IC at the junior high school level in Japan, students' self-reported changes in behaviour included increased cooperation, teaching among friends, having more positive attitudes towards English and greater empathy for others (Davis, 2019: 3–10). Related to FLA, other reported changes in behaviour were noted: 'I started to think I could do this before thinking I couldn't', and 'I could think about others more' (Davis, 2018: 6). The findings also showed a 'strong correlation between students' perception of their classmates' behaviour and their own' (Davis, 2018: 5). Essentially, students recognized that their changes in behaviour mirrored those of their classmates, which is what Murphey et al. (2014: 242–53) found.

Adding Ideal Classmates to my teaching approach came at a time when I was struggling to get students to gel in class. In an all-girls junior high English Conversation class, where students didn't know each other from the start, where they had to work together in class and practise outside of class and when class time was limited, it was a challenge to get students working well together quickly. After meeting Tim Murphey and his team, I was encouraged by the results they achieved from using IC. If students want to know how they should act and how others want them to act, they should ask each other. But discussions like that can be awkward and time-consuming, and likely to be unproductive for young, anxious learners facing a new class environment. The activity that will be explained in this chapter is straightforward, highly effective and not overly time-consuming.

Prior to using IC, it was not uncommon to have four or five students in a class of twenty refuse to participate in class activities. After IC, there were only one or two out of 100. Furthermore, I could see a change from the previous years in just how quickly students bonded and began cooperating in class. This allowed me to get students working faster together in class and making contact outside of class. Students spoke up more in class and could understand better that if they didn't support one another, making conversation in class was not really possible. Shy and anxious students tried harder, I believe, because they knew (after reading their classmates' responses) that making mistakes was natural and that their classmates were not going to laugh at them. Being aware through reading their classmates' IC responses and observing in class that they were acting in the same manner as their IC responses noted seemed to have eased the anxiety of participating for most students.

# Activity

## *Aims*

The aim of IC is to offer students the opportunity from the outset of the course to share, anonymously, what their classmates could do to help them learn better and have fun. By doing this, students actively participate in the shared imaginings, which can lead to actual lived experiences with and among their peers in the classroom.

- **Level:** Any.
- **Materials:** The activity itself requires either an online form (such as Google Forms or Survey Monkey) or photocopied handout. First, the paper form will be explained, and then the digital format will follow.
- **Time:** This activity needs to be carried out over at least two classes, but does not need to take up the whole class time.

## Photocopied handout procedure

1. To begin, create a simple worksheet with the following statement in both English and the first language of the students. You may change the word 'English' to suit whatever language you are teaching. It is recommended that several bilingual people check the translation to ensure the most meaningful prompt. Below the prompt, put five to six blank lines for students to write their responses.

> *Describe a group of classmates that you could learn English well with. What would you all do to help each other learn better and more enjoyably? (Students' native language follows here.)*

At the beginning of the first lesson, even before class introductions, hand out one sheet to each student. Read the prompt aloud to the students. In a foreign language classroom, students should answer in their native language. In a second language classroom, this might prove difficult if there are several different native languages, so it might be best to encourage students to write in English (with the aid of a translation program such as DeepL or Google Translate – while not ideal, it might be helpful for some students).

Tell them this is an individual exercise and it is anonymous, so do not write their name. Give students five to ten minutes to write their answers. Collect the papers, clip them together and note the day/time of the class to avoid mixing up responses from other classes. Proceed with your lesson as planned. Table 5.1 contains common responses from students.

2. Before the next class, photocopy one set of all of the responses for each student (be sure to check there are no names on the responses), so they can read what each of their classmates wrote. This is the most time-consuming part, but necessary for the next step.

**TABLE 5.1** Top 16 responses from students to the IC questionnaire

| | |
|---|---|
| 1 | Help each other |
| 2 | Get actively involved |
| 3 | Enjoy English |
| 4 | Listen to the teacher |
| 5 | Do your best |
| 6 | Speak English a lot |
| 7 | Do the important things first |
| 8 | Give your opinion |
| 9 | Try to teach friends |
| 10 | Get to know each other |
| 11 | Apply English to real life |
| 12 | Think about others |
| 13 | Don't be afraid to make mistakes |
| 14 | Smile when talking |
| 15 | Talk with the teacher |
| 16 | Don't laugh at others' mistakes |

3. In the second lesson, remind the students of the activity and hand out one set of responses to each student. Ask them to read through the responses quietly for four to five minutes (maybe longer for second language learners who are not reading in their native language).

Then have students discuss the responses in small groups and talk about how they might act upon the ideas their classmates wrote. Some questions you can pose to students who have trouble getting the discussion going are, 'What can you do to encourage your classmates who are shy or anxious to speak? In what ways is our own behaviour helpful or hurtful in the classroom?' Finally, take up some answers so the entire class can share their ideas. In total, depending on the talkative nature of the class, this might take about fifteen to twenty minutes.

## Digital format procedure

1. In digital form, the same prompt instructions are given to the students on the first day of class. Instead of a paper form, share an online form (Google Forms or Survey Monkey) with the students (either via email, QR code or AirDrop). If you are doing this activity with several classes, it is recommended to add a class code or day/time question to the form so you can sort each class's responses easily. Ask students to submit their answers and continue the lesson as planned. If students do not have a tablet, smartphone and/or Wi-Fi, you can give them a paper copy or ask them to complete the form later.

2. Before the second lesson, download the responses into a spreadsheet format so all responses can be read easily, and save it as a PDF file in addition to the spreadsheet. Saving it as a PDF makes it easier to share as some smartphones or tablets may not have a spreadsheet app. At the beginning of the lesson, remind students of the activity and share the PDF file (either via email, QR code or AirDrop) with every student. It is recommended to have a few paper copies on hand in case students do not have their tablets or phone. Ask them to read through the responses quietly for four to five minutes. Then have students discuss the responses in small groups and talk about how they might act upon the ideas their classmates wrote. Finally, elicit some answers so the entire class can share their ideas. In total, depending on the talkative nature of the class, this might take about fifteen to twenty minutes. In a second language setting where several different native languages are at play, students should be able to copy and paste the responses into DeepL or Google Translate to help with understanding.

## Follow-up tasks and suggestions

- Periodically throughout the semester, ask students to check their progress by giving them a few minutes to think about what they have been doing to help their classmates learn better and more enjoyably. Ask students to discuss this in small groups. Then elicit some answers on the board and discuss them as a class. This step has been very useful in classrooms where cooperation, collaboration and participation are noticeably lacking.

- An additional activity for younger learners (elementary to junior high) is to have them create a group (or class) vision board. If there is space on the walls for one or more poster displays, students can be creative (and use English) to make a visual representation of the ideas they came up with after reading their classmates' responses. These posters can include self-made rules, goals and/or encouragements. Photos of the students can also be included, giving them ownership over their ideas. If wall space is not available, you can instead put students in small groups (or teams) and have them create a small vision board to be displayed in the centre of their group desk during class. This display can be made using an A4-sized piece of cardboard (ones used to ship books are handy and sometimes readily available at the start of the school year when textbooks are delivered). Using a box knife, perforate the cardboard so it can be folded into a tent. Give students a piece of blank paper (the same size as the cardboard) and have them write in English (and their native language if desired) their group rules, goals and encouragements. Have them come up with a group name and use as much colour and creativity as they can. Ask them to display their vision board at the start of each class and rotate the responsibility among group members of keeping the vision board until the next class. Some examples of vision boards can be found on the Ideal Classmates online resources page.

- For older learners (high school and above), you can ask students to keep a class journal reflecting on their feelings about each lesson (their own behaviour and attitude, their classmates' behaviour, their level of enjoyment, etc.). This activity gives students writing practice and helps the teacher better understand the group dynamics and levels of interaction and cooperation. Teachers should collect the notebook and reply with encouraging comments and advice every two to four weeks to keep students actively writing and reflecting. If you notice frequent discord among students, it may be helpful to facilitate short discussions using the responses from the second lesson to encourage students to get back to helping each other learn better and more enjoyably.

# Recommended reading

Davis, W. (2019), 'Fostering a positive learning environment through ideal classmates' in T. Yearley (ed), *Proceedings from the 2018 Tokyo ETJ Expo [Special Issue], Accents Asia*, 12 (1): 1–56.

This article gives a statistical analysis of the action research conducted at the junior high school from which this chapter is based. For teachers who are looking for data that supports the author's belief in the power of Ideal Classmates, this is a short and easy-to-understand research article.

Fukada, Y., T. Fukuda, J. Falout, J. and T. Murphey, (2017), 'Collaboratively visualising possible others', *Learner Development Journal*, 1 (1): 78–93.
This article comes from the team that created Ideal Classmates and will thoroughly explain the background and theoretical basis behind the activity. For those teaching at the university level, the paper covers various activities carried out in the researchers' classrooms. It has a thorough explanation of the critical participatory looping, which will help you find a deeper understanding of Ideal Classmates.

Murphey, T. (2013), 'Ideal Classmates and Reciprocal Idealising', National Foreign Language Resource Center, University of Hawaii. Available online: https://nflrc.hawaii.edu/publications/view/vd25/ (accessed 15 April 2023).
For more visual (or aural) learners (like myself), Tim Murphey has this engaging talk on YouTube going through activities and an explanation of his team's research.

# References

Davis, W. (2018), 'Raising Metacognitive Awareness Using Ideal Classmates', in J. Mynard and I. K. Brady (eds), *Stretching Boundaries. Papers from the Third International Psychology of Language Learning Conference*, IAPLL, 84–6.
Davis, W. (2019), 'Fostering a Positive Learning Environment through Ideal Classmates', in T. Yearley (ed) *Proceedings from the 2018 ETJ Expo*, Accents Asia, 12 (1): 3–10.
Dörnyei, Z. (2009), 'The L2 Motivational Self System', in Z. Dörnyei and E. Ushioda (eds), *Motivation, Language, Identity and the L2 Self*, 9–24, Bristol: Multilingual Matters.
Markus, H. and P. Nurius (1986), 'Possible Selves', *American Psychologist*, 41 (9): 954–69.
Murphey, T., J. Falout, T. Fukuda and Y. Fukada, (2014), 'Socio-dynamic Motivating through Idealizing Classmates', *System*, 45: 242–53.

# CHAPTER SIX

# Flowing classrooms:

# Incorporating principles of flow in classroom activities to reduce FLA

*Fernando D. Rubio-Alcalá*

I concur with Horwitz et al.'s (1986) view that the teacher is the cornerstone of the implementation of strategies and procedures that support anxious learners. Therefore, my approach consists of providing specific instructions for teachers that will lead to states of flow, reducing levels of FLA. One of the best classroom management techniques, strategies or activities to support anxious language learners is one that can be easily implemented in the classroom, and does not require psychological expertise, as ordinary teachers are not psychologists, nor therapists. Furthermore, techniques, strategies or activities should not require a lot of preparation, nor consume extra class time, as the language class syllabus has to cover a lot of material. Thus, teachers need to optimize class time by implementing activities that are designed with a double purpose: learning and enjoyment.

This chapter introduces how to design activities that revolve around techniques based on flow theory for teachers to use in their classrooms. Flow theory is usually encapsulated within the positive psychology current (Dewaele et al., 2019). One important principle of flow theory is that an optimal level of flow is unlikely to occur during an experience that makes learners anxious (Oxford, 2017). However, if flow is promoted in the classroom, students will likely enjoy the experience, reducing their anxiety. This chapter will help teachers to provide a more effective learning experience for students, where academic achievement and enjoyment interplay in the learning process. Cognition and affect are then intertwined in this approach. The key to this approach is for teachers to understand how flow can be promoted and to make some adaptations when preparing activities for the language classroom. As well as including a theoretical background for better comprehension of the topic, this chapter also provides practical advice for incorporating flow into regular classroom activities.

## Background to the approach

I have been working as a language teacher for twenty-seven years now, and for most of that time as a teacher trainer as well. Although time doesn't make me a better teacher, it does provide me with a lot of experience. I have learnt through the years that many language classrooms are full of fears, insecurities and lack of motivation. It is true that learning a foreign language can cause anxiety (Rubio-Alcalá, 2004), or as most researchers explain, language learning is an anxiety-provoking subject. But, conversely, it cannot be denied that not all language classrooms are necessarily anxiety-provoking. What makes a difference? I think that many factors may play a role, and surely one of them is flow.

I read several books written by Mihaly Csikszentmihalyi, one of the founders of flow theory, about twenty years ago, and I was fascinated that a name was given to that floating experience that I have when I am really focused on a task and feel as if I am in a different dimension. I then wondered if this could be applied in the language classroom. As the literature on flow theory at that time was scarce, I decided to make my own approach and take it into my classroom, and, of course, evaluate the learning experience to ascertain if my students experienced flow, the factors that intervened and the benefits arising from it. The basic procedure was to incorporate flow factors into the steps of a class activity. For instance, in order to create an environment where it was more likely that students lost track of time because they were engaged in the activity, I did not interrupt them to remind them of the time left. Also, in order to facilitate their awareness of their own progress, I provided a checklist of the activity's steps.

It was interesting to observe that flow could be experienced both in whole class interactions and group interactions. The results, which were published in Rubio-Alcalá (2011), were very positive about students' enjoyment and achievement. Obviously, I was also very satisfied and felt fulfilled with my teaching practice. Accordingly, I decided to share my experience with colleagues. So that other teachers could replicate this experience, it was important to make feasible pedagogical adaptations and employ techniques that teachers could easily implement in their classrooms. This chapter explains how to do this.

Language teachers can help lower anxiety levels in their classes by implementing direct and indirect strategies. Direct strategies are forms of training or counselling that directly address anxiety (e.g. Rational Emotive Therapy, Psycho-social Training), whereas indirect strategies refer to educational interventions (Toyama and Yamazaki, 2021) that are part of the instruction, such as classroom management, teaching methods, tasks instructions, teacher-student rapport and so on. My activity addresses indirect strategies and focuses on implementing flow instructional practices.

The role of flow and its influence on learning are of central importance to positive psychology (Csikszentmihalyi, 2014). Flow is a state of optimal experience characterized by intense focus and complete involvement in a task. Flow theory identifies several conditions for flow to occur (e.g. Csikszentmihalyi, 1975; Jackson and Marsh 1996): (a) a perceived balance of skills and challenge, (b) opportunities for intense concentration, (c) clear task goals, (d) feedback that one is succeeding at the task, (e) a sense of control over oneself and the environment, (f) a loss of self-consciousness, (g) a transformation of time, (h) merging of action and awareness and (i) the autotelic or enjoyable nature of the experience. Czimmermann and Piniel (2016) found that the key to generating flow experiences in the language classroom was providing learners with sufficient time to build concentrated engagement with motivating and manageable tasks, and giving learners sufficient autonomy to execute them without teacher interference (in Dewaele et al., 2019).

Conditions (a) and (i) are particularly connected with reducing anxiety. Firstly, when the balance of skills and challenge does not meet because the challenge is high and the skills are low, the learner may experience anxiety (Csikszentmihalyi, 1975). Csikszentmihalyi (1990) explained how different emotional states arise from the interaction of challenge and skill level:

- A high task challenge and a low skill level lead to anxiety.
- A high task challenge and moderate skill level lead to arousal.
- A high task challenge and a high skill level lead to flow.
- A moderate task challenge and low skill level lead to worry.
- A moderate task challenge and high skill level lead to control.
- A low task challenge and a low skill level lead to apathy.
- A low task challenge and a moderate skill level lead to boredom.
- A low task challenge and a high skill level lead to relaxation.

Secondly, the autotelic experience is intrinsically rewarding, and naturally inverse to experiencing anxiety (i.e. you cannot feel safety and fear simultaneously). When an individual is in flow, a strong focus is directed to the task at hand, and the loss of self-consciousness prevents negative feelings towards oneself from arising. For example, when a student is in flow, they tend to only pay total attention to doing the task, and possible negative feelings that might interfere are minimized. Additionally, the recognition of gradually succeeding at the task facilitates positive feelings of competence and boosts energy to accomplish the task. Furthermore, when students savour their positive performance there is an increase of psychological well-being, and negative emotions decrease (Bryant and Veroff, 2019). Enjoyment has also been found to outweigh anxiety (Dewaele and Alfawzan, 2018). In sum, the flow experience can be an effective filter for anxiety.

Flow can happen in many different classroom situations. In fact, flow studies have shown that flow can happen in the realization of different skills. Therefore, the possible classroom applications are quite varied. For instance, flow was reported in reading (McQuillan and Conde, 1996), writing (Abbot, 2000), speaking (Rubio-Alcalá, 2011), listening (Toscano Fuentes and Fernández Corbacho, 2010) and doing computer activities (Trevino and Webster, 1992). Furthermore, Rubio-Alcalá (2011) and Sparling and MacIntyre (2023) observed that flow can be experienced in groups. My students have indeed reported experiencing flow when doing different tasks. So, rather than describing a specific activity, I am going to go through the steps of how to incorporate flow in a typical class speaking activity, in this case one which involves searching for song lyrics. The steps will fit any activity with a similar structure or purpose. This is to act as a guide when lesson planning and creating materials, and to give ideas on making flow a regular feature in your classes.

# Activity

## *Aims*

How to set conditions to optimize flow in the classroom.

- **Level:** Language can be adapted to the level
- **Materials:** Checklist and table for self-assessment
- **Time:** n/a

## 1 Preparation

Divide the class into groups of three or four students. Try to make mixed-ability groups, and pay special attention to the level of difficulty of the tasks, as a **perceived balance of skills and challenge** should be met. In the design of tasks, likewise, grade the level of difficulty from LOTS (lower order thinking skills: defining, classifying, finding, labelling ...) to HOTS (higher order thinking skills: evaluating, hypothesizing, creating ... ; cf. Bloom's taxonomy).

## 2 Preliminary instructions

Explain to your students the working objectives and learning outcomes of the activity. All objectives should be listed and handed out (whether paper or digital) to every group in a checklist format so that students can **have clear task goals** and **feedback of the accomplishment** of those steps (or tasks), as Figure 6.1 shows. Provide specific websites or platforms where students can find the information to help focus and avoid wandering around other non-relevant sites (for Step 3).

In order to cater for collaborative learning, propose roles for the members of the group to choose from. I usually suggest the *director* (to energize and manage work, and to control the time), the *writer* (to record and write the

**FIGURE 6.1** *Checklist with clear task goals to provide progress feedback (my own elaboration).*

| | Instructions | Tick when accomplished |
|---|---|---|
| 1 | Once you are assigned to a group, decide the role (director, English sheriff, writer, speaker). | |
| 2 | Calculate and allocate the time you need for the following steps (total time: 30 minutes). | |
| 3 | Look for songs on the internet and select one song that relates to the class topic. | |
| 4 | Read the lyrics carefully, underline specific mentions to the matter, and choose vocabulary and expressions. | |
| 5 | Evaluate your performance (role performance and contribution to the group). | |
| 6 | Hand in/upload your group's work. | |
| 7 | Presentation stage: play the song to the class and show the lyrics to your classmates (vocabulary, expressions and non-verbal aspects). | |

FIGURE 6.2 *Table for self-assessment.*

| Names | Roles | Mark for role performance (0–5) | Mark for contribution (0–5) | Total mark |
|---|---|---|---|---|
| | Director | | | |
| | Writer | | | |
| | English sheriff | | | |
| | Speaker | | | |

product), the *speaker* (to report the product to the class) and the *language sheriff* (to encourage L2 production and control voice volume). You could encourage the learners to do this part of the activity in the target language too. Make sure they understand the roles, and include a table in handouts where students have to include their names next to their role. The table could also contain a space for writing an evaluation for both effort and role performance, as shown in Figure 6.2.

Control external noise and other possible distractions as much as possible so that **opportunities for concentration** are provided. Also, make clear the time allotted for the activity (or subtasks) at the beginning, and avoid giving reminders about how much time the students have left, so that the **experience of transformation of time** is sustained. Note that activities usually take longer than expected, and so allow a reasonable amount of time, especially for exploration and discovery activities (as Ghani and Deshpande, 1994, point out, students reach flow in tasks where they need to explore or discover). Also, avoid competition among the groups, as competition may cause anxiety (Andrés and Arnold, 2009; Gilbert et al., 2009). This would prevent **the autotelic or enjoyable nature of the learning experience** to occur.

## 3 During the activity

In order to maintain **concentration** avoid too many class announcements and provide explanations and queries privately to the groups. You can then take advantage and provide **positive and sincere feedback** on the work, but not addressed to individual students, as we pursue a **loss of self-consciousness**.

## 4 Students report their findings

Before students report to the class, prepare an activity for the student listeners to be active while the groups are presenting – try to avoid passive listening. For instance, in this example of searching for lyrics students have to guess if the songs ascribe to a particular world view. Also, you could tell them to note specific related vocabulary or structures found in songs. You may also ask students to vote for the best song they heard. Finally, ask for opinions and offer conclusions about the matter. You may include groups' evaluations of the presentations or oral reports and promote positive praise from the classmates.

Rubio-Alcalá and Tamayo-Rodríguez (2012) note that a source of anxiety is found in the confusion that students have when the teacher's methodology is based primarily on the development of oral skills but the assessment consists mainly of a written exam. Consequently, ensure you give the project a reasonable overall mark.

Students' output errors can be dealt with altogether at the end of the reports so that the focus is not the students but the language. Accordingly, take notes while students are reporting instead of interrupting.

Horwitz et al. (1986) indicate that the fear of being evaluated is one of the three major causes of anxiety in the FLC, together with oral interaction inhibition and fear of exams. In order to develop a sense of security and naturalness when students have to perform in front of classmates, explain to your students that oral inhibition may come naturally as part of a self-defence mechanism to protect their egos. Thus, students are able to understand the process, be aware of it and accept the feelings that may result. This learning experience will help them cope with communicative difficulties and develop the ability to speak in public.

All these 'ingredients' will likely lead to creating flow, which will surely enrich your students' learning experience, and in turn, your teaching practice.

## Recommended reading

Rubio-Alcalá, F. D. (2011), 'Optimal Experiences in the Foreign Language Classroom: Flow States in Speaking Tasks'. *Anglistik. International Journal of English Studies*, 29 (1) (2011): 63–80. Available online: https://www.researchgate.net/publication/358404277_2011_anglistik_flow_speaking_activities (accessed 21 April 2023).
This article gives a clear overview of the effect of flow in the language classroom. It includes an account of flow theory and language learning and how flow interacts with the different skills. The article includes a study of flow and speaking activities in which students worked in groups under specific methodological instructions, which can serve as an example for implementation.

Rubio-Alcalá, F. D. (2017), 'The Links Between Self-Esteem and Language Anxiety and Implications for the Classroom', in C. Gkonou, M. Daubney and J. M. Dewaele (eds), *New Insights into Language Anxiety: Theory, Research and Educational Implications*, 198–216, Bristol: Multilingual Matters.
This book chapter studies self-esteem and anxiety and their effects in the language classroom. It shows that both factors are inversely

correlated: the higher the self-esteem level, the lower the anxious experience. It also applies theory into practice by proposing ways to cope with anxiety, for instance, by proposing a learner-centred methodology, by improving teachers' rapport or by introducing activities designed with a twofold purpose: language learning and authentic self-esteem generation.

# References

Abbot, J. (2000), '"Blinking out" and "Having the Touch": Two Fifth-Grade Boys Talk about Flow Experiences in Writing', *Written Communication*, 17: 53–92.

Andrés, V. de and J. Arnold (2009), *Seeds of Confidence: Self-Esteem Activities for the EFL Classroom*, Innsbruck: Helbing Languages.

Bryant, F. B. and J. Veroff (2017), *Savoring: A New Model of Positive Experience*, Mahwah, NJ: Lawrence Erlbaum Associates.

Csikszentmihalyi, M. (1975), *Beyond Boredom and Anxiety*, San Francisco: Jossey-Bass.

Csikszentmihalyi, M. (1990), *Flow: The Psychology of Optimal Experience*, New York: Harper and Row.

Csikszentmihalyi, M. (2014), *Flow and the Foundations of Positive Psychology*, New York: Springer.

Czimmermann, E. and K. Piniel (2016), 'Advanced Language Learners' Experiences of Flow in the Hungarian EFL Classroom', in P. D. MacIntyre, T. Gregersen and S. Mercer (eds), *Positive Psychology in SLA*, 193–214, Bristol: Multilingual Matters.

Dewaele, J. M. and M. Alfawzan (2018), 'Does the Effect of Enjoyment Outweigh that of Anxiety in Foreign Language Performance?', *Studies in Second Language Learning and Teaching*, 8 (1): 21–45. Available online: https://doi.org/10.14746/ssllt.2018.8.1.2 (accessed 21 April 2023).

Dewaele, J. M., X. Chen, A. M. Padilla and J. Lake, (2019), 'The Flowering of Positive Psychology in Foreign Language Teaching and Acquisition Research', *Frontiers in Psychology*, 10: 2128, 1–13.

Ghani, J. A. and S.P. Deshpande (1994), 'Task Characteristics and the Experience of Optimal Flow in Human—Computer Interaction', *The Journal of Psychology*, 128 (4): 381–91.

Gilbert, P., K. McEwan, R. Bellew, A. Mills and C. Gale (2009), 'The Dark Side of Competition: How Competitive Behaviour and Striving to Avoid Inferiority Are Linked to Depression, Anxiety, Stress and Self-Harm', *Psychology and Psychotherapy*, 82 (Pt 2): 123–136.

Horwitz, E. K., M. B. Horwitz and J. Cope (1986), 'Foreign Language Classroom Anxiety', *The Modern Language Journal*, 70 (2): 125–32.

Jackson, S. A. and H. Marsh (1996), 'Development and Validation of a Scale to Measure Optimal Experience: The Flow State Scale', *Journal of Sport and Exercise Psychology*, 18: 17–35.

McQuillan, J. and G. Conde (1996), 'The Conditions of Flow in Reading: Two Studies of Optimal Experience', *Reading Psychology: An International Quarterly*, 17: 109–35.

Oxford, R. L. (2017), 'Anxious Language Learners Can Change Their Minds: Ideas and Strategies from Traditional Psychology and Positive Psychology', in C. Gkonou, M. Daubney and J. M. Dewaele (eds), *New Insights into Language Anxiety: Theory, Research and Educational Implications*, 177–97, Bristol: Multilingual Matters.

Rubio-Alcalá, F. D. (2004), *La Ansiedad en el Aprendizaje de Idiomas*, Huelva: Universidad de Huelva.

Rubio-Alcalá, F. D. (2011), 'Optimal Experiences in the Foreign Language Classroom: Flow States in Speaking Tasks', *Anglistik. International Journal of English Studies*, 22 (1): 63–80. Available online: https://www.researchgate.net/publication/358404277_2011_anglistik_flow_speaking_activities (accessed 21 April 2023).

Rubio-Alcalá, F. D. (2017), 'The Links between Self-Esteem and Language Anxiety and Implications for the Classroom', in C. Gkonou, M. Daubney and J. -M. Dewaele (eds), *New Insights into Language Anxiety: Theory, Research and Educational Implications*, 198–216, Bristol: Multilingual Matters.

Rubio-Alcalá, F. D. and L. Tamayo-Rodríguez (2012), 'Estudio sobre Prácticas Docentes en Evaluación de la Lengua Inglesa en la ESO', *Revista de Currículum y Formación del Profesorado*, 16 (1): 295–316.

Sparling, H. and P. MacIntyre (2023), 'A Tartan Weave: Connecting the Experience of Flow in Traditional Music and Gaelic Language in Pursuit of Heritage Language Survival', *Journal of Multilingual and Multicultural Development*, DOI: 10.1080/01434632.2022.2146124.

Toscano Fuentes, C. M. and A. Fernández Corbacho (2010), 'Desarrollo del Estado de Flujo a través de Actividades de Capacidad Auditiva en la Clase de Lengua Extranjera', *Proceedings of the International Symposium 'Evaluación y calidad en la Universidad'*, Universidad de Huelva, 553–62.

Toyama, M. and Y. Yamazaki (2021), 'Classroom Interventions and Foreign Language Anxiety: A Systematic Review with Narrative Approach', *Frontiers in Psychology*, 12: 1–15.

Trevino, L. and J. Webster (1992), 'Flow in Computer-Mediated Communication: Electronic Mail and Voice Mail Evaluation and Impacts', *Communication Research*, 19: 539–73.

# CHAPTER SEVEN

# Making speaking tasks emotionally engaging:

# Incorporating flow principles in task design

*Haydab Almukhaild*

Many language teachers would agree that high levels of anxiety can have a detrimental impact on students' language learning experiences. Students who are apprehensive about speaking in a class discussion can struggle to enjoy or focus on the task at hand as they become vulnerable to anxious thoughts that can hinder their focus or engagement in the task. Anxiety can steal their attention and disrupt their focus. Although foreign language anxiety (FLA) is inevitable in the classroom and none of our students is immune, we can help students to manage anxiety and lessen its negative impact. Researching Saudi English as a foreign language (EFL) learners who often put a ton of pressure on themselves, I have found that providing these students with classroom meaning-based tasks or activities that meet selected elements of *flow* (Csikszentmihalyi, 1990; e.g. interest, control) can make students feel less anxious and encouraged to speak. I have witnessed moments where these anxious students were focusing on what they were doing and enjoying the task at hand. Some of these students told me that they lost track of time at some point during their oral performance and wanted more time to continue speaking about personally relevant tasks that were also at their perceived level of language proficiency. Let me clarify one point here: some of these anxious students were able to experience flow. Flow, a state of optimal experience, generates enjoyment; that pleasure enhances anxious students' relaxation and performance. If you try flow-based activities regularly, not only the quality of your classes may noticeably improve but you may also increase the likelihood of anxious students getting near to a state of flow which may, in turn, help these students engage in positive task-relevant emotions (e.g. enjoyment). Who would not want their students to experience such a high level of engagement in speaking activities?

This chapter offers a wonderful way to bring the spirit of flow into classroom speaking tasks. While drawing on existing research in educational psychology and language education, I will take a deliberately applied approach in discussing selected doable conditions of flow, illustrated by a carefully planned and adapted activity that meets the proposed engagement principles. The suggested activity was implemented in my research exploring the emotional dimension of engagement through the lens of flow among Saudi university learners with FLA.

## Background to the approach

The proposed activity is based on flow theory, which suggests that engagement can be promoted through well-designed or adapted tasks, with four factors being essential: (1) *challenge-skill balance*, (2) *interest*, (3) *control* and (4) *clear goals* (Csikszentmihalyi, 1990; Egbert, 2003). Language education research has demonstrated the powerful influences of these flow conditions on the planning of emotionally engaging learning experiences (e.g. Egbert, 2003). These flow principles could be integrated into your everyday classroom tasks, thus helping learners with FLA cope with anxiety on a regular basis. Considering these factors for learners with FLA can also have a strong impact on their levels of interest and willingness to take part in a speaking task. Different conceptualizations of these principles can help us translate these factors into practice in the context of classroom meaning-based speaking tasks.

The first important condition for facilitating the flow experience is establishing the balance between the *perceived challenge of a task and the learner's skills*. According to Csikszentmihalyi (1990), when individuals perceive the challenge of a task to be beyond their capability, anxiety is most likely to be experienced. This anxiety then shifts attention to the self, creating self-conscious thoughts that hinder engagement and flow (Nakamura and Csikszentmihalyi, 2009). If the challenge is deemed too low, boredom is most likely to be experienced. The flow channel occurs between anxiety and boredom where the perceived challenges are balanced with learners' perceived levels of skills.

Practically, you should plan speaking tasks that could be perceived by anxious learners as neither too difficult nor too easy. Although it is difficult to ensure that all students would perceive the task as matching their levels of skills, three main factors can easily be integrated into task design or task selection to influence learners' perceived level of task difficulty: (1) the number of steps involved in task completion, (2) familiarity of information and (3) the time available to the learner (Nunan, 1989; Abbott, 2019). Firstly, a task that involves many steps could be relatively more challenging than one that contains only a few elements. For example, in classes with mixed levels of students, high-level learners may be given four examples of a group holiday. They are required to determine which holiday was most appropriate for the whole group and then compare the provided cost and information to make suitable choices. Less proficient learners could be asked to discuss two examples of a group holiday and have learners focus merely on the cost of the holiday, thus making the task less difficult. Secondly, learners' familiarity with the task topic is an important consideration to foster a desirable level of task difficulty. A task that requires learners to engage with an unfamiliar topic can be more challenging than one in which the topic is known. Finally, you would not want your students to get anxious due to the limited time available to complete the tasks. Time pressure or time limits can affect students' perception of task difficulty (i.e. as pressure increases, difficulty increases). Therefore, the time available for learners to complete a certain task should match the level of task difficulty and accommodate different student skill levels.

Flow theory suggests that *interest* is also crucial to initiate and maintain positive task experiences. This means that a speaking task should offer opportunities for authentic communication on topics that are familiar to students' knowledge and experiences. Hence, you can create a positive emotional appeal by linking the task topic to students' personal or relevant interests (Renninger and Hidi, 2019). A positive emotional atmosphere is highly unlikely if the task topics are perceived by learners as irrelevant or unappealing. In contrast, when learners have an interest in a certain topic, they are more likely to focus on the task at hand and continue to persevere. By means of illustration, a task that asks learners to tell an anecdote that they think is personally interesting is likely to be more emotionally engaging than a task that asks learners to discuss anecdotes that are irrelevant to students' knowledge and personal experiences. In my experience, learners with FLA reported feeling focused on the task at hand when the task topics were perceived as personally relevant and familiar (e.g. personal stories and problems, holidays, favourite food) which subsequently contributed to their enjoyment. Topic familiarity also determined anxious learners' participation and contribution to the discussion tasks as they found it easier to understand the task content. While you might think that asking students to discuss interesting, personally relevant topics is a very common teaching practice, I would like to emphasize that when students delve more deeply into such task topics, they are more likely to get excited about the task at hand because it taps into their passion. You might also wonder about the feasibility of integrating such a principle in a context where you are required to follow a certain textbook. If you are required to follow the content themes in a certain textbook, it may be valuable to give your students the opportunities and options to generate their own task content. I further explore learners' control over the task content in the following section.

Another powerful element of flow is *control*. While language education research on flow has not been able to determine what kind of control has the most powerful influences to facilitate learners' flow experiences, studies which have focused on examining the affective dimension of engagement have shown that promoting learners' control or choice over the task content is very much likely to increase learners' emotional engagement, particularly in terms of enjoyment and focus on the task at hand (e.g. Lambert and Zhang, 2019; Phung, Nakamura and Reinders, 2021). To clarify, when learners are encouraged to bring their own ideas to the discussion based on their personal choice rather than relying merely on fixed task content supplied by teachers or material writers, students are likely to perceive the task's level of difficulty as matching their level of ability. This in turn can allow learners to adjust or manipulate the complexity of vocabulary and level of background knowledge required to carry out the task, thereby facilitating their task performance. This content, which is based on students' personal choice, creates emotional needs that are very much likely to enhance learners' task experience. In this way, learners are more likely to focus on the task at hand, thus reducing task-irrelevant thoughts such as fear of negative evaluation for making mistakes that have been documented as increasing levels of anxiety (e.g. Horwitz, Horwitz and Cope, 1986).

Of course, you would not expect anxious learners to perceive a task as emotionally engaging without the teacher's intervention such as *clarifying the goal* of the task, which is another important prerequisite for facilitating the flow experience (Csikszentmihalyi, 1990). This means that the task goal should be well articulated so students know what is expected from them, what their roles are and how they should proceed step by step. Having a clear goal will help learners to focus on the task at hand, which, in turn, contributes positively to their emotional responses to the task at hand. Contrastingly, when the task's goal is not clearly defined, it is less likely that learners with FLA would accomplish the task successfully. Hence, teachers should use an appropriate level of the target language that would be easily comprehensible by learners (Mercer and Dörnyei, 2020). In other words, the task goal should be clear, concise and succinct. This sounds obvious but it can make a difference to students' task experience.

To some teachers perhaps, the idea of incorporating flow principles in communicative activities is the norm. However, in many learning contexts, including the Saudi EFL classroom, students are rarely given the opportunity to work on meaning-based learning activities. The teachers tend to dominate classroom interactions and offer limited opportunities for student input. Along with the teacher-centred instruction, the focus on exam preparation rather than communicative use of language has left many students to focus on memorizing grammatical rules and vocabulary items. Rather than mechanical activities, learners with FLA are very much likely to appreciate the opportunities given to them to engage in authentic conversations. Once anxious learners recognize that meaning-based tasks can facilitate their language learning process, greater engagement should occur. These authentic conversations can, in turn, increase the likelihood of students entering a state of flow.

Although I am optimistic that carefully selected or adapted communicative tasks that meet the engagement principles of flow will result in greater enjoyment that would counterbalance the negative levels of anxiety, there are some challenges, including assessing task difficulty and learners' lack of familiarity with communicative tasks. Firstly, in a class of students with different levels of proficiency, you might find it challenging to determine the difficulty of tasks so students of different levels of proficiency are faced with tasks that are perceived as appropriate. While there is still no unified theoretical framework for assessing task difficulty (Ellis et al., 2020), there is some evidence that a range of potential task features, which have been described previously, can be effective to determine the difficulty of tasks in practical settings. Even so, it is worthwhile to remember that the difficulty of a task does not only depend on manipulating the task features (e.g. familiarity of information), but it is vitally important to consider the support provided to students. For instance, you can provide students with a list of words or phrases to help them complete the task or a model of the expected task outcome (Snyder 2018). Secondly, in different teacher-centred learning contexts, some students – and perhaps even the teacher – are unfamiliar with the nature of communicative tasks where students are asked to work in pairs or groups, which can lead them to feel reluctant to speak or feel anxious to take part in the task. Under such circumstances, it is vital to guide students so they know how they should complete learner-centred activities.

While you might be tempted to ask, 'If there are some challenges of using such activities, why bother?' I believe, as previous research has shown (see e.g. Egbert, 2003), that challenging tasks that match learners' current levels of ability, are personally appealing to students and provide options for students to explore multiple discussion options, and can enhance learners' emotional states, increase enjoyment and reduce anxiety in language classrooms. To illustrate how this might work, let us consider an example of a communicative task that was adapted to meet the engagement principles of flow theory, including (1) challenge-skill balance, (2) interest, (3) control and (4) clear goal.

# Activity

## *Aims*

This activity is a problem-solving task adapted from Klippel (1984). It requires learners to share a challenging problem or situation and take turns to suggest ways to help with the problem. The goal of the activity is to provide conditions for anxious students to reach a state of flow, thereby reducing anxiety and increasing engagement.

- **Level:** Intermediate
- **Materials:** None required
- **Time:** Thirty minutes

### Part 1. Pre-task

1. Preface the activity by explaining its goal. Each student describes a challenging situation or a problem that they have experienced inside or outside the classroom (e.g. not being able to focus during classes, feeling anxious during speaking and oversleeping). The others should try to suggest ways and means of helping with the problem.

2. Ask students to form groups of three to four students. Groups with a high number of students with low proficiency levels are asked to think about only a problem that they would like to share, whereas the groups which include students who are relatively more proficient are asked to think about multiple problems in the same length of time (ten minutes). This simple adjustment may help students to perceive the task as matching their current level of skill.

3. Next, tell students a problem that you have faced with language learning. This normalizes sharing challenging situations and helps students see a possible outcome of the task.

4. To provide opportunities for learners to control or tailor the task content, students are allowed to choose a problem(s) that they would like to discuss from examples in a pre-prepared list, or they might want to discuss another topic that is not included in the given task.

5. Encourage students to choose a problem topic based on their interests. Remind students that the topic of the problem or the situation should concern them.

6. Remind students that they have ten minutes to prepare for the task, so they are able to complete the task within the allotted time. Students are

reminded to discuss the task freely and think of it as an opportunity to talk to their peers.

## Part 2. During-task

1. As students take turns to share and discuss their problems or situations, pay close attention to the support students may need. Students should be able to know what is expected from them at all times.

2. Remind students to concentrate on communicative success rather than language form. Do not correct students' mistakes as this could cause students to feel hesitant during their oral performance.

## Part 3. Post-task

Elicit students' responses from each group in plenary mode. Each group should select those problems or situations that they would like to share. This kind of practice in which the teacher and students share their views may not only facilitate positive teacher-student relationships but also help students to become acquainted with each other.

# Follow-up tasks and suggestions

- Provide opportunities for students to reflect on their task experience by asking them to describe the reasons why their oral performance was deemed positive or negative (e.g. how would you describe your feelings towards speaking in the target language after completing this task?). These questions could be shared orally with classmates or completed individually in the form of written self-report sheets. Because learners' emotions are dynamic and vary across different timeframes, it may be necessary to integrate such reflection activities on a regular basis, ideally after each task. Such self-reflective activities may help students recognize their emotions, which may in turn allow them to move forward in their language learning process.

- An engaging activity requires developing a positive teacher-student relationship so that anxious learners are not afraid to speak up and feel confident that their oral performance will not be negatively evaluated by the teacher. It is important, therefore, to ensure that the activity is completed within a supportive atmosphere. To establish and maintain such an atmosphere, I have found it vital to demonstrate that your students' contribution to the task is valuable by listening attentively to their talks, valuing their ideas and frequently asking for their thoughts. You also need to show your trust; show that students can speak without fear of being negatively

- evaluated for making mistakes. This simple act of communication between you and your students can enhance your students' confidence in how they are speaking in the classroom, something that I found works especially well in Saudi Arabia.

- Setting time limits for completing this activity is important, but it is also vital that the time available matches students' level of proficiency. In my experience, I noticed that the limited time available for task completion led some anxious students to complain about the difficulty of the task which, in turn, led them to avoid the task as they felt nervous and scared. On the other hand, for other anxious learners who are relatively more proficient in the target language, the time available for task completion was considered too long, which led them to feel bored. As suggested previously, you might find it useful to ask lower proficiency students to complete a certain part of the activity (e.g. focusing on a problem), whereas learners who demonstrate relatively higher proficiency levels would have the same time to complete several parts of the activity (e.g. discussing two problems).

- You might find it useful to do a survey to find out more about task topics that provoke students' interest at a personal or individual level. This survey can include problems that they would like to solve or questions that they would like to answer. You can use these interests to inform the selection of tasks you choose for your class.

- To promote an appropriate level of task difficulty, it is necessary to consider the task conditions that are likely to influence learners' perceived level of task difficulty. One way in which you can manipulate the level of task difficulty is by varying the number of steps required to complete the task. For example, in the task above, groups with students who are relatively proficient may be asked to provide two problems along with justifications and explanations for their decision to focus on certain problems or situations. To reduce the number of steps for groups with less proficient learners, teachers could ask learners to focus merely on one problem without requiring students to provide an explanation for their decisions.

# Recommended reading

Mercer, S. and Z. Dörnyei (2020), *Engaging Language Learners in Contemporary Classrooms.* Cambridge: Cambridge University Press.
Although this book is not aimed at tackling language anxiety, it provides a great number of engaging principles for teachers who work with disengaged students such as anxious learners. The publication is a teacher-friendly resource that

provides theoretically grounded and practical approaches that can be adopted to foster language learner engagement in different learning contexts.

Oxford, R. L. (2017), 'Anxious Language Learners Can Change Their Minds: Ideas and Strategies from Traditional Psychology and Positive Psychology', in C. Gkonou, M. Daubney, and J. M. Dewaele (eds), *New Insights into Language Anxiety: Theory, Research, and Educational Implications*, 177–97, Bristol: Multilingual Matters.
This chapter, written by a highly regarded scholar, presents interesting interventions to deal with language anxiety. Drawing on positive psychology, Oxford proposes that increasing positive emotional states such as flow, agency and optimism can undo the negative effects of anxiety in language classrooms.

# References

Abbott, M. L. (2019), 'Selecting and Adapting Tasks for Mixed-Level English as a Second Language Classes', *TESOL Journal*, 10 (1): 1–14.
Csikszentmihalyi, M. (1990), *Flow: The Psychology of Optimal Experience*, New York: Harper Perennial.
Egbert, J. (2003), 'A Study of Flow Theory in the Foreign Language Classroom', *The Modern Language Journal*, 87 (4): 499–518.
Ellis, R., P. Skehan, S. Li, N. Shintani and C. Lambert (2020), *Task-Based Language Teaching: Theory and Practice*, Cambridge: Cambridge University Press.
Horwitz, E. K., M. B. Horwitz and J. Cope (1986), 'Foreign Language Classroom Anxiety Scale', *The Modern Language Journal*, 70 (2): 125–32.
Klippel, F. (1984), *Keep Talking: Communicative Fluency Activities for Language Teaching*, Cambridge: Cambridge University Press.
Lambert, C. and G. Zhang (2019), 'Engagement in the Use of English and Chinese as Foreign Languages: The Role of Learner-Generated Content in Instructional Task Design', *The Modern Language Journal*, 103 (2): 391–411.
Mercer, S. and Z. Dörnyei (2020), *Engaging Language Learners in Contemporary Classrooms*, Cambridge: Cambridge University Press.
Nakamura, J. and M. Csikszentmihalyi (2009), 'Flow Theory and Research', in S. J. Lopez and C. R. Snyder (eds), *Handbook of Positive Psychology*, 195–206, Oxford: Oxford University Press.
Nunan, D. (1989), *Designing Tasks for the Communicative Classroom*. Cambridge: Cambridge University Press.
Phung, L., S. Nakamura and H. Reinders (2021), 'The Effect of Choice on Affective Engagement: Implications for Task Design', in P. Hiver, A. H. Al-Hoorie, and S. Mercer (eds), *Student Engagement in the Language Classroom*, 163–81, Bristol: Multilingual Matters.
Renninger, K. and S. E. Hidi (2019), 'Interest Development and Learning', in K. A. Renninger and S. E. Hidi (eds), *The Cambridge Handbook of Motivation and Learning*, 265–90, Cambridge: Cambridge University Press.
Snyder, B. (2018), 'Creating Engagement and Motivation in the Japanese University Language Classroom', in P. Wadden and C. C. Hale (eds), *Teaching English at Japanese Universities*, 137–43, London: Routledge.

**PART THREE**

# Cognitive Techniques: Thinking through Anxiety

# CHAPTER EIGHT

# Stoic sayings for alleviating anxiety:

# Epictetus, Stoic philosophy and the art of cognitive distancing

*Ian Gibson*

There's a humorous observation attributed to the German philosopher Georg Hegel that one thing we learn from history is that we never learn from history. Well, no offence to Hegel but, in a slight rebuttal, I have learned something from history, some very valuable ancient wisdom, drawn from the precepts of Stoic philosophy, and I think this wisdom merits sharing here. It has proved extremely helpful in addressing anxiety both for me and for the students in my classes. As (mea culpa) a rather over-anxious person at times, I personally found these teachings very useful in combating anxiety in everyday life when I first read about them. I then had a slight epiphany and thought it worked for me, so why not extend these principles to my classes? This chapter introduces some activities I have found successful.

The works of Epictetus (Hard and Gill, 2014) were particularly poignant and introduced the concept of cognitive distancing to me: that is, finding space between one's anxiety and the ability to perform the task at hand. Epictetus, a Greek Stoic philosopher (c.50–c.135 CE), was born a slave, later freed and became a highly influential philosopher and teacher. He proved an important philosophical mentor to the Roman Emperor Marcus Aurelius, and Marcus drew reference to Epictetus' instruction many times in *Meditations,* Marcus' classic personal journal (Aurelius, 2013). Epictetus taught his students that anxiety or 'troubling impressions' were products of our own minds. Paradoxically, our own minds were also sources of dealing with these troubling impressions. Additionally, Epictetus taught that if properly trained by memorizing key expressions, students, in turn, could effectively distance themselves from these impressions. One of Epictetus' most famous examples found in his *Enchiridion,* or 'handbook' of dealing with a troubling thought, was to respond to this thought by saying, 'You're an impression and not at all what you appear to be' and to dismiss the thought by declaring, 'That's nothing to me' (Hard and Gill, 2014: 287).

The Stoic precepts for combating anxiety are relatively easy to understand and very effective. Stoicism has many 'laconic' phrases, 'memorable sayings eminently quotable' that helped Stoics to commit key philosophical ideas to memory as a way of coping with 'adverse circumstances' (Gill et al., 2015). When someone complained to the Stoic founder Zeno of the brevity of these philosophical teachings, he replied, 'they were supposed to be concise and that if he could he'd abbreviate the sound of the syllables as well!' (Gill et al., 2015). A good phrase for gaining cognitive distance when dealing with a criticism that you don't feel was justified would be, 'That is how it seemed to [them]' (Hard and Gill, 2014: 300) or it seemed right to them.

As an example of cognitive distancing, I explain to my language classes that when we prepare for a presentation we are often anxious about its success, but in reality, we are more worried about the reception, that is, the reaction of the people we are giving the presentation to, on which we have no control over. Instead, we should prepare well, and whatever the reception is, it is out of our hands, as Epictetus put it, beyond our control. We have, after all, done our work, and we have prepared well; the rest (how our work or task is received) is not up to us.

## Background to the approach

In the 1950s, the psychotherapist Albert Ellis began to adapt the work of Epictetus and others of the Stoic School into what became Rational Emotive Behavioral Thinking (REBT). Later through the work of Aaron T. Beck and his colleagues, Ellis' ideas, drawing on the Stoics, were incorporated into cognitive behavioural therapy (CBT) (Robertson, 2020). Ellis took Epictetus' guiding principle – it is not things in themselves that disturb us, but how we think about these things, as a starting point in treating his patients' emotional distress. Ellis' work followed on from the Swiss psychiatrist Paul Dubois, who employed Socratic questioning with his patients, teaching them the basic principles of a Socratic and Stoic philosophy of life. Here 'a *rational* approach' to psychotherapy emerged, 'which held that many emotional and psychosomatic problems were caused by negative self-talk or autosuggestions, which could be amenable to rational disputation' (Robertson, 2019).

Indeed, the Stoic philosophy (the name taken from the *Stoa Poikile* or 'painted porch' in Athens where the founder, Zeno of Citium, first used to teach) has recently enjoyed a popular revival through such work as the University of Exeter's 2012 project, *Stoicism Today*, and the writings of people such as Donald Robertson, a cognitive behavioural psychotherapist. The Stoic philosophy is an ancient (and modern) source of practical virtue ethics and well-being. It is also a highly functional method for combating anxiety and emotional distress. The work of Epictetus and others of the Stoic school provides compelling techniques for dealing with stressful and emotionally challenging situations as well as a practical guide to living a good life.

For the above reasons, I have chosen to adapt some of these Stoic principles in this chapter. They are easy to implement in classes and highly effective for both students and teachers. As well as teaching several language classes of varying English language ability, I teach peace and conflict studies and civic engagement. These students are fluent or near fluent in English, and the class content is delivered in English. Initially, I found that a lot of the issues in the civic engagement and peace and conflict classes lent themselves to Stoic thought, and I began to underscore key points or learnings with references from the Stoic school.

Over the years, students have remarked that they felt uneasy presenting in front of people or that they were unwilling to speak up in group work. Taking the idea that 'cognitions play a central role in determining our emotions' (Robertson, 2019) and the 'Stoics considered [people's] conceptions (or misconceptions) of events rather than the events themselves as the key to [their] emotional upsets' (Beck 1976: 3 quoted in Robertson, 2019), I started to explain Stoic cognitive distancing ideas to the students showing in the Stoic maxims and with the activities below how one might overcome feelings of anxiety when, for example, speaking out in classes or in public.

At the beginning of term with new language classes, I now take the students carefully through some key Stoic cognitive distancing learnings. I demonstrate that even I, as an instructor, am nervous when speaking in front of a class, so how can I feel more comfortable when speaking? By adding humour such as pointing to my head and pulling a face, I can show that I am nervous about what they (pointing at them) are thinking. I then ask out loud, can I change your thinking? Well, up to a point maybe, I say, but not really, so the important thing is not to worry so much about others but to prepare well, to practice well, and if you do this properly, then your work is done. What others think is up to them; you have done your part, you have prepared and the rest is out of your hands. So why worry?

In many of my language classes, the textbooks give end-of-unit tests in the form of research presentations. Many students make a face, and when I ask them why, they say I am nervous speaking in front of the class. At this point, I might offer up the idea of mentors as a way of objective help as in 'What would so-and-so do or say?' and use the idea of giving ourselves advice using the second-person voice, for example 'You are now feeling nervous, what would so-and-so say to you perhaps?' – he or she might say, 'Do your preparation well, practise and people are here to listen to you, they are interested in what you have to say, and no one wants you to do badly' (and if they do, then that is their problem, not yours).

The Stoic principles began to take on a more personal meaning when the Covid-19 pandemic forced university classes online. Students were required to send in weekly journal submissions based on the class content (reflective journaling, as suggested by Marcus Aurelius, proved to be very helpful and revealing for the class). Many students, given a more personal way of communicating with the instructor, opened up and journaled their own anxiety problems. While I stress I am not a counsellor and anyone with mental health issues should seek professional help, anxiety arising from the Covid-19 pandemic, giving a presentation, speaking up in class or being hesitant in voicing an opinion are dealt with very effectively from a Stoic school standpoint. Whenever a student voiced concerns about group work or presentation work when online, I directly communicated with the student through the journal, giving some Stoic hints, or some appropriate Stoic Maxims (also below). In the lectures, I continued to hone and illustrate examples from the Stoic texts, which I will explain in the activity section below. During 2020 at the height of the Covid-19 pandemic, I had a class of over seventy students doing the civic engagement class online. Many wrote in their journals how they were failing to cope both with the move online and in their lives in general. By careful feedback on their individual issues, I was able to convey Stoic strategies to combat anxiety, strategies that had worked for me in the past both in the online lectures and in personal responses to their reflective journals. One example of the latter was when a student felt that she couldn't contribute to a weekly online group discussion. I explained that everyone felt like this at times (including me), and by, again, outlining Epictetus' ideas of things up to us and things beyond our control, I showed her that she was more worried about how other people would view her, which is really out of her own control. She wrote back and said that this had really helped her, and although difficult, she was trying to overcome her nervousness and just say what she thought in the group discussions. The following are activities I have developed over time that illustrate cognitive distancing techniques and have proved very helpful to students.

# Activity: Epictetus and the lyre player

## *Aims*

How to prepare for a presentation or speech if you are feeling anxious.

- **Level:** Language can be adapted to the level
- **Materials:** None required
- **Time:** About twenty minutes

1. Find a picture of a lyre. Explain that a lyre player like any musician is one who practises to be good. Practice applies to anyone wishing to improve: baseball players, cooks or language learners – practice makes perfect, and if not perfect, then certainly better than yesterday. At home, the lyre player plays beautifully, but on stage, the lyre player becomes nervous, why? (students can contribute here).

2. Depending on the level of the class, write on the board: *Some things are within our power, while others are not. Within our power are opinion, motivation, desire, aversion and, in a word, whatever is of our own doing; not within our power are our body, our property, reputation, office and, in a word, whatever is not of our own doing* (Epictetus *Enchiridion* 1.1 in Hard and Gill, 2014: 287).

3. Stress the 'within our power' part. Elicit student feedback and comments. As examples of things not in our control, not up to us, explain that in the case of our body, we can of course go to the gym, eat well, etc., but we cannot stop our heart or make our blood go around our body in a different way (you can choose your own examples if need be – our SNS profile on Twitter or Instagram is not up to us although we might presume so, and is a source of much SNS disturbance for many). Things not up to us are out of our control; they are, therefore, 'externals' or 'indifferents'.

4. After explaining the Stoic example, students could then choose their own image/allegory, etc., aside from the lyre. This would personalize it for the students and extend the activity, helping them to think more deeply about the Stoic ideas. They could then share their pictures with classmates.

5. Again, depending on the language level of the class, explain that people get nervous, it's natural, but let's not snowball (to illustrate: enact or draw a large snowball rolling down a hill on the board if necessary with a person in the snowball). While we can focus our attention on how we play the lyre, we cannot control how our lyre playing is received by an audience. Our practice is key, preparation counts and *that's the important part.* How people receive our lyre playing (our presentation, our speech) *is up to them.* We have

no control over people's reactions or their opinions or their judgements. Nor should we care. We have done our part in our practice, and in our preparation. What others think is up to them not up to us. Furthermore, Epictetus (*Discourses* 2. 13, see Hard and Gill, 2014: 98) also explains that the lyre player is relaxed at home but wants to perform well and wants to receive approval. However, again, this is out of the musician's control, and so irrelevant to the performance (or class presentation).

6. Depending on the language level of the class you can show this quote from Epictetus:

> If the things, then, that lie outside the sphere of choice are neither good nor bad, and those that lie within the sphere of choice are subject to our control, and no one can either take those away from us or impose them on us *unless we wish it*, what room is left for anxiety?
> (Hard and Gill, 2014, emphasis mine)

## Activity: Cicero's archer

### *Aims*

This activity is designed to alleviate student anxiety regarding presentations, group work and speaking in front of people. Cicero, although not a Stoic, was sympathetic to the Stoic philosophy and translated many of the Greek Stoic works into Latin, making them accessible to a Roman audience.

- **Level:** Language can be adapted to the level
- **Materials:** None required
- **Time:** About twenty minutes

1. I usually draw a bow and arrow and target (badly) on the board. The bad drawing usually gets a laugh and as mentioned I have found humour to be a great help in alleviating stress or anxiety. I ask the question, what is the aim of the archer? Answers are usually to hit the target, to hit the bullseye, win a prize, etc.

2. I explain that this is the intention but what about gusts of wind, the bow snapping, someone walking near the target and suddenly distracting the aim, the target falling over, etc. (again one can demonstrate by illustrating these incidents on the board).

3. I suggest once the arrow leaves the bow it is out of the archer's control. The task is done. A good presentation is all in the preparation. We cannot

control the response; responses are therefore to be disregarded, by preparing well we have done our work.

4. I ask students, "Is this correct? Do you agree, if so why/why not?" I again suggest that to hit the target is preferred but is not certain. Just as an audience's response is not certain but the audience at least is there to hear what you say, they are interested, so 'aim' (pun intended) for that idea.

5. The following is the background explanation from Cicero, and depending again on the language level of the class you can explain as you wish:

Cicero in *De Finibus Bonorum et Malorum*, III.22 explains his archer metaphor:

> If a man were to make it his purpose to take a true aim with a spear or arrow at some mark, his ultimate end, corresponding to the ultimate good as we pronounce it, would be to do all he could to aim straight … Yet, although he did everything to attain his purpose … the actual hitting of the mark would be in our phrase 'to be chosen' but not 'to be desired'.
> (Pigliucci, 2015)

Here intention is everything. One prepares carefully, and carries out the action to the best of one's ability. The rest is not up to us, we cannot decide the outcome, but we have carried out our task (our intention) with care and accuracy.

## Follow-up tasks and suggestions

- I've used the following Stoic maxims and affirmations (see below) often in my peace and conflict classes and civic engagement classes at key points in the semester to highlight certain points in the teaching units. In the peace and conflict class, for example, they have proved useful in explaining and gaining inner and outer peace, as well as excellent methodology when engaging in conflict resolution. I have also used these expressions for discussion in language classes at certain times of the courses depending on language levels. Beginner classes have proved difficult, but these maxims are surprisingly good in intermediate and upper intermediate classes for stimulating discussion. I usually write a few on the board and ask groups to offer explanations, explain what they think the sayings might mean, whether they agree or disagree and so on. They work very well as critical thinking exercises.

- **Stoic Maxims and Affirmations** (Gill et al., 2015). The Stoics appear to have repeated certain key phrases or maxims to themselves in order to memorize them and have them constantly 'ready-to-hand', especially in the face of a crisis. They are very good for discussion, excellent for critical thinking and great tools for building resilience and coping with anxiety.

- **From the Handbook (Enchiridion) of Epictetus:**
  - 'You are just an appearance and not at all the thing you claim to represent.' (Response to a troubling impression.)
  - 'Some things are up to us and other things are not. Things up to us are opinion, desire, aversion, our own actions. Things not up to us are body, property, reputation, whatever are not our own actions.' (Response to things not under your control.)
  - 'What is beyond my control is indifferent to me.'
  - 'If you want any good, get it from within yourself.'
  - 'Don't demand that things go as you will, but will that they happen as they do, and your life will go smoothly.'
  - 'Sickness is a hindrance to the body, but not to the will.'
  - 'Never say of anything "I have lost it" but "I have returned it."'
  - 'It seemed right to them.' (Response to someone whose actions seem disagreeable to you – *Classic advice for SNS or difficult people*!)
  - 'Everything has two handles, and can be picked up and carried either wisely or foolishly.'
  - 'People are upset not by things but by their judgements about things.'
- It is important to remember that we are human and a work in progress. We forget our learnings or do not always employ them successfully, and so we are often anxious about outcomes. The vital precept, as Epictetus explained, is to keep repeating these maxims (rather as I have done throughout this chapter) until they become internalized or second nature, just as a musician or a language learner keeps practising until they become more confident and more proficient (see also the Massimo Pigliucci, 2020, link below for a wider discussion on this). By focusing on the task rather than focusing on the reaction to the task our actions become centred and up to us, not up to others.

# Recommended reading

Aurelius, M. (2013), *Marcus Aurelius: Meditations, Books 1–6*. Oxford: Oxford University Press.

Hard, R. and C. Gill (2014), *Epictetus: Discourses, Fragments, Handbook*. Oxford: Oxford World's Classics.
These two books are classic Stoic texts. Very accessible and endlessly rewarding, I have recommended them to students whether in English translations or in their own language.

# References

Aurelius, M. (2013), *Marcus Aurelius: Meditations, Books 1–6*, Oxford: Oxford University Press.

Gill, C., P. Ussher, J. Sellars, T. Lebon, J. Evans, G. Garratt and D. Robertson (2015), 'HC Stoic Week Handbook-v1.2'. Available online: https://modernstoicism.com/wp-content/uploads/2021/06/Stoic-Week-2015-Handbook-Stoicism-Today.pdf (Accessed 8 August 2021).

Hard, R. and C. Gill (2014), *Epictetus: Discourses, Fragments, Handbook*, Oxford: Oxford University Press.

Pigliucci, M. (2015), 'What Would a Stoic Do? The Stoic's Decision Making Algorithm'. Available online: https://howtobeastoic.wordpress.com/2015/12/08/what-would-a-stoic-do-the-stoics-decision-making-algorithm/ (Accessed 17 August 2021).

Pigliucci, M. (2020), 'Updating Epictetus and Stoicism for the 21st Century by Massimo Pigliucci'. Available online: https://modernstoicism.com/updating-epictetus-and-stoicism-for-the-21st-century-by-massimo-pigliucci/ (Accessed 10 August 2021).

Robertson, D. (2019), 'Stoic Philosophy as a Cognitive-Behavioral Therapy'. Available online: https://medium.com/stoicism-philosophy-as-a-way-of-life/stoic-philosophy-as-a-cognitive-behavioral-therapy-597fbeba786a (Accessed 10 August 2021).

Robertson, D. (2020), *The Philosophy of Cognitive-Behavioural Therapy: Stoic Philosophy as Rational and Cognitive Psychotherapy (Second Edition)*, London: Routledge.

# CHAPTER NINE

# Boosting your students' confidence in second language learning:

# The confidence-building diary

*Jo Mynard and Scott J. Shelton-Strong*

When learning a new language, we can often lack confidence and feel anxious about using this language in ways that reflect who we are and how we wish to communicate in it. The confidence-building diary (CBD) represents a tool that draws on positive psychology and scaffolds opportunities for self-discovery and reflection on self-chosen examples of actual language use and learning tasks. It is designed to help students build confidence and to generate and regulate positive feelings towards their language learning and use. Results of our research (Shelton-Strong and Mynard, 2018, 2021) indicate that the process of choosing activities, keeping the diary and, later, reflecting on the ways it was motivating and the feelings that arose can be a powerful learning experience. The diary can be used by any language learner but can be especially helpful for learners experiencing foreign language anxiety (FLA) as they set their own tasks within their comfort zones. When completing and reflecting on activities, students experience feelings of success that can trigger positive emotions and a sense of competence and confidence.

The initial planning and the final associated reflection tasks can be done during class, where students can reflect on positive experiences occurring both inside and outside class. In fact, it may be beneficial for them to focus mainly on things they do outside the classroom in order to broaden their scope of experiences and personalize the task. The activity requires minimum preparation for the teacher and is easy to implement and adapt to a wide range of learner proficiency levels, ages and class types.

## Background to the activity

A version of the CBD was first used at our institution in 2004 (before either of us joined) as part of a self-directed learning module. This module was called 'The First Steps Module', an optional course designed to introduce students to key self-directed learning skills that they could apply in order to effectively manage their own autonomous language learning (Shelton-Strong and Mynard, 2018). Over the years, generations of learning advisors working in the self-access learning centre (SALC) have adapted the module and its contents based on learners' needs, updated learning outcomes and perceived success of the activities contained within the module (Thornton, 2013).

The CBD has remained a key part of the module, but the tool itself has evolved and can be used to motivate learners and help them overcome foreign language anxiety. The latest iteration of the activity includes opportunities for ongoing and retrospective reflection of exploring what happens when a learner consciously chooses to record activities related to language learning from a positive point of view and keeps this diary for a week. The activity asks learners to focus intentionally on activities that make them feel good or positive about themselves or their language learning. Learners are likely to choose tasks where they experienced success, either through completing something challenging or through experiencing positive emotions such as joy and satisfaction. Reflecting on this success can help students change their perceptions and interpretations of their abilities, leading to increased confidence. For example, a person who feels anxious about being understood in the language they are learning can overcome this feeling by noticing evidence of how successfully they communicated with others. Learners write how they felt about each activity, which adds an affective dimension. This provides an opportunity to recognize and name an emotion, and associate it with a positive learning activity.

Our research helped us to understand students' experiences of using the CBD (see Shelton-Strong and Mynard, 2021), and the results showed that students chose to focus on a range of personally meaningful learning activities, the majority of them taking place outside the classroom. In terms of emotional responses, learners expressed a diverse range of feelings; the majority were positive, and, in general, students experienced a sense of achievement and feelings of volition, satisfaction and competence. Appendix 4 provides an intact excerpt from one of the participants and shows how the student pushed themselves to do a speaking activity outside the classroom, which initially made them feel nervous. However, the learner wrote in their CBD that they enjoyed the activity overall and even *'forgot the time'*. Similarly, another student shared two incidents in their CBD that they would not normally have challenged themselves to do due to language anxiety. The first challenge was to speak up in class, and the second was to join a language exchange activity. The student expressed feelings of nervousness but also enjoyment and happiness. In the final reflection, this student wrote *'writing my activity which positive makes me confidence'*. In sum, all thirty-nine participants from our study felt that the CBD activity was beneficial and contributed to their motivation and confidence for English language learning and use. In follow-up interviews five months later with seven of the students, we found that all of them continued to intentionally engage in positive activities in order to continue to experience feelings of competence, fulfilment or optimal challenge.

The CBD has its roots in positive psychology, a scientific theory and approach which looks at what goes right in life (Peterson, 2006). It focuses on people's strengths and when they are at their best (Biswas-Diener, 2010). At its core, positive psychology is concerned with enhancing our understanding of the conditions, positive emotions and social contexts which enable people to flourish. It focuses on the positive experiences that provide the psychological nourishment people need to thrive and grow in increasingly integrated ways, and what it is about our own nature that helps us do that (Seligman, Steen, Park and Peterson, 2005; Sheldon and Ryan, 2011). However, as Dewaele et al. (2019) mention, positive psychology is not necessarily the absence of negative emotions but rather the creation of a balance by harnessing the power of positive emotions. Positive psychology research applied to language learning shows how it has a positive influence on learners' experiences that enhance linguistic progress (Dewaele et al., 2019).

The CBD is an example of a positive psychology intervention (PPI), which is how the theory of positive psychology is applied to practice in people's lives. PPIs are direct and purposeful attempts to raise awareness of the benefits of focusing on positive emotions, thoughts and intentions as they relate to activities, beliefs and ideas which people experience, hold and are involved in. In language learning, these can be, for example, activities or tasks which focus on building on one's strengths, noting personal examples of growth and development, and expressions of thankfulness and acceptance (MacIntyre, Gregersen and Mercer, 2019), which the CBD gives learners the opportunity to do.

Positive emotions are important in learning for several reasons. Firstly, maintaining a positive outlook when learning a language can lead to perseverance and the overcoming of difficulties or challenging circumstances (Oxford, 2015). Enjoying a task may trigger intrinsic motivation (Ryan and Deci, 2017), whereas experiencing negative emotions such as anxiety, worry or boredom may lessen intrinsic motivation. By focusing on positive experiences in language learning (such as noting one's strengths and accomplishments in a diary), a PPI such as this can help to build a learner's confidence and decrease anxiety as they reflect on and become more self-aware of their ability to enjoy success and notice learning progress.

Secondly, when someone experiences positive emotions and these are nurtured in the learning process, this has a beneficial effect on learning (Forgas, 2000). Jin and Dewaele (2018) investigated the effect of learners' positive orientations on foreign language anxiety in a study of 144 Chinese EFL university students. The results showed that levels of anxiety were significantly lessened when students were positively oriented; this is something that the CBD aims to do.

Confidence is defined as a belief in ourselves or in our abilities and can play a key role in language learning. If we believe that we can be successful at a certain task, this enables us to reflect on the reasons for the success and feel confident in our abilities (Oxford, 2016). Our confidence and self-belief play a significant role in our expressions of agency, or our drive to do something. We can be driven to engage in continued efforts towards reaching our goals despite the challenges we face, such as when we experience feelings of anxiousness or insecurity about our abilities as we learn and attempt to use a new language. In other words, experiencing success contributes to confidence and an internal strength to persevere. A key factor in experiencing and maintaining this inner strength and vitality is the need for engagement in learning tasks to be accompanied by a sense of autonomy. As Ryan and Deci (2017:95) explain, 'to develop a true sense of perceived competence, people's actions must be perceived as self-organised or initiated, or in other words, people must feel ownership of the activities at which they succeed'. The CBD introduced in this chapter is designed to support the learner's autonomy as they choose the learning experiences and tasks to focus on in a positive light and reflect on their experience.

The CBD has the potential to address challenges associated with language anxiety, and we recommend it for all language learners, either as part of a self-directed learning course or within a language class. Supporting the learners' autonomy to choose the activity provides the appropriate degree of scaffolding to reduce or completely eliminate situations that are too anxiety-inducing. On the other hand, learners should be encouraged to challenge themselves (at their own pace) rather than choose activities that may be understimulating. This can be facilitated through reflective questions on the task sheet, semi-guided peer discussions in class and one-to-one advising.

## The activity

The CBD was originally designed as a self-directed learning activity or an out-of-class task, but the steps below provide guidelines for introducing the CBD to students in class as well. It benefits from dialogue and reflection, so no matter which way it is introduced to students, after the task has been completed, students should have the opportunity to write their reflections and engage in dialogue with others.

Optimally, the CBD would be introduced and explained and a rationale for doing it provided, and students would have a choice as to whether they would take part or not. A related but different activity (a text to read, a short video to watch and comment on) might be offered as an alternative.

The following steps are suggestions for (i) the in-class version and (ii) the self-directed version.

# Activity: The confidence-building diary (CBD)

## Aims

The activity is designed to help students to build confidence while engaging in activities related to language learning and use. The CBD is a way for students to complete, record and reflect on achievable tasks, which help them to generate and regulate positive feelings and feel motivated.

- **Level:** Any
- **Materials:** Make copies of the activities (see appendices), example CBD
- **Time:**
    1   Optional pre-activity – Confidence questionnaire (fifteen minutes)
    2   The CBD (ten minutes to explain, one week to complete)
    3   Post task reflection sheet (twenty minutes, maybe more)

## i. In-class version

Optional pre-activities

1. Invite students to share what some important factors for success in language learning are (e.g. aptitude, confidence, motivation, grammatical knowledge, personality, good memory, opportunities … ). Explain that in this lesson, they will focus on confidence – one very important factor.
2. Ask students to reflect on times when they feel anxious when speaking a foreign language and times when they feel confident (either write a reflection which you can respond to in writing or discuss these questions with classmates).
3. Explain that keeping a positive outlook and experiencing success are important to improving confidence and sustaining motivation for language learning over a long period of time. Invite them to think about what positive things they do as part of their language learning (either write a reflection or discuss with classmates).

The CBD activity

1. Explain that students will have the opportunity to keep a confidence-building diary for one week in order to experience and reflect on positive experiences in language learning.
2. Distribute the CBD (Appendix 2) and ask students to read the introduction. If necessary, show students an example from your own language learning or from another student (with permission). (Appendix 4 is an authentic example that is free to use or adapt if needed.)
3. Give students a few minutes to read, plan and ask questions.
4. Negotiate the number of entries (at least three) and the deadline together – usually one week. This supports the learner's need to experience some control over what and how much they choose to do. Some may feel ready to do more, while others may prefer to begin with a goal of noting down three positive reflections, to begin with, and have the option to keep going if they wish. For those who suffer from stronger anxiety, this can lessen the pressure. It's important that students know they can choose what to do.

Reflection tasks

1. Invite students to share some of the activities they wrote in their journals either as a whole class activity or in small groups. Demonstrate the variety of activities and emotions, highlighting that this activity is highly individualized and personal.
2. Explain that in order to understand the benefits of the CBD, it is important to reflect on the process and on how they felt about doing them. Distribute the post-diary reflections (Appendix 3) and ask students to read all of them.
3. Depending on the students and the group dynamics/context, some of the questions can be completed individually, and some can be done with other students in pairs or small groups while they discuss them together. There is no one correct way, but it is beneficial for students to be able to discuss their experiences with others and also learn from their classmates.
4. After the reflection and group/pair discussions, elicit some responses from the groups to demonstrate the variety of benefits and ways to maintain a positive outlook.
5. Invite students to continue this diary (have some spare copies of the blank CBD to hand).

## ii. Self-directed/out-of-class version

Optional pre-activities

1 Provide an open-ended question for students to think about or write a response to:
   - What are some important factors for success in language learning? (e.g. aptitude, confidence, grammatical knowledge, personality …).
2 Provide an explanatory paragraph/video:
   - The following activities focus on confidence – a very important factor in language learning. If you feel nervous about using English, knowing that you can choose what to do to notice and think about in a positive light can help you feel less anxious. Complete the activities alone before going on to the reflection tasks.
3 Ask students to complete a confidence questionnaire (Appendix 1).
4 Provide an open-ended question for students to think about or write a response to:
   - Reflect on times when you feel most/least confident.
   - Keeping a positive outlook and experiencing success are important for feeling confidence in language learning over a long period of time.
     i What positive things do you do as part of your language learning?

The CBD activity

1 Explain in text/video:
   i You will have the opportunity to keep a confidence-building diary for one week in order to experience and reflect on positive experiences in language learning.

2 Distribute the CBD (Appendix 2) and ask students to read the introduction. If necessary, provide the students with an example from your own language learning or from another student (with permission). (Appendix 4 is an example that is free to use or adapt if needed.)

3 Ask students to decide the number of entries (at least three) and the deadline for submission – usually one week.

Reflection tasks

Students complete the post-diary reflections (Appendix 3). Question 3 requires interviewing other students, but the whole activity could be done with other students in pairs or small groups.

Follow-up (essential for the self-directed version and recommended for the in-class version)

Respond to individual students' responses by writing in the final box – and also on the activities themselves. While this may take extra time depending on the number of students you have, it can be very meaningful for the learners to feel their teacher is interested in them and cares about how they feel. Here are some tips for giving good responses (see Kato and Mynard, 2016 for more examples):

- Respond to each individual uniquely, depending on what they write, who they are and what they have done
  - Avoid using generic phrases; refer to what students have said.
  - Don't correct any language mistakes.
  - Don't evaluate the responses.
  - Don't judge the choice of activity.
  - Don't make assumptions; i.e. ask reflective questions rather than assume you have understood something.
  - Ask questions to try to understand students' choices.
  - Ask reflective questions to help students think more deeply about the experience.
  - Ask questions that you are genuinely interested to know about.
  - Share your own experiences (or that of another student), but only if it is useful for the learner.
  - Meet the learners where they are (but gently encourage them to challenge themselves).
  - Use caring and non-threatening language.
  - Give positive feedback, but make sure it's relevant and specific to each learner.
  - For anxious students, ask them how they feel they are perceived by others. Did they find anything concrete to indicate that they need to worry about their speaking skills?

## Recommended reading

Biswas-Diener, R. (2010), *Practicing Positive Psychology Coaching: Assessment, Activities, and Strategies for Success*. Hoboken, NJ: John Wiley & Sons.
This book shares strategies, interventions and tools for applying positive psychology in practice. It was originally designed for use by coaches but can be adapted for use in language teaching and learning.

Dewaele, J. M., X. Chen, A. M. Padilla and J. Lake (2019), 'The flowering of positive psychology in foreign language teaching and acquisition research', *Frontiers in Psychology*, 10: 2128.
This article provides a summary of the impact positive psychology has had on the field of applied linguistics and, in particular, the growing recognition of the important role of emotions in language learning.

Shelton-Strong, S. J. and J. Mynard (2021), 'Promoting positive feelings and motivation for language learning: The role of a confidence-building diary', *Innovation in Language Learning and Teaching*, 15 (5): 458–72.
This article gives details of a study which looked at language learners using the CBD and the emotions and motivation they experienced during and as a result of using it.

## References

Biswas-Diener, R. (2010), *Practicing Positive Psychology Coaching: Assessment, Activities, and Strategies for Success*, Hoboken, NJ: John Wiley & Sons.
Dewaele, J. M., X. Chen, A. M. Padilla and J. Lake (2019), 'The Flowering of Positive Psychology in Foreign Language Teaching and Acquisition Research', *Frontiers of Psychology*, 10: 2128.
Finch, A. (2004), *English Reflections: An Interactive, Reflective Learner Journal*, Daegu, South Korea: Kyungpook National University Press.
Forgas, J. (2000), 'The Role of Affect in Social Cognition', in J. Forgas (ed), *Feeling and Thinking: The Role of Affect in Social Cognition*, 1–28, Cambridge, MA: Cambridge University Press.
Jin, Y. X. and J. M. Dewaele (2018), 'The Effect of Positive Orientation and Perceived Social Support on Foreign Language Classroom Anxiety', *System*, 74: 149–57.
Kato, S. and J. Mynard (2016), *Reflective Dialogue: Advising in Language Learning*, New York, NY: Routledge.
MacIntyre, P. D., T. Gregersen and S. Mercer (2019), 'Setting an Agenda for Positive Psychology in SLA: Theory, Practice and Research', *The Modern Language Journal*, 103 (1): 262–74.
Oxford, R. L. (2015), 'Emotion as the Amplifier and the Primary Motive: Some Theories of Emotion with Relevance to Language Learning', *Studies in Second Language Learning and Teaching*, 5 (3): 371–93.

Oxford, R. L. (2016), 'Toward a Psychology of Well-Being for Language Learners: The "EMPATHICS" Vision', in P. D. MacIntyre, T. Gregersen and S. Mercer (eds), *Positive Psychology in Second Language Acquisition*, 10–87, Bristol, UK: Multilingual Matters.

Peterson, C. (2006), *A Primer in Positive Psychology*, Oxford, UK: Oxford University Press.

Ryan, R. M and E. L. Deci (2017), *Self-Determination Theory: Basic Psychological Needs in Motivation, Development, and Wellness*, New York, NY: Guilford Press.

Seligman, M. E., T. A. Steen, N. Park and C. Peterson (2005), 'Positive Psychology Progress: Empirical Validation of Interventions', *American Psychologist*, 60 (5): 410–21.

Sheldon, K. M. and R. M. Ryan (2011), 'Positive Psychology and Self-Determination Theory: A Natural Interface', in V. I. Chirkov, R. M. Ryan and K. M. Sheldon (eds), *Cross-Cultural Advancements in Positive Psychology: Human Autonomy in Cross-Cultural Context: Perspectives on the Psychology of Agency, Freedom, and Well-Being*, 33–44, Dordrecht, The Netherlands: Springer.

Shelton-Strong, S. J. and J. Mynard (2018), 'Affective Factors in Self-Access Learning', *Relay Journal*, 1 (2): 275–92.

Shelton-Strong, S. J. and J. Mynard (2021), 'Promoting Positive Feelings and Motivation for Language Learning: The role of a Confidence-Building Diary', *Innovation in Language Learning and Teaching*, 15 (5): 458–72.

Thornton, K. (2013), 'A Framework for Curriculum Reform: Re-designing a Curriculum for Self-Directed Learning', *Studies in Self-Access Learning Journal*, 4 (2): 142–53.

# Appendix 1. Confidence questionnaire (adapted from Finch, 2004: 42)

## Confidence Questionnaire

Circle the number that best suits you to find out how confident you are.

| How confident am I? | Disagree....MAYBE...Agree | | | | |
|---|---|---|---|---|---|
| 1. I have the ability to learn English. | 1 | 2 | 3 | 4 | 5 |
| 2. If I do my best, I will achieve my learning goals. | 1 | 2 | 3 | 4 | 5 |
| 3. I will improve if I continue to study. | 1 | 2 | 3 | 4 | 5 |
| 4. I like to speak English in class. | 1 | 2 | 3 | 4 | 5 |
| 5. Trying to speak English is more important than accuracy. | 1 | 2 | 3 | 4 | 5 |
| 6. I like to study with my group members in class. | 1 | 2 | 3 | 4 | 5 |
| 7. My contribution is as important as anyone else's. | 1 | 2 | 3 | 4 | 5 |
| 8. I participate even if I am embarrassed or nervous. | 1 | 2 | 3 | 4 | 5 |
| 9. I ask the teacher for help when needed. | 1 | 2 | 3 | 4 | 5 |
| 10. I participate in all the activities in class. | 1 | 2 | 3 | 4 | 5 |
| 11. If I don't understand, I say so. | 1 | 2 | 3 | 4 | 5 |
| 12. I do my best, whatever the situation. | 1 | 2 | 3 | 4 | 5 |
| 13. I keep trying to learn, even if I am nervous. | 1 | 2 | 3 | 4 | 5 |
| 14. It is OK to make mistakes when trying a new language. | 1 | 2 | 3 | 4 | 5 |
| 15. I do not worry about what other students think of my English. | 1 | 2 | 3 | 4 | 5 |
| 16. I do not worry about what the teacher thinks of my English. | 1 | 2 | 3 | 4 | 5 |
| 17. I believe in myself. | 1 | 2 | 3 | 4 | 5 |
| 18. I trust my feelings and emotions. | 1 | 2 | 3 | 4 | 5 |
| 19. I think about my learning (e.g. "How am I doing?"). | 1 | 2 | 3 | 4 | 5 |
| 20. I am a good language learner. | 1 | 2 | 3 | 4 | 5 |
| | TOTAL (____/100) | | | | |

❖ Add up your answers from statements 1-20. Draw your own flag ( ) below to show the total points.

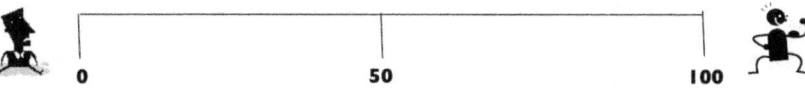

0                          50                        100

**Low confidence**                        **High confidence**

# Appendix 2. Confidence-building diary (adapted from Kanda University of International Studies n.d.)

*(Activity sheet for distribution to students – adapt this for other languages and add or subtract the number of days.)*

## Confidence-Building Diary

Our confidence and motivation can go up and down. Telling yourself every day about something **GOOD** and **POSITIVE** you have done using your English will <u>increase your confidence, give you a boost when feeling nervous, and motivate</u> you to continue through even the most difficult times.

In this diary, write something good and positive about learning and using your English that you noticed this week. This can include anything (online, offline, alone, with others), *even an area you might be worried about.* Consider how this makes you **feel** about your ability to use and learn English successfully. Make an effort to see the positive results of the learning activities you decide to focus on.

example

**Day 1**: *"I <u>went</u> to the conversation area and enjoyed talking with a teacher."*
*"I <u>was able to</u> use new words I had learned in class in the conversation!"*
*"I **felt happy** because I could really notice my progress from two weeks ago!."*

| | "GOOD" & "POSITIVE" experiences using and learning English |
|---|---|
| **Day 1** | Activity: <br><br> Feelings: |
| **Day 2** | Activity: <br><br> Feelings: |
| **Day 3** | Activity: <br><br> Feelings: |

# Appendix 3. Post-diary reflections (adapted from the original used at KUIS)

## **Post-diary Summary**

1. Did the Confidence-Building Diary help you feel less nervous about using English? Why or why not?

2. Other than the Confidence Building Diary, what can you do to maintain positive feelings and the confidence to use more English?

3. Interview your friends – What do they do to maintain their positive perspective?

## **Reflection**

1. What did you find out about your **confidence** related to learning and using English by keeping the confidence-building diary?

2. How can you use this experience of focusing on the positive feelings you have about using English to help you become a more active and effective language learner?

# Appendix 4. An example confidence-building diary (data excerpt from a participant in Shelton-Strong and Mynard's (2021) study)

|  | **"GOOD" & "POSITIVE" experiences using and learning English** |
|---|---|
| **Day 1** | Activity:<br>I went to the SALC to communicate with a teacher in English. (Actually I made a reservation). At the beginning of the conversation was about our hobbies, but later on it changed to works (overworking, salary, etc.)<br><br>Feelings:<br>I'm very happy to have been able to talk with foreign teachers. I was nervous a little when we started to talk, however our talk continue a lot, what was more, we forgot the time. 15 minutes!! Next time, I want to have a discussion to interact more. |
| **Day 2** | Activity:<br>I participated in a volunteer activity called "Yamathon." I used English to confirm runners and give them instructions.<br><br>Feelings:<br>I could get more confidence to speak English with foreign people. But, I couldn't interact with Japanese people including seniors and students. (In reality, they need Japanese...) |
| **Day 3** | Activity:<br>As an assignment of another English class, I collaborated with some seniors (students = 3rd year-students) after the class. We discussed an easy topic such as Japanese education, music, hobbies, etc.<br><br>Feelings:<br>If I continued to have a discussion, I felt comfortable and very tired. I don't know my progress, but I can mention that I became to be able to put into words in British English with an appropriate pronunciation. I yearn for having an ability of speaking in British English fluently. |

## CHAPTER TEN

# Facing worries head on:

# Discussions for raising awareness and tackling communicative anxiety

*Amelia Yarwood*

Dialogue is powerful. Some of the deepest insights we have about ourselves come from conversations with a friend, teacher or mentor. This discussion activity capitalizes on the power of dialogue by inviting learners to collaboratively reflect on areas of concern and work together to find personally relevant solutions. The use of discussions to tackle communicative anxiety may sound counterintuitive at first, but by creating a supportive environment where fears are acknowledged, experiences are shared and strategies are developed together, learners often realize that they are not alone and that dealing with anxiety does not have to be a solitary endeavour.

The foundation for this activity lies in my experience as a learning advisor (LA). The role of an LA is to collaboratively reflect and support learners in becoming confident, autonomous language learners. During my time as an LA, speaking concerns featured heavily in advising sessions. In our conversations, students often acknowledged the need to take control of their own learning but they faced worries which included:

- Initiating an interaction – How do I phrase my invitation to have a conversation? What if I interrupt them from something important and they get angry at me? What if we don't understand each other?

- Awkward conversations – What if my pronunciation is bad or I can't think of any questions? What do I do if there is silence for too long? What if I accidentally offend the other person with my questions or comments?

- Building and maintaining relationships – How can I make conversations fun? Where do I find conversation partners who want to talk to me each week? What if we don't get along? What if the other person asks me about personal information? What do I say if I feel offended or scared?

My students knew what they wanted (to speak English), but their sense of competence (knowing what to say and how) and relatedness (supportive relationships) were missing. Conversations with students also revealed that they were afraid of being negatively evaluated by their peers, many of whom they perceived to be in possession of greater linguistic resources. Even high-performing students active in English-speaking communities or who were top of their classes expressed similar concerns. One student shared her anxiety over becoming a second-year student because of the pressure she felt to speak accurately after having studied at the university for a year (Hooper, Mynard, Sampson and Taw, 2019). Stories like these show that students, regardless of experience or proficiency, can benefit from a change in perspective to realize they are not alone in their experiences.

## Background to the approach

The activity is grounded in supporting learners' need for autonomy (self-endorsed, valuing of choices), competence (a sense of mastery) and relatedness (belonging to a group). These three needs come from a theory of human well-being known as self-determination theory (SDT) (Deci and Ryan, 1985; Ryan and Deci, 2017). These needs will be connected to the three main features of the activity: (a) structured prompts, (b) experience-centred and (c) peer-collaboration.

### *Structured prompts*

Autonomy in SDT centres on informed choice and the endorsement of tasks. If students value a task because it is relevant to their situation, then their need for autonomy can be satisfied. By combining student-elicited topic suggestions and teacher-designed follow-up questions, teachers play a supportive role. To illustrate further, primary questions (e.g. Do you fear making mistakes in English?) structure the discussion as a whole, while follow-up questions (e.g. When others make mistakes, how do you feel?) invite personal opinions and experiences. In this way, anxious learners are guided towards making personally relevant contributions which can add to their sense of individual autonomy and competence. Of course, not all prompts will be relevant to students; some of the contributions may even cause discomfort. Explicit acknowledgement of these potential outcomes can act as a 'form of inoculation' (Lee, 2021) to ameliorate discomfort and promote a respectful environment in which differences are acknowledged, normalized and addressed. Valuing tasks because they are beneficial to others is thus encouraged.

## *Experience-centred*

The activity centres on sharing individual and shared experiences. Through co-constructing an understanding of potential setbacks to learning and formulating strategies, students are able to (re)evaluate past experiences and imagine potential future ones. In doing so, they are also able to develop self-awareness, an integral component to making self-determined choices. All learners bring with them unique experiences, knowledge, skills and expertise that can help them collaboratively understand and cope with shared psychological and situational phenomena (Hämäläinen and Vähäsantanen, 2011). In coming to an understanding of fears, worries, concerns and setbacks, learners become engaged in the question of 'why'. Why do I feel fear? Why is it harder to speak up in front of my peers? Why don't I feel close to my classmates in online classes? These 'why' questions have significant relevance to their lives which gives them ownership and control over their collaborative investigation into concerns. The pursuit of goals for autonomous, learner-centred reasons has been demonstrated to be positively associated with value endorsement, conceptual understanding, positive coping and experiencing internal motivation (Deci and Ryan, 2000; Hämäläinen and Vähäsantanen, 2011). Naturally, self-disclosure can be daunting. As such, the third element in this activity focused on relatedness which in SDT encompasses peer-to-peer relationships.

## *Peer-collaboration*

Supportive peer relationships are central to reducing different forms of anxiety, including communicative anxiety. Our classrooms are shaped relationally in an adaptive manner based on what individuals do and how those actions are perceived and responded to (Joe, Hiver and Al-Hoorie, 2017). This means students need to feel a sense of relatedness – that they are a team working together without judgement. The honest disclosure of experiences facilitates stronger communities in which every voice can be heard, ambient (classroom) values are made known and perceptions of peers can be transformed. Individuals tend to accept as their own the values and practices of those whom they feel connected to (Niemiec and Ryan, 2009), and for many language students, the people they want to connect to most are their peers. For learners with relatively fixed beliefs about language learning, who worry about the validity of their efforts, or who perceive judgement from their peers, listening to the experiences of their peers can offer new perspectives. These new perspectives then open up opportunities to engage in meaning-making with respect to their own personal values and motivations. For some students, this may lead to the transformation of external motivations into ones that are in line with their own values (Deci and Ryan, 2000). While the teacher is viewed as an expert, language learning peers walk the same path. It is these individuals with whom an anxious learner can often best relate, empathize and strategize with.

The activity outlined here has been the subject of several intervention studies and student workshops. When conducting this activity with language learners from multiple departments in a university specializing in foreign languages (Yarwood, Rose-Wainstock and Lees, 2019), it was found that learners were modestly supported in developing a range of personally relevant strategies for dealing with issues they were experiencing. The biggest change, according to this initial study, was the change in the classroom environment. With negative emotions related to language learning being openly shared, acknowledged and normalized, a space for the non-judgemental exploration of thoughts, feelings and experiences was created, embraced and sustained over a single semester. The benefits gained and the ease in conducting the activity led to a second study (Yarwood and Bennett, 2021) in the following academic year, which took place after classes moved online due to the Covid-19 pandemic. This study was longitudinal and covered the entire academic year, and by the end of the academic year, a 'relationship of trust' had developed and issues surrounding not knowing 'who' or 'what kind of person' were largely resolved thanks to the students' decisions to use free time for bonding over shared interests and day-to-day stories, active efforts to reciprocate in more detail, and making better use of body language by turning on cameras. Positive appraisals of interactions were also recorded. Students who were unable to formulate opinions about positive coping solutions were still able to share their experiences. Even if struggles persisted, they were glad to still be able to offer support and encouragement. Overall, the intervention appeared to have successfully bridged the gap between competency-based learning objectives and socially oriented, relatedness-based interactions.

# Activity

## Aims

- **Level:** Intermediate and above
- **Materials:** Prompts
- **Time:** See timeline below

The aim of this activity is to raise learners' self-awareness of their past experiences, needs and future desires while simultaneously encouraging jointly constructed, personally relevant strategies to be developed. Rather than something to be hidden away and avoided, negative thoughts and experiences are transformed into objects for discussion through which worries, failures and struggles are normalized as part of the learning process. Once normalized, learners are then able to focus on developing strategies to overcome their concerns. An illustrative timeline of the activity over the course of a thirteen-week semester is shown in Figure 10.1.

## Preparation

The preparation phase should take place at the beginning of a new unit or semester.

FIGURE 10.1 *Activity timeline.*

| | | | | | ↓ Out-of-class ↓ | | | | | | | |
|---|---|---|---|---|---|---|---|---|---|---|---|---|
| Prep | | | | Strategy Testing | | | Strategy Testing | | | Strategy Testing | | |
| Prep | A | A | B | A | A | C | A | A | B | A | A | C |
| | | | | | ↑ In-class ↑ | | | | | | | |
| 1 | 2 | 3 | 4 | 5 | 6 | 7 | 8 | 9 | 10 | 11 | 12 | 13 |
| | | | | | Weeks | | | | | | | |

*Note:* A: In-class discussions; B: In-class planning for strategy use; C: In-class reflecting on strategy use

## Step 1. (In-class, once)

1.1. Prompt development

- Each student writes down on a sticky note the language learning concerns they (a) have experienced or (b) fear experiencing.
    - e.g. I am scared to make a mistake when giving a presentation in class.

1.2. Sharing

- Sticky notes are collected.
- As a class, categorize the sticky notes based on commonalities
    - e.g. Fear of mistakes, Pronunciation, Starting a conversation.
- If necessary, break the categories down further.
    - e.g. Fear of mistakes with classmates vs. Fear of mistakes with native speakers.
- Rank each category based on the number of sticky notes. Use this ranking system to choose which categories will become discussion prompts.
    - e.g. The category with the most sticky notes is ranked #1.
- *Alternative*: Students vote on which categories they would like to discuss in future classes.

## Step 2. (Post-class, once)

2.1. Formalizing the prompts

- Based on the categories selected in Step 1, the teacher creates prompt/cards/presentation slides (see examples in Figure 10.2 below).
    - Each prompt should start with a general question or scenario followed by additional questions to help structure the discussion so it (a) defines the cause of the concern, (b) encourages the sharing of personal thoughts and experiences and (c) explores relevant strategies.

## *Discussions*

The discussions should take place once or twice each week over the course of a unit or semester. Where possible, discussions should take place at the beginning of lessons and outside of examination periods to reduce cognitive fatigue.

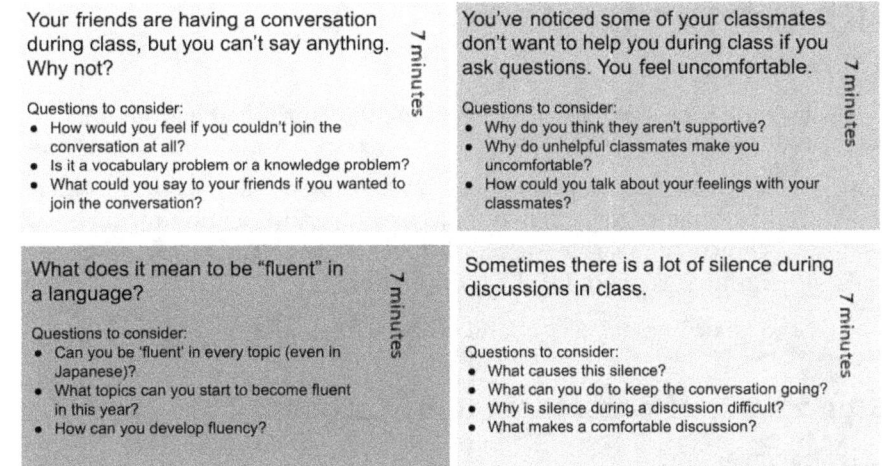

**FIGURE 10.2** *Example prompts used in a Japanese English university classroom.*

## Step 1. (In-class, weekly)

1.1 Discussion

- Divide the class into groups of three to four students.
  - Provide each group with a prompt (depending on purpose, the same or different prompts could be used).
  - Groups discuss their prompts for ten to fifteen minutes.

1.2. Sharing

- Representatives from each group share the main discussion points and conclusions with the class.
  - Strategies for dealing with, or overcoming the issue can be made tangible through (a) writing the strategies on the board, (b) adding them to a shared document or (c) asking students to create strategy posters for display around the classroom.

## *Testing strategies*

Testing strategies is necessary for students to actively investigate the effectiveness of strategies or ideas gained from the discussions. Replace a discussion with one of the activities in Step 1 and Step 2 as per the illustrative timeline.

## Step 1. (In-class, periodically)

1.1. Preparation

- Provide each student with a template to record their actions and reflections.
  - The template should include (a) ONE issue they wish to tackle, (b) what strategy they wish to use, (c) a justification for this choice, (d) a space to record three to five attempts, (e) a five-star rating system and (f) final evaluation.
- Students complete (a), (b) and (c) on the template.

## Step 2. (Out-of-class, three to five attempts)

2.1. Strategy testing

- Students attempt the strategy they wrote down in (b) three to five times and record their actions in (d).

## Step 3. (In-class, periodically)

3.1. Reflection

- Students complete (e) and (f) and share their thoughts with their group for ten minutes.

# Potential Concerns

## *Linguistic*

1. *Emotional vocabulary* is often neglected from language curriculum leading to the absence of robust, descriptive adjectives and phrases to accurately describe the emotions experienced. To overcome this concern, depending on their level, provide students with bilingual vocabulary lists to help them accurately name their feelings, or alternatively, you can use the L1.

2. *Explaining feelings* is difficult in your own language, and twice as difficult in a foreign language. The frustration of not being able to communicate the intricacies of an emotional experience may act as a trigger for anxious learners. Where possible, scaffold basic cause-effect dialogue (e.g. First, ... happened. This made me feel .... and because I felt ... I then .... In the end I ...). The use of online translators and limited L1 use to support the sharing process is also advised depending on classroom rules.

## *Psychological*

1. *Fear of ridicule* is natural when disclosing personal experiences. Anxious learners may refrain from sharing during initial discussions, but often these individuals feel emboldened by the knowledge that their peers have been through, or are going through similar experiences. Set the tone of the discussions in the first class by disclosing your own embarrassing mistake – when the students laugh, laugh with them to demonstrate that what can be terrifying or mortifying in the moment can be reframed as a fond memory later.

2. *Solidary preferences* may be demonstrated by students experiencing heightened anxiety in social situations. Although this activity encourages self-disclosure and exposure to some psychological discomfort as a form of inoculation, it is wise to keep an eye out for students who need a break from spoken participation in group work. Summarizing the discussion in note form in a language most comfortable for the student can help them participate in group work from the periphery while also experiencing a sense of competence.

# Modifications

## *Strategy archive*

Physical or digital archives of strategies can be maintained, modified and shared with learners to help with choosing appropriate strategies. They can be paired with action logs.

*Best used with:* Beginner to intermediate learners; Learners worried about which strategies to try; Learners who need external resources; Learners with limited autonomous learning experiences; Learners seeking external advice.

1.1. Preparation

A minimum of five strategy sheets should be created by the teacher to open the archive. Ensure each strategy sheet includes the following sections:

i  A Best-Used-For statement: A statement outlining scenarios in which the strategy may be most appropriate.
ii  How to: An outline of how to use the strategy.
iii  Modifications: For suggestions and adaptations as created by the students.
iv  User feedback: For students to contribute their feedback on the effectiveness or ease of use. (If using an online platform, user feedback can take the form of student comments/posts.) If possible link to a demonstration video using QR codes or shortened URLs.

## 2.1. Implementation

Direct students' attention to the archive during the first discussion. Let them know they can view the strategy sheets during or after their discussion if necessary. Invite students to contribute to the strategy sheets if they have previously used the strategy, or after they test it out for a week or two.

If students have their own strategies they wish to contribute to the archive, provide them with access to the strategy sheet template. Encourage free rein to add to and create new strategies.

Alternatively, several lessons over the course of a semester can be dedicated to creating new strategy sheets, modifying old ones and adding user feedback. If using an online document or platform, giving students editing rights can support their sense of ownership.

## Recommended reading

Reeve, J. (2018), 'Chapter 6. Psychological needs', in J. Reeve (ed), *Understanding motivation and emotion*, 123–50, New Jersey: John Wiley & Sons.
Focusing on human motivation, this text delves into recent findings in psychology while also providing replicable interventions for enhancing motivation and emotional understanding. Chapter 6 provides the reader with an overview of psychological needs, how these needs are supported or frustrated, and how relationships and social contexts support an individual's needs. Easy to read and well-structured, this chapter is perfect for practitioners wanting to apply SDT theories to their classroom practices.

Yarwood, A. and P. A. Bennett (2022), 'Engendering WTC in online learning spaces: Peer connectivity is more important than we may think', in C. N. Giannikas (ed), *Transferring Language Learning and Teaching from Face-to-Face to Online Settings*, 227–46, Pennsylvania: IGI Global.
To see how the activity described in this chapter was used as part of an action research project, please read this article. Using both self-determination theory and willingness to communicate frameworks, this article highlights the importance of relatedness when implementing discussion-based interventions in online classrooms. For teachers who struggle with silent online classrooms, this article offers several pedagogical suggestions for creating a positive, mutually supportive and aware social climate.

## References

Bennett, P. A. and A. Yarwood (2021), 'A Case for Scaffolding Self-Reflection', *PanSIG Journal*, 6 (1): 55–64.
Deci, E. L. and R. M. Ryan (1985), *Intrinsic Motivation and Self-Determination in Human Behaviour*, New York: Plenum.

Deci, E. L. and R. M. Ryan (2000), 'The "What" and "Why" of Goal Pursuits: Human Needs and the Self-Determination of Behaviour', *Psychological Inquiry*, 11 (4): 227–68.

Hämäläinen, R. and K. Vähäsantanen (2011), 'Theoretical and Pedagogical Perspectives on Orchestrating Creativity and Collaborative Learning', *Educational Research Review*, 6 (3): 169–84.

Hooper, D., J. Mynard, R. Sampson and P. Taw (2019), 'Shifting Identities in a Social Learning Space', *Learner Development Journal*, 1 (3): 26–43.

Joe, H. K., P. Hiver and A. H. Al-Hoorie (2017), 'Classroom Social Climate, Self-Determined Motivation, Willingness to Communicate, and Achievement: A Study of Structural Relationships in Instructed Second Language Settings', *Learning and Individual Differences*, 53: 133–44.

Lee, W. W. S. (2021), 'Relationship between Beliefs about Collaboration and Epistemic Emotions in Collaborative Learning: An Explorative Study Among Secondary School Students', in *Emotions in Learning, Teaching, and Leadership*, 18–28, London: Routledge.

Niemiec, C. P. and R. M. Ryan (2009), 'Autonomy, Competence, and Relatedness in the Classroom Applying Self-Determination Theory to Educational Practice', *Theory and Research in Education*, 7: 133–44.

Ryan, R. M. and E. L. Deci (2017), *Self-Determination Theory: Basic Psychological Needs*, New York: Guilford Press.

Yarwood, A., C. Rose-Wainstock and M. Lees (2019), 'Fostering English-Use in a SALC through a Discussion-Based Classroom Intervention', *Studies in Self-Access Learning Journal*, 10 (4): 256–378.

# CHAPTER ELEVEN

# Positive attributions:

# Using attributional retraining techniques to reduce students' speaking anxiety

*David McLoughlin*

Speaking anxiety, along with its accompanying fear of negative evaluation, is recognized as a major component of foreign language classroom anxiety (FLCA) (Aida, 1994). One source of FLCA is learner beliefs about language learning (Young, 1991). For example, Cheng, Horwitz and Schallert (1999: 436) found that 'learners' beliefs about their English speaking and writing capabilities were found to be a better predictor of their anxiety levels than what they were actually capable of accomplishing'. We may all know students whose negative beliefs about past performance in, say, speaking English can have a debilitating effect on their future motivation and performance. Such students can be caught in a spiral of self-doubt that may prevent them from improving their performance in the future. The activity described in this chapter helps students to interpret and explain their unsatisfactory past speaking performances in ways that can reduce their anxiety about speaking in English. The activity draws on techniques used in an educational intervention known as attributional retraining.

The activity comes from my experience teaching a course in presentation skills to university EFL students in Japan. While the activity could be used for any type of speaking course (or courses focusing on other skills), it is especially useful in academic speaking courses, such as presentation, debate or academic discussion. This is because effective performance in these genres of speaking depends to a great extent on learning and practising discrete communication skills, such as organizing main points clearly, providing supporting details or responding to questions. As I will show in this chapter, focusing on such strategies can help students modify their beliefs about their past speaking performances. The students in my context are in their second year at university, but the activity can be done with students in any year. The course I teach is a required course for second-year students, and it is the first time these students have studied English presentation skills at university, having taken more general conversation and discussion courses in their first year. My students tend to have a high proficiency in English, but many still lack confidence in their speaking skills. They also tend not to have much experience in giving presentations in English, so they can be somewhat anxious as they embark on this course. For example, some may have general anxiety about standing in front of the class and speaking, while others' anxieties are more specific: not being heard because they speak too quietly, not being understood because of pronunciation problems and not remembering what to say at critical moments.

The activity presented in this chapter can be done in one class period, preferably three or four weeks into the course, so that students will have already done some presentations in class. For this activity, students reflect on the presentations they have given in the course, focusing on those in which they did not do as well as they would have liked. They think about and discuss why they felt their performances were unsatisfactory. The goal is for students to get into the habit of seeing the causes of less successful performances in public speaking as malleable and controllable, thus making them less likely to experience anxiety.

## Background to the approach

Causal attributions are the explanations we assign to events and outcomes in our lives. The search for explanations is most common after outcomes that are negative and/or unexpected (McLoughlin, 2007). The attribution theory of achievement motivation and emotion, as presented by Weiner (1985, 2000), examines how people explain their achievement outcomes, as well as how their attributions have consequences for their subsequent motivation, emotional states and achievement.

People can make many different attributions, but the most common are attributions to ability and effort. A key insight of attribution theory is that attributions can be categorized along three dimensions (Weiner, 1985). The *locus* dimension refers to whether a cause is seen as internal or external to the individual. For example, effort and ability are internal, but luck would be seen as external. The *stability* dimension categorizes an attribution according to how likely it is to change over time. So, ability tends to be seen as stable (though this is not always the case, as I will discuss later), whereas effort is unstable. The final dimension is *controllability*, which reflects how much control people feel that they had over an outcome. For example, two students who have got good scores on a foreign language test may view their success very differently. One may attribute success to hard work and effort, while the other might attribute success to the fact that the exam was easy. The difference between the two attributions is that effort is under an individual's control, whereas task characteristics (e.g. an easy test) are often seen as something beyond one's control. Or consider two students who have done poorly in an English presentation. One might attribute failure to a lack of ability, which is often seen as stable, while the other explains the failure by attributing it to a lack of effort (an unstable cause).

The important point about the examples in the previous paragraph is that people can attribute similar outcomes to very different causes. According to attribution theory, our attributions influence our emotional states and our expectancies for future success (Weiner, 1985). Thus, whether we see a cause as internal or external affects our pride and self-esteem, our perception of the stability of a cause may lead to feelings of hopelessness or hopefulness, and how much control we feel we have over an outcome is linked to feelings of guilt or shame. Meanwhile, expectancies for future success are linked with the perceived stability of a cause. For example, attributing failure or poor performance to a stable cause like lack of ability can lead to low expectations for future success and increased feelings of hopelessness. On the other hand, attributing poor performance to an unstable cause, such as insufficient effort, is more likely to increase feelings of hopefulness and expectancies for future success.

Attributions, therefore, can be adaptive (having positive consequences) or maladaptive (having negative consequences). A real problem emerges if a student gets into the habit of making maladaptive attributions. The persistent use of maladaptive attributions 'can result in a downward spiral wherein negative emotional states contribute to continued poor academic performance, which then further undermines emotional functioning, and so on' (Haynes et al., 2009: 234). Falling into such a cycle of maladaptive attributional thinking can contribute to anxiety (Haynes et al., 2009).

The realization that maladaptive attributional thinking can have detrimental effects on emotional states, motivation and future achievement prompts the question, can we help our students develop adaptive attributional thinking styles? When tackling this question, we need to consider what types of attributions would be adaptive. Overall, students should be 'encouraged to attribute unsatisfactory academic outcomes to internal/unstable/controllable factors such as effort and strategy in place of external attributions such as luck, or uncontrollable factors such as ability' (Haynes et al., 2009: 237). Getting students to make more adaptive attributions is the aim of an education-based treatment known as attributional retraining, which is concerned with 'highlighting the controllable factors and downplaying uncontrollable factors following failure' (Haynes et al., 2009: 253). Although the main purpose of attributional retraining is to improve academic achievement, it has also had success in lowering test anxiety among first-year college students in the United States (Ruthig et al., 2004). The principles and some of the techniques of attributional retraining can be adapted for the foreign language classroom, and the activity described in this chapter draws on attributional retraining protocols (Haynes et al., 2009).

While attributing poor past performance to a controllable and unstable factor like lack of effort seems to have positive effects on future achievement, 'encouraging individuals to accept more responsibility for their actions might result in increased anxiety' (Haynes et al., 2009: 259). However, some research into the relationship between attribution theory and mindset theory suggests that attributing poor past performance to a lack of ability may be adaptive depending on what the learner believes constitutes ability. Zhang et al.'s (2022) review of forty-seven attributional SLA studies found that L2 learners do not always assume ability/aptitude to be stable. For example, people with a fixed mindset tend to categorize ability as stable. For them, 'failures are regarded as indications of aptitude inadequacy' (Zhang et al., 2022: 163). On the other hand, people with a growth mindset see ability as unstable and failures as temporary setbacks. Consequently, as Lou and Noels (2019: 547) state, 'fixed mindsets are linked to maladaptive emotional tendencies', such as language anxiety and fear of failure, whereas learners with growth mindsets tend to report less language anxiety.

Therefore, encouraging students to think of ability in terms of specific skills and strategies can help them make more adaptive attributions since any attribution that is seen as unstable 'could have the same positive effects as an attribution to lack of effort' (McLoughlin, 2007: 36). This is realistic in a presentation course with many specific skills and strategies that students can learn and practise.

# Activity

## Aims

This activity encourages students to reflect on an unsatisfactory speaking performance (in this context, giving presentations in English) and to interpret a disappointing performance in positive ways, with the aim of reducing students' anxiety about presenting in English. Students learn to make adaptive attributions, either to effort (an internal, unstable and controllable factor) or to ability in terms of strategy and skills development (also internal, unstable, and controllable). Although I have used this activity in a presentation course, it can be adapted for use in other types of speaking courses, such as academic discussion or debate courses.

- **Level:** Intermediate
- **Materials:** None required
- **Time:** Seventy to eighty minutes in one class period (plus a follow-up activity of twenty to thirty minutes)

## *Preparation*

Early in the semester (week one or two), have students discuss how they feel about doing presentations (or, depending on the type of speaking course, participating in discussions, etc.) in English. They can share any experiences they have of giving English presentations and what emotions they experienced. They can also share how they feel about the prospect of doing presentations almost every week in English.

After each practice presentation in the first three or four weeks of the semester, get students to write a few sentences about how they think the presentation went. The teacher can use these reflections to decide whether to do the activity and, if so, whether to modify it in any way.

## *Procedure*

1. Thinking about and discussing performance in past presentations (twenty-five to thirty minutes)

   - Give students time to reflect individually on presentations they have done in the course in which they feel their performance was unsatisfactory. This step is inspired by the *causal search activation* stage of a typical attributional retraining protocol (see Haynes et al., 2009). Students write short answers to the following questions:
     i *In which presentation(s) this semester did you not do as well as you wanted?*
     ii *Why did you not do as well as you wanted?*
   - After about ten minutes, ask students to form small groups and discuss their answers for ten minutes.
   - Finally, there is a brief (five minutes) class feedback session. Briefly explain the meaning of the term 'attribution' ('explanation for why things happen') and write some examples of student attributions on the board.

2. Thinking about adaptive and maladaptive attributions (fifteen minutes)
This next step introduces adaptive and maladaptive ways of viewing past performance. It draws on an attributional retraining method known as attribution retraining induction (see Appendix A in Haynes, Perry, Stupnisky and Daniels, 2009).

- Give students a handout (see example below and in the online materials) to read individually. The handout gets students to think about the controllability and stability of attributions.

- After students have read the handout (see Table 11.1 below), go through it with the class. The explanations on the left are maladaptive, while the ones on the right are adaptive. Explain the concept of adaptive and maladaptive attributions.

TABLE 11.1 Attribution handout (adapted from Haynes, Perry, Stupnisky and Daniels, 2009)

| When a presentation did not go well, did you think like this? | How about thinking like this instead? |
|---|---|
| I am not good at speaking English/doing presentations in English.<br><br>The presentation assignment/topic was too difficult.<br><br>It was bad luck/I had a bad day/I had tech problems.<br><br>I was too nervous/anxious. | I can improve if I work at it. For example, I can:<br>• review what was covered in the textbook<br>• practise my presentation before I do it in class<br>• work with another student<br><br>I can improve certain important presentation skills that I find challenging, such as:<br>• time management<br>• using transitions<br>• organizing my presentation into an introduction, body section, and conclusion<br><br>Perhaps I should have reviewed the relevant content in the book to better understand the assignment. I need to give myself enough time to think about the topic and plan what I am going to say in my presentation. I should have focused on certain presentation skills like the ones listed above.<br><br>Things like this happen to all of us occasionally. I can make sure I am well prepared and have a backup if things go wrong (a paper handout in case the projector doesn't work, for example).<br><br>There are ways to deal with nerves and anxiety. For example, I could break the presentation into more manageable parts (attention-getter, preview etc.) when I prepare it. |

- Explain how the maladaptive attributions focus on causes that are seen as fixed and uncontrollable (bad luck, anxiety, lack of ability, task difficulty) while the adaptive attributions focus on causes that are seen as changeable and controllable. Also, point out that ability can be viewed in different ways: as something stable or as something we can improve through practice and skill development (unstable).

3. Explanation (fifteen minutes)

Next, give a simple explanation of some key concepts that students need to understand about attributions. This can be done by preparing some simple slides that present the key concepts (please refer to the slides in the online materials). Include the following information:

- the main types of attribution (ability and effort)
- the classification of attributions (locus, stability and controllability)
- the consequences of attributions on our cognitions, emotions, motivation, behaviour.

These three bullet points have been explained in this chapter, and there is no need to go into greater detail when explaining them in class. You can also use the recommended reading listed in this chapter when preparing your explanation. I find it best to start with a concrete example of failure (real or imagined). The example could be from student life, but it does not need to be. A simple example would be two people who have failed their driving test. By describing how each person tries to explain their failure, you can introduce the idea of effort and failure attributions quite clearly. Likewise, the classification and consequences of attributions can be explained by describing how the people in the example situation feel and behave.

As you explain these points to students, check comprehension and answer any questions they may have. Students should start to think about how to apply the principles of attribution theory to their own experiences.

4. Group discussion (fifteen to twenty minutes)

Put students into groups to analyse the explanations (attributions) they discussed in step 1, classifying them in terms of locus, stability and controllability. They should also discuss whether their own attributions are adaptive or maladaptive and what would be the best type of attribution to make after failure or poor performance. Students then share their ideas with the whole class.

5. Follow-up writing activity

This is done outside class, and students should take at least twenty to thirty minutes to work on it. It is based on a technique from attributional retraining in which students recall an unsatisfactory academic performance, describe how they felt (and still feel) about the event and how they have reinterpreted it in a more positive and adaptive way (Haynes et al., 2009). Give a writing prompt such as the following (adapted from Appendix B in Haynes et al., 2009: 272):

> *Think about a presentation you have made in this course in which you did not do as well as you expected. How did your performance make you feel? How have you learned to think about your performance in a more positive way? How will this help you when you make presentations in the future?*

You can discuss this activity with individual students later in the semester. It is important to notice that the writing prompt asks students to think about their emotional responses and to focus on future presentations as well as past ones. These questions give students an opportunity to write about their emotional states, such as anxiety, and this is something you can pick up on in your discussions with them.

Students should keep the handout from Step 2 and refer to it when reflecting on their performance in future presentations. This can become a regular component of post-presentation reflection for the rest of the course.

This activity is not a one-size-fits-all approach. The way it is presented here may not be suitable for all contexts. The advantage of doing these activities a month or so into a course is that the teacher has the chance not only to see how students perform in their presentations but also to learn how the students interpret their performances. Therefore, teachers can tailor these activities to suit their own contexts. It should be noted that students will vary in how quickly they start to make more adaptive attributions. One way to help students who find it difficult to think more adaptively about their past performances is to encourage them to focus on specific components of the speaking task. In the case of presentations, for example, students can focus on how to improve the introduction to a talk. By breaking down the larger speaking task into smaller components, it is easier for students to see that they can improve their performance.

If you consider using a form of this activity, you might want to consider a couple of questions. The first is: *What if some of my students feel that all their presentations went well?* A modification of this activity could ask students to give reasons for both satisfactory and unsatisfactory presentation performance. The idea of adaptive and maladaptive attributions applies to both success and failure attributions. For example, attributing successful performance in presentations to ability (seen as a stable construct) may boost self-efficacy; on the other hand, it may lead to complacency (Graham, 2004) and possibly poorer performance in more challenging future presentation assignments. Therefore, it may be more adaptive to attribute successful performance to effort and/or knowledge of specific strategies (McLoughlin, 2012).

The second question is: *What if some of my students are already making adaptive attributions?* Unlike the situation I described in the previous paragraph, this could apply to students reflecting on either successful or unsuccessful past performances. If they attribute either type of performance to effort or ability in terms of learnable skills, then we can say that their attributions are already adaptive. This activity is still useful for such students. Making adaptive attributions in one area of language learning is not a guarantee of adaptive attributions in all areas of language learning, let alone in other subjects. Therefore, this can be a useful awareness-raising activity that students can apply to other aspects of their learning.

## Recommended reading

Haynes, T. L., R. P. Perry, R. H. Stupnisky and L. M. Daniels (2009), 'A review of attributional retraining treatments: Fostering engagement and persistence in vulnerable college students' in J. C. Smart (ed), *Higher Education: Handbook of Education and Research*, 227–72, Berlin/Heidelberg: Springer Science + Business Media B. V.
This article provides a clear overview of the key insights of attribution theory and then gives a thorough explanation of the principles of attributional retraining. In particular, the protocol for attributional retraining, which I drew on when designing these activities, is very useful.

Weiner, B. (1985), 'An attributional theory of achievement motivation and emotion', *Psychological Review*, 92 (4): 548–73.
Weiner's work on attribution theory is essential reading. He has written a huge amount on it, so it can be difficult to know where to start. This article is a clear presentation of the fundamentals of the attribution theory of achievement motivation and emotion, so it's a good one to read first.

Zhang, X., N. M. Lou, K. A. Noels and L. M. Daniels (2022), 'Attributions and Mindsets', in T. Gregerson and S. Mercer (eds), *The Routledge Handbook of the Psychology of Language Learning and Teaching*, 161–77, New York: Routledge.
This article is a very good exploration of the connections between attribution theory and mindset theory. It gives a concise outline of the key elements of attribution theory and shows how having a growth mindset view of ability can lead to adaptive attributions that can reduce anxiety.

## References

Aida, Y. (1994), 'Examination of Horwitz, Horwitz, and Cope's Construct of Foreign Language Anxiety: The Case of Students of Japanese', *The Modern Language Journal*, 78 (2): 155–68.

Cheng, Y., E. Horwitz and D. Schallert (1999), 'Language Anxiety: Differentiating Writing and Speaking Components', *Language Learning*, 49: 417–46.

Graham, S. J. (2004), 'Giving Up on Modern Languages? Students' Perceptions of Learning French', *The Modern Language Journal*, 88 (2): 171–91.

Haynes, T. L., R. P. Perry, R. H. Stupnisky and L. M. Daniels (2009), 'A Review of Attributional Retraining Treatments: Fostering Engagement and Persistence in Vulnerable College Students', in J. C. Smart (ed), *Higher Education: Handbook of Education and Research*, 227–72, Berlin/Heidelberg: Springer Science + Business Media B. V.

Lou, N. M. and K. A. Noels (2019), 'Language Mindsets, Meaning-Making, and Motivation', in M. Lamb, K. Csizér, A. Henry and S. Ryan (eds), *The Palgrave Handbook of Motivation for Language Learning*, 537–59, London: Palgrave Macmillan.

McLoughlin, D. (2007), 'Attribution Theory and Learner Motivation: Can Students be Guided Towards Making More Adaptive Attributions?', *OnCUE Journal*, 1 (1): 30–8.

McLoughlin, D. (2012), 'Attribution Theory as an Advising Tool', in J. Mynard and L. Carson (eds), *Advising in Language Learning: Dialogue, Tools and Context*, 151–63, New York: Routledge.

Ruthig, J. C., R. P. Perry, N. C. Hall and S. Hladkyj (2004), 'Optimism and Attributional Retraining: Longitudinal Effects on Academic Achievement, Test Anxiety, and Voluntary Course Withdrawal in College Students', *Journal of Applied Social Psychology*, 34 (4): 709–30.

Weiner, B. (1985), 'An Attributional Theory of Achievement Motivation and Emotion', *Psychological Review*, 92 (4): 548–73.

Weiner, B. (2000), 'Intrapersonal and Interpersonal Theories of Motivation from an Attributional Perspective', *Educational Psychology Review*, 12 (1): 1–14.

Young, D. J. (1991), 'Creating a Low-Anxiety Classroom Environment: What Does Language Anxiety Research Suggest?', *The Modern Language Journal*, 75 (4): 426–347.

Zhang, X., N. M. Lou, K. A. Noels and L. M. Daniels (2022), 'Attributions and Mindsets', in T. Gregerson and S. Mercer (eds), *The Routledge Handbook of the Psychology of Language Learning and Teaching*, 161–77, New York: Routledge.

# CHAPTER TWELVE

# Looking for evidence: Using CBT-based activities for FLA

*Neil Curry*

This activity is based around techniques used in cognitive behaviour therapy (CBT). One important component of CBT is searching for evidence (or more precisely, a lack of) to prove or disprove anxiety-inducing beliefs. Activities which encourage anxious learners to address whether their worries about speaking are actually justified by evidence; that is, they are an excellent means by which they can begin to form more rational, and ultimately more positive, beliefs. Rather than reacting with negative emotions and beliefs regarding a perceived lack of speaking skills, they can learn to develop a more realistic appreciation of their abilities, which leads to greater confidence. The activity is simple to implement and effective in both presenting anxious students with options to allay their individual concerns, and also as a means by which a class can become more at ease with each other, as they are able to confront FLA together.

## Background to the approach

The foundations, development and usage of CBT are too broad to go into extensive detail here, but I will give a brief outline of its key concepts in order for you to understand how it works and how it can match the needs of anxious language learners. I need to point out though that in my experience, sometimes when other educators hear the word 'therapy' they associate it with the professional help provided by trained psychologists and psychoanalysts, and fear that to engage with CBT techniques would risk straying into areas in which they have no place being. After all, we are educators, not counsellors. Sometimes we may be put in the position where students may confide in us their personal problems or issues, which may or may not relate to their mental and emotional health. Such students should always be encouraged to talk to a specialist if they are not already seeking help.

It is therefore important to make it very clear that in a language learning context, using activities derived from CBT techniques is simply to encourage students to reflect on and question their existing beliefs about their language skills, and if they find that these beliefs are detrimental to their linguistic progress and enjoyment of speaking in a foreign language, they now have a means by which these beliefs can be re-evaluated. This process of re-evaluation leads to CBT's description 'as the psychology of common sense' (Wilding, 2012: 10); the core idea here is that we are simply asking our learners to think about their skills rationally and objectively, instead of in emotional terms.

CBT has been shaped by a number of ideas through its development to its present form (see Stallard, 2019), but a recurring thread in the literature is that the studies of Aaron Beck, especially regarding his use of cognitive therapy (CT) to treat depression, have perhaps been the main influence (Stallard, 2002; Wright, Basco and Thase, 2006; Westbrook, Kennerley and Kirk, 2011; Wilding, 2012; Stallard, 2019). CT comes from the premise that 'maladaptive thoughts about the self, the world and the future (cognitive triad) result in cognitive distortions which create negative effect' (Stallard, 2002: 3). CBT is also influenced by behavioural theory (BT), and its principle that our behaviour is affected by conditions and consequences, and if these consequences are positive, then that behaviour will be reinforced. Additionally, our behaviour is influenced by our thinking, and so by changing our thinking, our behaviour can change too (Stallard, 2002).

Most relevant to the CBT approach is the focus on emotions and how they affect our cognitive processes. Wilding states that 'it is the feelings that our thoughts engender that have the most power over us' (2012: 6). Simply, if an event creates negative cognitions, this will lead to negative emotions and subsequent behaviour reflecting those emotions, and may result in negative outcomes. Learning to think about an event differently, so that we can develop more positive emotions and subsequently modify our behaviour, is the key to CBT. But it is important to note, as Wilding does, that 'an individual's current thinking style may have developed more from faulty perceptions than from actual events' (2012: 9). Specifically, the fears that students express to me (being negatively evaluated by others, experiencing breakdowns in communication, potential embarrassment) are often not the result of lived experiences but rather what the students think might happen. This is why it is essential to have students look for evidence of their successes, which points to their fears often being largely groundless and which enables them to adopt more positive beliefs.

Another important factor in CBT is core beliefs or schemas, which are formed by experiences (sometimes in childhood), and which can be activated by events, leading to the development of assumptions, which in turn produces automatic thoughts concerning the cognitive triad (Stallard, 2002). If a belief is negative, say, in regards to how a person thinks they will be viewed by others if they make a mistake speaking an FL, the subsequent assumptions will be dysfunctional. Westbrook, Kennerley and Kirk (2011) state that dysfunctional assumptions (DAs) are often constructed as conditionals (e.g. *'if I make a mistake, I'll be thought badly of'*) and are over-generalized. In my context, we do see this kind of generalizing occurring when students make statements like *'what if I don't get my point across properly?'*: the assumption being that problems will inevitably occur. The resulting automatic thoughts are likely to be self-critical and lead to uncomfortable emotions 'and unhelpful behaviours such as social withdrawal or avoidance' (Stallard, 2019: 3), which can be seen in this example from one of my students: *'I feel anxious about whether I am correct or not though I'm enthusiastic to speak.'* As automatic thoughts can often be plausible, they can be accepted as true and go unquestioned, becoming generalized statements about the self (Westbrook, Kenerley and Kirk, 2011), and the underlying issues are not challenged. I believe that this is a good explanation for why some students find themselves unable to participate in speaking activities, and don't seek out opportunities to communicate and practise outside of the classroom, and of why conducting activities like the one described below is necessary.

Here I'll describe how CBT works in practice, namely the skills and concepts used to help people reassess their negative core beliefs. What makes CBT a good fit for the language classroom is that it utilizes the same kinds of skills that we are often trying to encourage in our students – those of setting achievable goals, collaborating, improving critical thinking and encouraging self-reflection and autonomy.

One important characteristic of CBT is that it adopts a 'here-and-now focus' (Stallard, 2009: 15); rather than being too concerned about why the problem developed, it focuses on finding a solution and improving the situation. CBT therapists will set goals with their clients, 'focusing on how they would like their life to be different and the targets they would like to achieve' (Stallard, 2019: 16). This approach is motivating and empowering for students; they can change their own situation by becoming more in control of their feelings, and gain a more positive attitude towards their own speaking abilities. Goal-setting is a fairly common technique in language education too; although students often need some guidance in how to do it well, they are often familiar with it.

With CBT, critical thinking regarding the self is enhanced. Users gain the ability to recognize beliefs which are unhelpful and not necessarily representational of reality. This is accomplished through *psycho-education* where the connection between beliefs, emotions and actions is explained, and those undergoing therapy are trained to become aware of how they react in anxiety-provoking situations and to recognize maladjusted thinking processes (Stallard, 2019). This is why during my activity, I present the CBT cycle (see online materials) – showing the relationship between beliefs, emotions and behaviour – and explain to the students why they may have produced negative thoughts during speaking activities. I usually find that they understand very quickly, and it gets them thinking about their own experiences and thinking processes.

CBT is notable for the high degree of collaboration between the therapist and the client. Wright, Basco and Thase (2006: 19) describe the relationship 'much as an investigative team, developing hypotheses about the accuracy or coping value of a variety of cognitions and behaviours'. The therapist instructs on the use of CBT techniques, and the patient assumes responsibility for practising these methods in their daily lives and giving feedback. One-to-one collaboration of this type can be difficult for a classroom teacher, which is why it is useful to encourage students to share their thoughts about their worries of using the FL, and to look for evidence together following completion of the classroom activity below.

Another feature of CBT is its use of the Socratic method – questioning in order to arrive at new perspectives. Posing this kind of question enables clients to consider new possibilities and views regarding their thoughts. For students, this can aid critical thinking abilities and encourages reflection. Overall, the goal of the therapist is to train the patient to learn how to ask these questions to themselves, becoming independently equipped to examine their own beliefs. Encouraging this skill in our students helps them not only with anxiety issues but also with challenging other aspects of their language learning beliefs and practices – essential for becoming an effective, autonomous learner.

Having encountered anxious students from my first days of teaching, it led me to research FLA for my TESOL MA, and try to develop ways in which students could decrease their anxiety and speak with more confidence. A mention of CBT in McLoughlin (2013) and the possibility of its use to change students' negative attributions led me to begin to research its uses. My sister is also a CBT counsellor, so I had a rudimentary understanding of it, and so I decided to conduct research with individual students as described in Curry (2014). The activities I have tried out are based on and highly influenced by the work of Paul Stallard in using CBT with young people, and I highly recommend reading his workbook *Think Good, Feel Good* (2002). This particular activity is also a development of the Rational-Emotive approach described by Foss and Reitzel (1988), who also ask students to identify irrational beliefs which may be causing anxiety, and ask them to consider what evidence exists to support those beliefs. The Rational-Emotive approach must be very effective I believe; however, I don't want to tell students that their fears are *irrational* – it's perfectly normal to fear embarrassment, and I just suspect that most people don't want to be told in front of others that they are being irrational. I think it's more effective to ask them whether their beliefs are *helpful* or not; if you have a belief about yourself which is unhelpful and acts as a barrier to achieving your goals, then why not change it? I also find that the practical aspect of actually having the students actively search for the existence of evidence is more effective than just discussing it. Lastly, I hope that students might remember aspects of the activity such as the cognitive cycle and how negative thoughts are formed, and apply this knowledge to other anxiety inducing activities in their lives.

In my role as a learning advisor, I meet students on an individual basis to discuss questions and issues regarding their learning, using reflective dialogue (Kato and Mynard, 2016). I help them to think about such matters as what are appropriate learning strategies and resources for their own individual needs, how to set and plan for learning goals, how to use time effectively and how to create opportunities to practise their foreign language. Inevitably during the semester, I will talk to students about affective issues, which often relate to FLA. I often hear students comparing their own perceived lack of linguistic abilities with their peers, with such generalized statements as *'everyone else is better than me'*. This kind of comparison can be seen with students in their very first semester, when it is the first time for them to be surrounded by peers whose English proficiency is possibly higher than that which they have previously experienced, and which usually does not account for differences in learning experiences. It often results in a negative self-evaluation and a sense of inferiority, leading to a notion that the learner is not equal to their peers and therefore cannot meaningfully contribute to classroom conversations and discussions. As a result, they tend to speak far less than they would ideally like. I have found that such students can benefit from adopting a more objective view of their abilities, redirecting their focus to the gains they have made in their own progress since beginning their learning journeys, rather than concentrating on what they perceive they lack.

The activities used with individual students take several forms, ranging from advising using Socratic questions to get the student to challenge their beliefs (Curry, 2014) to highly structured evidence-gathering tasks (seen in this volume). As I also teach courses on self-directed learning skills to help students become more effective autonomous language learners, I wanted to adapt my approach with individual students to something that would work with a group. As students in my context often express concern about what their peers are thinking regarding their speaking abilities, I realized that it would be beneficial if students could do a confidence-raising task together, and share their worries in regards to what others are thinking. I believe that being confident to speak in another language is a skill that can be acquired, and is just as important as learning basics such as grammar or vocabulary. What is the point of learning the knowledge of how to speak in a foreign language if we don't have the confidence to do so?

# Activity

## *Aims*

This activity is particularly useful both as a class bonding exercise and as a means for anxious students to develop a more positive mindset. Students are able to see that they are not necessarily alone with their fears, and that, in fact, the worry that mistakes are something which classmates frown upon is not a widespread sentiment.

- **Level:** Any
- **Preparation:** Sticky notes, questions for discussion and analysis, CBT cycle explanation slides, follow-on 'Challenge your Beliefs' activity
- **Time:** Sixty to ninety minutes

## Part 1

1. Discussion

Divide the class into small groups of three or four students. Ask them to discuss what concerns they have when they are speaking English in class. In my context the speakers are all fluent in Japanese, so I ask them to discuss in their native language to allow them to express themselves clearly. Sticky notes are provided so that the groups can write down their thoughts. As I monitor the class, I ask the groups to explain to me the reasoning behind their thinking, so that we can fully understand the situation. This is an early point where it is possible to encourage students to spot any gaps in their thinking and to start considering whether their worries are justifiable or not.

2. Sharing

The sticky notes are placed on the whiteboard or some other focal point. What is noticeable about the collected thoughts is that they usually contain very similar thoughts and worries. In summary, I can expect to see such sentiments as:

- Fear of mistakes and embarrassment – arising from fear of negative evaluation by peers.
- Lack of confidence – on further investigation this often arises from a perceived lack of vocabulary, so that students fear that they will be unable to make their thoughts clear. This in turn can lead to a fear of being misunderstood, which will be problematic and embarrassing.

**Note** – It's very important at this point to draw explicit attention to the similarity of the concerns; students need to know that they are not alone in their worries, and that in fact they are widely shared.

3. Explanation

At this point, present the CBT cycle using the slides (based on Stallard, 2002: 37 – see online materials). Explain that our beliefs about a situation influence how we feel about it, which in turn affects the actions we take. This cycle can be positive or negative. However, if we have a negative belief, we can change it into a positive one if we challenge it.

4. Conversation and analysis

The object of this part of the activity is for students to practise communicating, and then to reflect on their performance in terms of whether they felt they were able to communicate effectively, and if the experience was enjoyable. The conversation serves as an opportunity to get evidence that while mistakes might occur, the students are generally still able to keep the conversation going, and that their conversational partner doesn't react negatively to errors.

   i  Provide a short question and answer handout on a topic of your choice. Giving them around ten questions is fine. It's best to choose a topic which you know students should be able to talk about without requiring any specialist knowledge, for example food, films and school life. You might find one from a conversation textbook or prepare your own. For example, if the topic is films, then questions could include items such as 'What's the last movie you saw' or 'What genre of films is your favourite?' Students participate in pairs for around ten minutes, but if you find that they are enjoying the conversation and expanding it, it can go on for longer.

   ii Following this, provide them with these questions to analyse the conversation. Have them write their answers so that you can collect and share:

   1  *Did you make a mistake?*
   2  *Did anyone laugh because you made a mistake?*
   3  *Did anyone else make a mistake?*
   4  *Did you laugh because they made a mistake?*
   5  *If others make a mistake, do you think they are stupid?*
   6  *Could your partner understand you?*
   7  *How do you feel about the conversation you just had?*
   8  *Do you think your partner enjoyed it?*

Whenever I have done the activity, the answers provided are almost always as shown in Table 12.1 below:

**TABLE 12.1** Common answers

| No. | Answer | Comment |
| --- | --- | --- |
| 1 | Yes | |
| 2 | No/ Yes | In exploring 'yes' responses, it's important to determine that the wrong answer may have been amusing, thus eliciting laughter |
| 3 | Yes | |
| 4 | No/ Yes | Again, the humorous aspect needs to be examined |
| 5 | No | |
| 6 | Yes | |
| 7 | Variations on 'good' | |
| 8 | Yes | |

iii. Collect the answers and present them to the students. This can be done simply by reading them out loud to the class. This confronts anxious learners with the fact that there is little evidence to support some of the concerns expressed in the initial discussion, and therefore they should begin to re-evaluate any core beliefs they might have. Encourage them to make this kind of evidence gathering and reflection a habit; critically evaluate their speaking performances in terms of whether you could mostly successfully say what they wanted to say or not, how others reacted (or not) when mistakes were made and whether misunderstandings led to a breakdown in communication. They will begin to think more in terms of being relatively successful communicators who are improving with practice, rather than thinking in generalized assumptions about how their speaking skills are consistently inadequate.

5. Follow-on activity

The activity might provide sufficient evidence for some students, but it is beneficial to add a follow-on task, again looking for evidence (or lack of) to support any negative belief. This activity, 'Challenge your Beliefs', is adapted from Stallard (2002) and can be found with the online materials.

The activity requires students to put into practice what they have learned through the class activity. It asks them to select their main negative belief and over the following week look for any evidence that suggests it's not necessarily true. For example, if a student thinks that people will laugh when they make a mistake, they should record how often this does/doesn't happen. At the end of the activity, they are asked to write a new, more balanced belief.

By the time that this activity is finished, students should now have the means by which they can critically examine and reappraise their concerns about speaking in class, and develop a more balanced, evidence-based viewpoint. If a student requires further help, the confidence-building diary described in Chapter Nine is a very useful tool for the longer-term.

Be sure to check with students who do any follow-up activities to see if they have been able to reassess their belief and see if they are feeling more confident about speaking. I always revisit the initial confidence activity at least once later in the semester with a reflection to ask the students how confident they are feeling now about speaking English.

## Recommended reading

Stallard, P. (2002), *Think Good – Feel Good: A Cognitive Behavioural Therapy Workbook for Children and Young People*. UK: John Wiley & Sons.
This book gives an approachable overview of cognitive behavioural theory and ideas for practical application but focused on working with children and young people. For those who are interested in using a CBT-based approach with these age groups, Stallard explains how the theory and skills can be applied and presented to them. Also, this book has a series of activities, attractive visuals and worksheets with guides for how to use them.

Mynard, J. and L. Carson (eds), (2013) *Advising in Language Learning: Dialogue, Tools and Context*, 151–63, Abingdon: Routledge.
This collected volume is an excellent introduction to learning advising, describing the development and different contexts of the approach. It also presents the tools and techniques that can be used in guiding students to become autonomous language learners.

## References

Curry, N. (2014), 'Using CBT with Anxious Language Learners: The Potential Role of the Learning Advisor', *Studies in Self-Access Learning Journal*, 5 (1): 29–41. Available online: https://sisaljournal.org/archives/mar14/curry/ (Accessed 26 April 2023).
Foss, K. A. and A. C. Reitzel (1988), 'A Relational Model for Managing Second Language Anxiety', TESOL Q, 22: 437–54.
Kato, S. and J. Mynard (2016), *Reflective Dialogue: Advising in Language Learning*, Abingdon: Routledge.
McLoughlin, D. (2013), '"Attribution Theory as an Advising Tool', in J. Mynard and L. Carson (eds), *Advising in Language Learning: Dialogue, Tools and Context*, 151–63, Abingdon: Routledge.

Stallard, P. (2002), *Think Good – Feel Good*, Chichester, UK: John Wiley & Sons.
Stallard, P. (2009), *Anxiety: Cognitive Behaviour Therapy with Children and Young People*, Hove, UK: Routledge.
Stallard, P. (2019). *Thinking Good, Feeling Better*, Chichester, UK: John Wiley & Sons.
Wilding, C. (2012), *Cognitive Behavioural Therapy*, London, UK: Hodder Education.
Westbrook, D., Kennerley, H., and J. Kirk. (2011), *An Introduction to Cognitive Behaviour Therapy: Skills and Applications*, Singapore: Sage Publications.
Wright, J.H., M.R. Basco and M.E. Thase (2006), *Learning Cognitive Behaviour Therapy: An Illustrated Guide*, Arlington, VA: American Psychiatric Publishing.

# CHAPTER THIRTEEN

# What makes you nervous?:

# A cognitive behavioural theory-based approach to identifying FLA triggers

*Kate Maher*

When language learners experience FLA, they can often become overwhelmed by their anxiety, as it can dominate how they perceive themselves as a language user. Anxiety tends to result in the use of unconditional statements (Kennerley, Kirk and Westbrook, 2017), such as 'I can't speak', 'I can't learn languages' or 'I always feel nervous when I speak', which can become internalized as beliefs (Hofmann, 2007). However, if anxious learners become more aware of what causes their anxiety, it may help them to develop a more balanced perspective and manage their anxious feelings. Language learners are rarely always nervous when they speak; rather, they become nervous in certain situations. So, by recognizing what causes their anxiety, in turn, they notice that they experience FLA in certain situations and what factors exist in these situations that cause them to feel nervous. Also, by recognizing what factors trigger their FLA, learners can better create effective goals to improve their speaking. Anxious people can struggle with setting goals as their anxiety often makes it hard for them to select what to focus on or how to choose appropriate coping strategies due to negatively biased thinking and being overwhelmed by negative thoughts (Hofmann, 2007). This can lead to learners selecting and relying on maladaptive coping strategies to avoid feeling anxious, such as not speaking in class (King and Smith, 2017). So, by supporting anxious learners to recognize that there are often specific factors that cause them to become nervous, they can create focused goals to deal with these factors, helping them to select coping strategies that are targeted towards their individual needs.

Without awareness of what specific factors trigger their anxiety, anxious learners are more likely to conclude that they are 'bad at speaking' and become overwhelmed by negative beliefs (Corrie, Townend and Cockx, 2016: 57), making it more challenging for them to take steps to improve their speaking confidence and ability. This chapter presents a cognitive behavioural theory-based activity to improve speaking confidence by increasing learners' awareness of their FLA triggers. Cognitive behavioural theory focuses on cognition and provides an individualized approach based on the insights gathered from the individual's perceptions of their anxiety (Kennerley, Kirk and Westbrook, 2017).

## Background to the approach

Most language teachers will know from experience that there are a multitude of factors that can cause students to experience FLA. These factors are often related to the type of learning task, the pedagogical approach and the classroom environment, which involves interpersonal relationships between the students, the teacher and other students (King, 2014). In addition, individual differences can also play a significant role, including how a student perceives language learning and being a language user, and how they participate in class (Gregersen and MacIntyre, 2014). The complex nature of FLA can make identifying causes a complex task, as this type of anxiety is not limited to the content-specific factors of learning a language, such as fears of making grammatical mistakes, being corrected and lacking specific skills such as listening (Yan and Horwitz, 2008). Context-specific factors resulting from the social performance required of students when they speak in the target language in the classroom can also play a role in FLA (King and Morris, 2022). While most subjects can be anxiety-inducing due to content and context-specific factors, due to the communicative and interpersonal nature of learning and using a language, students may feel that their social performance and language proficiency are both being judged (King and Smith, 2017) and struggle with not being able to present themselves 'authentically' (Horwitz, 2017: 42). Furthermore, FLA is dynamic, meaning that causes can change throughout the learners' language learning journey (Gregersen, MacIntyre and Olson, 2017). Therefore, while teachers should aim to make the classroom environment as supportive as possible, approaches that recognize individual differences can be a helpful way to enable students to manage their FLA and become more autonomous. If students can identify what underlying factors are causing them to feel nervous, they may be able to select and use coping strategies more effectively.

The activity in this chapter uses a cognitive behavioural theory-based approach. This approach focuses on a person's perceptions of situations when they experience anxiety and how their cognitive processes influence their feelings and actions. Through the insights gained by formulating the person's cycle of how their cognitive processes impact their emotions and behaviours, cognitive behavioural theory can be applied to create an individualized approach to examining and reducing their anxiety (Kennerley, Kirk and Westbrook, 2017). Cognitive behavioural theory is a well-established approach to understanding anxiety. Studies have shown the importance of examining a person's anxiety through their cognitive processes due to the interrelated nature of emotions and cognition.

Furthermore, cognitive behavioural theory has also demonstrated how anxious people tend to have negatively biased perceptions, which result in them being more likely to perceive events as anxiety-inducing situations (Heimberg, 2002; Hofmann, 2007). For example, in the case of the language classroom, a student who experiences FLA may be more likely to perceive participating in a speaking practice activity with a classmate as a risky situation where they will feel anxious and uncomfortable. In comparison, a more confident learner will be more likely to perceive the same activity positively, perhaps as something enjoyable and useful practice to develop their speaking skills.

Cognitive behavioural theory can be used to determine what factors potentially trigger an anxious person's negative perceptions or make negative thoughts more likely to occur (Corrie, Townend and Cockx, 2016). Common triggers that have been identified include (Kennerley, Kirk and Westbrook, 2017: 74–6):

- Situational factors, such as interpersonal dynamics with certain people
- Cognitive factors, such as particular topics
- Behavioural factors, such as performing specific tasks or actions
- Physiological factors, such as feeling tired or unwell (tired, hungry)

When identifying anxiety triggers, cognitive behavioural theory approaches tend to focus on the person's present situation rather than a history of their previous experiences (although these are factored in). So, from a cognitive behavioural theory perspective, a person's anxiety can be triggered multiple times a day (Corrie, Townend and Cockx, 2016). This means that an anxious language learner may become nervous on more than one occasion during a class. This cognitive behavioural theory perspective of FLA supports existing literature which has established FLA as a dynamic, situation-specific anxiety (Horwitz, Horwitz and Cope, 1986). In terms of supporting anxious students, this perspective adds to the argument that students need strategies to manage their FLA independently by being aware of what triggers it.

One cognitive behavioural theory approach to discovering factors that trigger a person's anxiety is using formulations. Formulations examine specific situations when the person experienced anxiety and what their thoughts, feelings and behaviours were before, during and after the moment they became anxious (Kennerley, Kirk and Westbrook, 2017). Firstly, by collecting evidence of their thoughts, emotions and behaviours, the person can become more aware of their negatively biased perceptions and how these influence what they feel and how they act, and how negative cycles of cognition, emotions and behaviours can emerge. Secondly, by comparing similar situations where they did not become anxious (or felt less anxious) and experienced a positive 'cycle', the person can recognize what factors made their perceptions and experiences of the situations differ (Corrie, Townend and Cockx, 2016). By using an adapted version of a formulation with anxious language learners, as introduced in the activity below, they can gain a deeper insight into how FLA influences their speaking performance and become aware of what factors may trigger negative thoughts, causing them to experience FLA.

The activity in this chapter was developed as part of an intervention study examining the relationship between low oral in-class participation and speaking-related anxiety. By comparing the positive and negative CBT formulations, participants noticed factors that could be targeted when designing the interventions to help them balance their negative thoughts. What also struck me was how some participants seemed to experience a confidence boost when they noticed that they were not always nervous when speaking in class; their anxiety and the effects of their anxiety were limited to certain situations and caused by specific factors, which were possible to find coping strategies for. For example, Eri, a participant in the study by Maher and King (2022), was very pessimistic about being able to build up her speaking confidence. She expressed feeling overwhelmed and was struggling to maintain her motivation to attend classes as she could not imagine how her situation could improve. After creating the CBT formulations, Eri became aware that she was not always nervous and did try to speak during classes. It also came to light how Eri felt nervous about speaking with a group of classmates, especially those she did not know well, but tended to feel less anxious about speaking with her teacher and during pairwork activities with a classmate she knew. Eri feared that classmates she did not socialize with would be more likely to evaluate her speaking skills negatively. By understanding her fears about speaking to less familiar classmates, in a follow-up study, we focused on developing coping strategies to help Eri improve her confidence in these situations.

# Activity

## Aims

The following activity can be used with individual learners or as a class group activity to promote peer bonding to encourage students to learn about each other while getting ideas for developing coping strategies. The activity is divided into two parts. The aim of Part 1 is to develop learners' awareness of how their thoughts influence their feelings and actions, and Part 2 is to help them identify triggers that set off a negative cycle of thoughts, feelings and behaviours related to speaking in the target language.

- **Level:** This activity works for any proficiency level, but L1 may be required for lower levels. The activity may be more suitable for students aged fourteen and over.

- **Materials:** Handouts adapted from the figures in this chapter (downloadable versions available online).

- **Time:** Part 1 should take about thirty minutes, and part 2 could be completed in forty-five minutes. However, time should be adjusted depending on the class size and how quickly the students understand the approach. Parts 1 and 2 should be carried out on different days to allow the teacher time to read and comment on the students' part 1 reflection. Ideally, ten to twenty minutes could be set aside in each class for the follow-up stages to support students in developing and evaluating their coping strategies.

## Part 1

1. To warm up, lead a class discussion to guide students towards recognizing how thoughts influence how we feel and what we do. The discussion will also prompt students to become aware that most classroom speaking situations are inherently neutral; that is neither good nor bad; rather, our perceptions decide. By understanding these ideas, students should notice that they can control how they think, feel and behave. Start by introducing the example of making a mistake when speaking in the target language. In pairs or small groups, get students to list negative and positive perspectives before getting them to give feedback to the class. Negative perceptions may include 'I will look stupid' and 'My ability is not good enough', and positive perceptions could be 'I can notice what I need to improve' and 'I learnt something new'.

- The negative perceptions list will probably be longer, and this discussion can be a helpful indicator of how your students perceive speaking in the target language.

- Acknowledge that there are positive and negative perspectives. Avoid telling students to be more positive, as the reality is that sometimes making a mistake is a negative experience, which is why students need coping strategies to know how to deal with those moments.

2. Introduce the CBT cycle (Figure 13.1) to demonstrate how thoughts influence our feelings and actions. Draw the cycle on the board titled 'Mistakes are bad'. In the 'Thoughts' circle, write down two to three negative thoughts from the discussion feedback. Then point to the 'Feelings' circle and elicit from the students how they would feel if they had these thoughts. Lastly, point to the 'Behaviours' circle and ask, 'If you had these thoughts and felt like this, how do you think you would behave in class?' Try to guide their answers towards responses such as 'I wouldn't speak much' or 'I would be too nervous to speak', to show how their negative thoughts and feelings impact their participation during in-class speaking activities. Figure 13.2 contains an example cycle.

3. Once students understand this relationship, demonstrate how the cycle continues by going through the cycle again. Ask questions such as 'If you don't speak much because you are worried and feeling bad about making mistakes, what other thoughts might you have?' (students may give responses related to self-doubt about their ability). Continue to 'Feelings' and 'Behaviours.'

4. Repeat Part 1 Steps 2 and 3 with the title 'Mistakes are good!' After completing the positive cycle, end by emphasizing how thoughts influence feelings and actions.

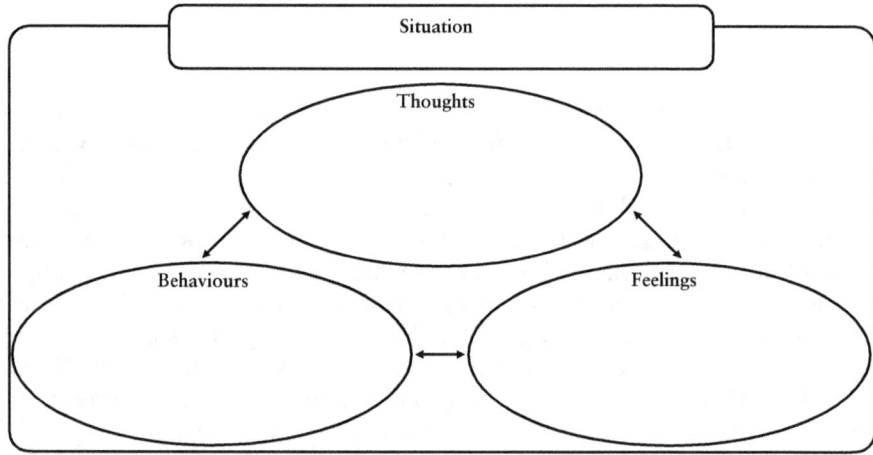

FIGURE 13.1 *CBT cycle*.

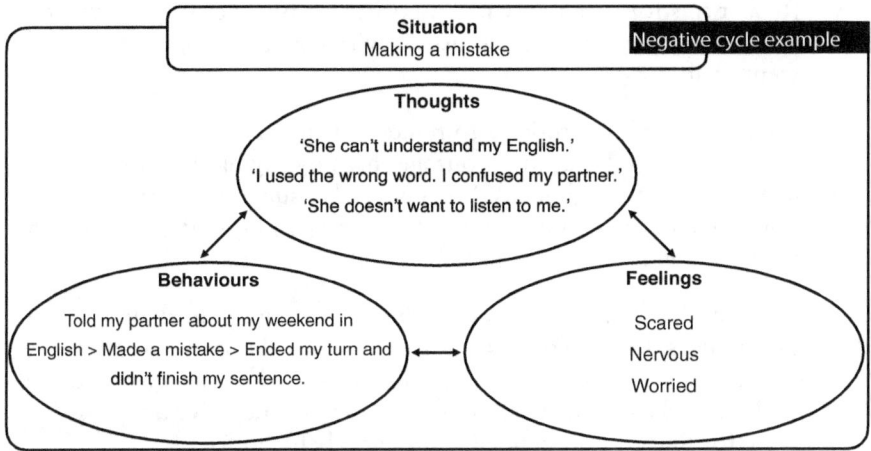

FIGURE 13.2 *Example CBT cycle.*

- CBT concepts may be unfamiliar to students, so it is important to spend sufficient time modelling the cycle. It may be necessary to demonstrate the cycle further, so have other speaking situations where there are negative and positive perceptions prepared, for example, 'My partner asked me to repeat what I said because they couldn't understand me' or 'Pausing because I forgot how to say a word'. Try to use specific situations such as these to model the level of depth you will want them to achieve, eventually, and away from catastrophizing thoughts such as 'I am always nervous when I speak'.

5. Ask students to individually complete a negative cycle for a recent in-class speaking situation when they felt nervous. They can draw the cycle, or you could adapt Figure 13.2 into a handout. Talk them through the steps:

  i  Choose a situation when they felt nervous, for example, a ten-minute discussion task with classmates.

  ii  What were they thinking during that situation? What were they worrying about? For example, 'I can't say my opinion clearly', 'I don't have enough vocabulary' and 'My classmates think my English is poor'.

  iii  How did this make them feel? For example, 'nervous', 'frustrated'.

  iv  What did they do during the situation? How did these thoughts and feelings affect them? For example, 'I only spoke once', 'I gave short answers' and 'I was busy looking up words I needed, so I just listened to my classmates' answers'.

v   Repeat this for when they had a positive experience of that type of situation, for example, a discussion with classmates when they felt it went well.

vi  It may be hard for students to remember in detail what they thought, felt and did, so encourage them by saying that it is fine to write down rough ideas. You could also suggest that they write down what they might typically think, feel and do. At this stage, the main aim is to help them become familiar with the cycle.

vii Some students may not be comfortable writing about their experiences, so you could suggest they write about hypothetical situations; for example, 'Shigeo felt nervous when the teacher called on him in class to answer a question. Draw a negative and positive cycle for Shigeo's thoughts, feelings and behaviours.'

6. Ask students to complete a written reflection about their CBT cycles, how thoughts can influence them and what they learnt about themselves as language learners.

## Part 2

1. In the next class, recap by modelling the cycle on the board, perhaps repeating a situation from the previous class. Then, if appropriate, ask students to share their cycles and reflections from part 1.

2. Using Figure 13.3 as the base for a handout, tell students that they are going to create their cycles for situations in which they feel less confident, for example, sharing their opinion, asking/answering questions, class debate and so on (part A of Figure 13.3). Ask them to complete the negative cycle first and then think of a positive experience for the positive cycle (part B in Figure 13.3).

- Each student will need two copies of the handout for each situation to complete a negative and positive cycle.

3. Have students consider what it is about those situations that may trigger the negative thoughts they wrote down in their cycle. For example, many students tend to feel anxious about giving presentations. However, to reduce this anxiety, they need to identify what it is about presentations that make them anxious. In the case of presentations, a student may feel nervous about speaking in front of a large group of peers, but encourage them to think more deeply about what makes them nervous about speaking in front of a large group of peers. Is it their facial expressions? Fear of negative evaluation by their friends? Having to speak loudly? Worries that their topic will be boring? To help them notice what specific factors might be triggering their negative thoughts, have the students compare their negative and positive

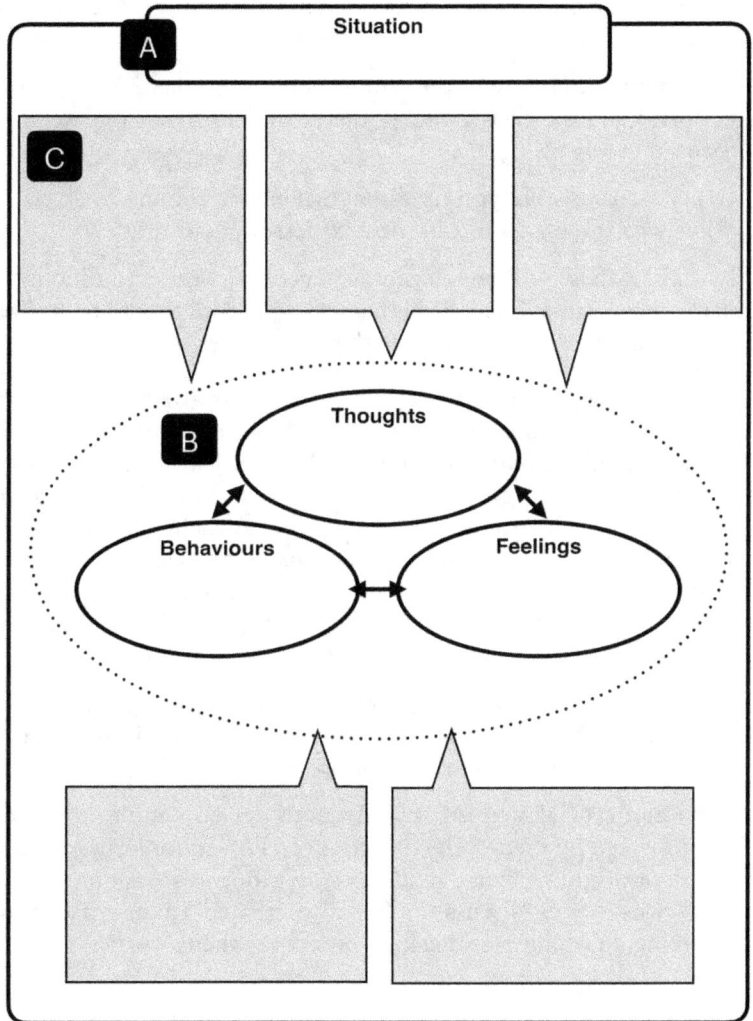

FIGURE 13.3 *Identifying triggers.*

cycles to see what factors were different. In the boxes around the cycles (part C on Figure 13.3), students write down possible triggers, for example:

- **What:** What was the topic? (Enjoyed it? Interested in it? Understood it? Chose it?). What was the type of task? (Evaluated? Long speech? Discussion?)
- **Who:** Who were you speaking to? (Teacher? Classmates? Classmates you knew well? One person or a group? The whole class?) What

was that person/people doing? (Listening carefully? Checking their notebook? Talkative or quiet? Correcting you?)

- **Environment**: How was the atmosphere in the class? What was happening in the classroom? (Quiet? Noisy? Classmates were focused or off-task?)
- **Other factors**: Were you tired/nervous before coming to class? Any other worries, e.g., a test in the next lesson, your grade?
- Not all of these will be relevant, so encourage them to fill out as many as possible. Encourage them to add more thoughts, feelings and behaviours to the cycles as they remember.

4. After identifying possible triggers, ask students to think about which one/s had the most significant influence and why. For example, Ayaka was a student who struggled to say her opinion in English. The negative experiences she recollected tended to be in group activities, and positive experiences of saying her opinion were often with a partner or a teacher. By comparing the two cycles and triggers, it became apparent that her anxiety was triggered by not knowing when to take her speaking turn in a group of people, especially when no one was speaking. However, when it was just her and her partner, she felt more confident taking risks and starting the discussion.

- If the class dynamics are appropriate, students can work in pairs or small groups to help each other by asking the questions in part 2 step 3 to prompt them to think more deeply.

5. The final and crucial step is for students to develop and evaluate coping strategies informed by their cycles and triggers. For example, in Ayaka's case, she worked on building her confidence for group discussions and taking more 'risks' to start the discussion. She also created a bank of expressions for introducing an opinion and asking others for theirs.

## Follow-up tasks and suggestions

- Once students have identified some triggers, support them with selecting, using and evaluating coping strategies. One approach is to have them create a 'strategy tracker'.
- Based on their triggers, get them to choose a coping strategy (the teacher should ideally provide some example strategies) and try using it for a week, recording how they used it, how effective they found it and why (or why not). Their records could be shared each week in class and used to build up a bank of strategies that others can try. A crucial element of this task is that students try and

evaluate a coping strategy for a sustained period. In my experience, students often know of strategies but do not test them out or only use them once without evaluating them.

- Care should be taken when introducing these activities to learners as some of the terminologies – anxiety, CBT and emotions – are sensitive due to their mental health implications. It is better to use less intimidating terms, such as 'increasing confidence' and 'controlling your nervous feelings'.

- Always have some hypothetical example situations to hand that can be used by students who prefer not to write about or share their own experiences. Hypothetical situations are used in CBT formulations to help with issues related to disclosure (Kennerley, Kirk and Westbrook, 2017). In a language classroom, hypothetical situations are also helpful for students who need more support to understand the CBT cycles before trying the approach for their own experiences.

- It may be hard to do this activity with a large class as you may need to provide frequent explanations and support as students become familiar with the CBT cycles. People with anxiety can become more anxious if they do not understand how the approach works or how to use it (Heimberg and Becker, 2002). However, by modelling example cycles to the class and providing feedback on written reflections, it is manageable with a larger group. In my experience, once students have seen a few example cycles, they tend to understand the key ideas.

- Some students may have strong beliefs that influence their thoughts in all aspects of their lives. For example, they may believe that 'mistakes are bad' because of a perfectionist trait, making it hard for the student to understand what causes their FLA. As a language teacher, it would not be appropriate to 'investigate' what underlying factors exist for that student. Instead, you could encourage them to focus on why those beliefs become stronger in certain situations or have them use hypothetical situations.

## Recommended reading

Maher, K. and J. King (2022), '"The Silence kills me.": "Silence" as a trigger of speaking-related anxiety in the english-medium classroom', *English Teaching and Learning*, 46: 213–34.
This study used a cognitive behavioural theory-based approach to examine language learners' perceptions of their speaking-related anxiety in the classroom. Semi-structured interviews were conducted using an interview schedule based on a CBT formulation to explore learners' thoughts and feelings

about their in-class oral participation and what factors triggered their anxiety. The findings revealed various triggers, including silent behaviours, such as extended pauses, short responses and using the L1. Participants described feeling uncomfortable and nervous about being unable to speak as much as they wanted to, as well as when their partner was 'silent', leading to fears of being negatively evaluated by classmates and self-doubt about their language proficiency.

Kennerley, H., J. Kirk and D. Westbrook (2017), *An Introduction to Cognitive Behaviour Therapy: Skills and Applications*. Singapore: Sage Publications. This comprehensive guide provides an introduction to cognitive behavioural therapy and key concepts of cognitive behavioural theory. While this text is aimed at people training to work in mental health, it is written in an approachable way, with plenty of example cases to demonstrate the ideas and techniques. Also, an online companion website contains additional materials and videos demonstrating how to use the techniques.

# References

Corrie, S., M. Townend and A. Cockx (2016), *Assessment and Case Formulation in Cognitive Behavioural Therapy*, 2nd edn, London: Sage Publications Ltd.
Gregersen, T. and P. D. MacIntyre (2014), *Capitalising on Language Learners' Individuality: From Premise to Practice*, Bristol: Multilingual Matters.
Gregersen, T. S., P. D. MacIntyre and T. Olson (2017), 'Do You See What I Feel? An Idiodynamic Assessment of Expert and Peer's Reading of Nonverbal Language Anxiety Cues', in C. Gkonou, M. Daubney and J. M. Dewaele (eds), *New Insights into Language Anxiety: Theory, Research and Educational Implications*, 110–34, Bristol: Multilingual Matters.
Heimberg, R. G. (2002), 'Cognitive-Behavioral Therapy for Social Anxiety Disorder: Current Status and Future Directions', *Biological Psychiatry*, 51 (1): 101–8.
Heimberg, R. G. and R. E. Becker (2002), *Cognitive-Behavioral Group Therapy for Social Phobia: Basic Mechanisms and Clinical Strategies*, New York: Guilford Press.
Hofmann, S. G. (2007), 'Cognitive Factors that Maintain Social Anxiety Disorder: A Comprehensive Model and Its Treatment Implications', *Cognitive Behaviour Therapy*, 36 (4): 193–209.
Horwitz, E. K. (2017), 'On the Misreading of Horwitz, Horwitz and Cope (1986) and the Need to Balance Anxiety Research and the Experiences of Anxious Language Learners', in C. Gkonou, M. Daubney and J. M. Dewaele (eds), *New Insights into Language Anxiety: Theory, Research and Educational Implications*, 31–48, Bristol: Multilingual Matters.
Horwitz, E. K., M. B. Horwitz and J. Cope (1986), 'Foreign Language Classroom Anxiety', *The Modern Language Journal*, 70 (2): 125–32.
Kennerley, H., J. Kirk and D. Westbrook (2017), *An Introduction to Cognitive Behaviour Therapy: Skills and Applications*, Singapore: Sage.

King, J. (2014), 'Fear of The True Self: Social Anxiety and the Silent Behaviour of Japanese Learners of English', in K. Csizér and M. Magid (eds), *The Impact of Self-Concept on Language Learning*, 232–49, Bristol: Multilingual Matters.

King, J. and S. Morris (2022), 'Social Interaction', in T. Gregersen and S. Mercer (eds), *The Routledge Handbook of the Psychology of Language Learning*, 311–22, Oxon: Routledge.

King, J. and L. Smith (2017), 'Social Anxiety and Silence in Japan's Tertiary Foreign Language Classrooms', in C. Gkonou, M. Daubney and J. M. Dewaele (eds), *New Insights into Language Anxiety: Theory, Research and Educational Implications*, 91–109, Bristol: Multilingual Matters.

Maher, K. and J. King (2022), '"The Silence Kills Me.": "Silence" as a Trigger of Speaking-Related Anxiety in the English-Medium Classroom', *English Teaching and Learning*, 46: 213–34.

Yan, J. X. and E. K. Horwitz (2008), 'Learners' Perceptions of How Anxiety Interacts with Personal and Instructional Factors to Influence Their Achievement in English: A Qualitative Analysis of EFL Learners in China', *Language Learning*, 58 (1): 151–83.

PART FOUR

# Visualization Techniques: Imagining Confidence

# CHAPTER FOURTEEN

# Imagine how I will face up to speaking anxiety:

# An imagery-focused mindfulness approach to preparing for speaking situations

*Sarah Ng*

In my teaching career, many colleagues and I have witnessed how some students came into class fully prepared for a speaking task but could not perform as expected because of anxiety. We often wish that they could go back in time, calm down and have another try. The good news is that the human brain is so powerful that it is possible for learners to transport themselves through time using mental imagery to practise self-soothing – what I call emotional rehearsals. With a background in neuroscience and mindfulness, I have been exploring how the two disciplines can be used to empower individuals to monitor and lower their foreign language anxiety levels. Apart from language skills, learners need effective emotional management to confidently navigate cross-linguistic and cross-cultural situations.

The activity in this chapter combines guided mental imagery with mindfulness. Mental imagery is a term 'variously used to describe a range of techniques from simple visualization and direct imagery-based suggestion through metaphor and story-telling' (Rossman, 2018: 930). It is a vivid way for learners to rehearse managing emotions, including anxiety. Mental imagery has been shown to lead to physiological reactions highly similar to those in the real situation, and therefore, it is used widely among athletes in psychological training for best performance. Mindfulness refers to the skilled use of attention 'on purpose, in the present moment, and nonjudgmentally' (Kabat-Zinn, 1994: 4). There are many types of mindfulness practices, and this activity focuses on the technique of body scanning. A body scan involves scanning your body for sensations linked to different emotions, such as anxiety.

## Background to the approach

Research evidence indicates that the more able a learner is in doing mental imagery rehearsals, the more motivated and the less anxious they tend to be in speaking a foreign language (Papi, 2010, Dörnyei and Chan, 2013). This is possible because imagination can be as effective as real stimulus in reducing perceived threat and anxiety, as revealed in brain-imaging studies (Lacey and Lawson, 2015, Reddan et al., 2018). Mental imagery is particularly powerful when it uses multiple senses in the mental 'picture' or 'video', including visual, auditory and tactile input. Through imagining an upcoming speaking situation, the learner experiences emotional and physiological responses similar to those they will have in the actual situation. This presents an opportunity for the learner to practise managing their anxiety using mindfulness.

Mindfulness, specifically the technique *body scan*, brings into learners' awareness their physiological reactions when they are anxious (e.g. faster heartbeat, sweaty palms, butterflies in the stomach). Non-judgemental observation of those reactions allows them to become curious and accepting of anxiety. In other words, they learn to face up to rather than suppress anxiety over time. With greater sensitivity and acceptance of anxiety as a natural response, learners will have a greater ability to manage the emotion. The better ability to notice and regulate anxiety means that they can be less dependent on others, such as their teachers, to improve their emotions. In other words, they become more autonomous in the aspect of emotion regulation in language learning.

In my research on emotion regulation in language learning, I identified evidence which shows that learners with low speaking anxiety are more emotionally aware and sensitive to their own bodily reactions (Ng, 2023). I also found that learners who suppress their anxiety paradoxically become more anxious over time. These findings echo those in established psychological research (e.g. Cameron and Overall, 2018, English and John, 2013). As you probably would agree, a teacher interaction strategy affects learners' anxiety and willingness to speak a foreign language (Lee and Ng, 2010). Apart from language skills, as an educator you may help by enhancing learners' capacity to face up to speaking anxiety, where imagination has been shown to be an effective psychological intervention (e.g. Landkroon et al., 2022). The guidance you give to your students in developing such an ability will pay off in the long term if the learners follow through on the practices.

I have used the technique with individual learners and small classes. In most cases, students reported a more relaxed state of mind, and there were cases of significant improvements in managing speaking anxiety. One example is a business student on a job search course who could not utter a word at the mock job interview because of fear in expressing themselves in English. In the following week, the student attended three short one-on-one sessions where I guided them to imagine attending a job interview with specific details described, for example, turning the door handle, taking a seat, feeling a faster heartbeat and looking at an expressionless interviewer. For each image, I invited them to scan their body for the *most* noticeable anxiety response, such as a lump in the throat or tightened shoulders. I suggested observing the response without self-criticism and then appreciating how the response was a way of their body trying to cope. I also proposed alternative self-talk to a potentially anxiety-provoking scene where cognitive bias is likely. For instance, the interviewer had a blank face, not because of boredom but because they were interested in the student's answers. After each session, the student would practise on their own and vary the situation, for example, the details of the interview and interviewers, sources of anxiety and alternative self-dialogue. In all the practices, whether with me or on their own, the objective was for the student to remain non-judgemental towards their emotional and physiological reactions. It was amazing that the student later reported a much better job interview performance than before.

The major challenge to achieving the intended outcomes of this activity stems from two commonly held beliefs:

1 Anxiety is a trait that cannot be changed at all. There are learners who refuse to believe that they have some control over the trait. This is understandable because they probably have failed many times to regulate their emotion. However, such a belief is unhelpful.

2 There is a quick fix to becoming a less anxious speaker. I have had many students who asked how they could become confident speakers with little time investment. While there have been promising cases that saw considerable improvement in a short time, change is most likely seen over months or even years of practice. However, with patience as well as considered and sustained practice, learners would very likely find that they are less reactive to stimuli they used to dread.

For both of the above cases, I find that it is most useful to share stories about myself and other students believing in change and repeated practice. To have a solid grasp of the steps before trying the activity with your students, you may want to experience the activity by doing it yourself beforehand.

It is also helpful to have students recall how they have successfully learned another skill by having a conducive self-belief and engaging in repeated, effective practices, such as playing a musical instrument or swimming. In the following, you will learn how to guide your learners to deal with anxiety symptoms should they arise when they speak a foreign language. However, they may be applied to situations involving other language skills, such as listening to a lecture.

# Activity

## *Aims*

The activity is for students to practise 'body scanning': becoming mindful of their bodily responses to help them manage anxiety in an FL communicative situation. The activity consists of two stages: pre-activity discussion and guided imagery-based mindfulness. The details are intended to be suggestions only. You are advised to adapt it according to the specific context you are working in. For example, for younger learners, you may want to simplify the language and use appropriate pictures, analogies and gestures to aid their understanding.

Body scan is backed by empirical evidence to be associated with better well-being and learning motivation; however, for their effects to be seen, continued practice is necessary (Hyland, Lee and Mills, 2015, McConville, McAleer and Hahne, 2017). The activity in this chapter is designed to be short so that it can be feasibly fitted into a lesson. The more your learners do them (e.g. before every speaking activity), the more likely they will build a mental habit that helps to lower their anxiety. However, please consider the specific context you are working in when deciding how often you would like to conduct the activities. Also, although mental imagery and mindfulness are generally safe, it is important to know that learners with disturbing or even traumatic experiences (e.g. being bullied for their accent) may not welcome or benefit from the activity. It is advisable to consider the learners' history, to issue a warning beforehand where appropriate, to make participation voluntary and to observe learners' reactions closely.

The activity can be held with an individual learner or a group of students, whether it is big or small. However, you are recommended to determine the size of the group by thinking about how many learners you will be able to closely observe for their facial and bodily reactions in your guidance process.

- **Level:** Any
- **Materials:** Pictures to induce positive and negative emotions, scripts
- **Time:** Sixty minutes

## Part 1. Pre-activity discussion (twenty to thirty minutes)

i First, it is important to acknowledge that anxiety is a natural response not to be ashamed of. Share with the class that there are many common reasons why we are nervous about speaking, e.g. fear of making mistakes and worry about being judged. Talking about it helps an individual to become aware of the emotion, which is the first step to processing it. If time allows, invite students to share how they have overcome anxiety in learning a new skill (e.g. learning a new football trick, or singing in a group).

ii As a lead-in activity, show two pictures of your choice one by one and ask students to focus on how their bodies react. The pictures should be intended to respectively induce positive and negative emotions (e.g. Picture 1 may show a calming, beautiful park at sunrise while Picture 2 illustrates a person about to speak in front of a crowd). The objective is to highlight the immediate responses of the body and to let students be more in tune with their own reactions in preparation for the main activity. Invite students to share their reactions. Most likely, students will report bodily reactions indicating pleasantness for picture 1 (e.g. relaxed arms), and unpleasantness in picture 2 (e.g. faster heartbeat). Be sure to focus the discussion on physical reactions (e.g. breathing, heartbeat, muscular tension) in addition to emotional experiences (e.g. feeling relaxed).

iii Then divide students into groups. In groups, students will share their most recent episode of feeling anxious when speaking a foreign language. The questions are as follows.
  1 When and where did it take place?
  2 Who was there? Did you know the audience well?
  3 How anxious were you overall? Assign a score on a scale of 10, 0 being the lowest. The meaning of a number differs across people, so just pick a score you feel best represents your anxiety level at that point.
  4 What was the *one* major cause of anxiety then? If you don't mind, please share how you knew you were anxious (e.g. racing heart, flushed face, sweaty palms).

It is advisable to invite but not nominate students to share their experiences with the class. The pre-activity discussion is a chance for you to enhance rapport with students by showing a non-judgemental attitude towards anxiety in speaking a foreign language. There may be a reluctance to open up or an 'awkward' silence when the discussion is had the first few times. However, a consistently open and accepting attitude will encourage students to share about themselves over time. If the class does not seem keen to share their thoughts openly, the activity may be turned into an anonymous activity in which students will read one another's written responses. Learning about others' experiences helps students to see the ubiquity of anxiety and to build mutual trust and support.

## Part 2. Imagery-based mindfulness (twenty to thirty minutes)

*Introductory stage*
Tell students that they will learn how to manage their anxiety by being mindful of (i.e. attentive to) their physical responses when speaking in a foreign language. They can do so by imagining a situation and noting their bodily responses. During the activity, they may feel as anxious or uneasy as they would in a real situation, but they will learn how to handle it and if they practise it regularly, they will likely feel less anxious in a similar situation.

The following is an example script of the introduction to the activity. As mentioned above, you are encouraged to adapt it to suit the cognitive, linguistic and motivational needs of your students. You may also make it more interactive by making some of the statements into questions if you wish.

### Do you like films?

Today, I'm going to show you how you can play a film where you're the screenwriter and director. That means you can decide what's going to happen!

The film is about presenting about [topic] in a foreign language to a group of people. Who's that person speaking to? You. Yes, you're the actor as well. But remember, you can direct how you do things, which will, in turn, change how you feel.

When you're told that you'd be speaking to people you don't know in a foreign language, your mind might already be wandering off. It is natural to feel anxious. You may think, 'Will I be making an embarrassing mistake?' Or an image of the audience may flow into your head. Even the most experienced speakers may feel nervous.

Here's the good news – we can do something to the imagery to help ourselves feel more relaxed. It helps your body to prepare for the actual speaking situation.

> The more detail we draw up in the imagery, the more likely it will work in the real situation. The method has been tested and shown to be useful in helping us to calm our nerves and to be more ourselves. Even if you don't usually feel very anxious speaking the language, it doesn't hurt to do a bit of imagination and relax ahead of a task, does it?

It is fine if a student wants to opt out, but where appropriate, invite them to join the experience.

Ideally, the activity is held in a quiet environment. Have everyone put away their electronic devices, including laptops and tablets.

An individual can do this activity practically anywhere, but they should ensure that they are in a safe position without risk of falling (e.g. falling from a chair). The teacher is expected to safeguard the learners by observing them closely during the mindfulness activity and reacting appropriately when seeing danger.

## Main stage

Invite students to sit in a safe and comfortable posture with their feet on the ground. Below is an example script to illustrate imagery-based mindfulness, using an oral presentation as an imagined scenario. It is recommended that the exercise be conducted in an instructional language the learners feel most comfortable with, which could be their native language. The rationale is to minimize distraction. I also recommend keeping the pace of speech slower than usual throughout the activity. I have suggested places to pause and closely observe learners.

> Very soon, I will invite you to close your eyes because that will help you focus on your imagination. You may open your eyes at any time, especially if you feel uncomfortable, and remember, you may withdraw at any time. If you do so, I would appreciate it if you can wait for others to complete the imagery unless there is something urgent that you need to tell me straight away.
>
> Now I'd like to invite you to close your eyes, although if you want, you may keep your eyes open. You are going to give an oral presentation in [the foreign language] very soon. You see that the last presenter has almost finished. You're seated and waiting for your turn. What is the colour of the desk you are at? Do you have a cue card in front of you? Are you reading it? Imagine what it's like. [pause and closely observe learners.]
>
> What is the biggest sign in your body that tells you you're anxious? Is it heavier breathing? Faster heartbeat? Tightened shoulders? A lump in your throat? [pause and observe.] This is a sign of your body trying to help you. There's no right or wrong. You may feel uneasy or even scared about the

sign. This is natural. There is no need to blame yourself. See if you can let the feeling be there. [pause and observe.] I'd like you to observe it. Be curious. What is the sign like? Does it change slightly over time? If so, how? [pause and observe.]

Excellent. I'd like to invite you to feel how your stomach is rising and falling as you breathe. You're breathing in and out. In and out. [pause and observe.] Your stomach is rising and falling. Rising and falling. Very good. I'd like to invite you to find something that gives you a feeling of comfort and safety. It can be inside you, like your stomach rising and falling or your lips touching each other. It can be something outside, like a sound you hear or your contact with the chair. [pause and observe.] Let's call it your safety spot. Can you feel it? [pause and observe.] You're doing very well.

Now, it's your turn to speak, and you're looking at your cue card one more time. What colour is the card? Is it white, yellow or what? It may be your favourite colour. [pause and observe.] How is your body responding? Which part tells you that you may be anxious? Your heart? Shoulders? Throat? Mouth? [pause and observe.] Again, it's okay. Allow yourself to gently accept the discomfort. You may put it in a cradle like a baby, look at it and give it warmth. [pause and observe.] How does the feeling change? Remember, feelings are temporary. They go away slowly when we gently let them go. [pause and observe.] Where's your safe spot? I'd like you to spend a little time there. Slowly feel how you feel supported or anchored there. [pause and observe.]

You're walking to the centre of the stage. The audience becomes quieter. You look at them. As you speak, you see a smiling face. Who's that? Is that your friend, the teacher or a friendly person you don't know? Whoever that is, what does that person look like? Look at how they are smiling. How does that make your body feel? [pause and observe.] Which part of your body gives you the biggest sign that you're feeling positive? Is it that your lips curl up a bit? Or are your shoulders a bit more relaxed? Or is it your face? [pause and observe.] Enjoy the relaxation. [pause and observe.] You may feel unsure if it's okay to feel happy at this moment. You may think that'll take away your concentration. [pause and observe.] Or you fear that the enjoyable feeling will slip away. [pause and observe.] It's fine to feel like this. Like you did before, try to sit with the feeling. At the same time, gently focus on the good feeling you have. It's acceptable to feel both anxious and positive at the same time. [pause and observe.]

The four key principles embedded in the script include the following.

- Describing the details and giving students liberty over some of the images, e.g. colours in the setting, people and physical reactions, because the more detailed and authentic the simulation is, the better the effect.

- Directing attention and promoting acceptance of physiological reactions
- Highlighting that negative and positive emotions can co-exist
- Encouraging acceptance and letting go of negative emotions and nurturing of positive emotions.

## Recommended reading

Dornyei, Z. and M. Kubanyiova (2013), *Motivating Learners, Motivating Teachers: Building Vision in the Language Classroom*. Cambridge: Cambridge University Press.
This book is among the few that provide a range of practical principles and techniques that can be implemented in the language classroom. The ideas have strong empirical support in not only foreign language acquisition but sports and psychology, making it convincing, easy to read and highly useful in different aspects of life apart from language learning.

Jeffers, S. (2014), *Feel the Fear and Do It Anyway*. London: Ebury Publishing.
First published more than thirty years ago, the book outlines simple but powerful beliefs that are conducive to managing anxiety. The beliefs are what all kinds of learners, including language learners, need to develop to step out of their comfort zone.

Landkroon, E., E. A. Van Dis, K. Meyerbröker, E. Salemink, M. A. Hagenaars and I. M. Engelhard (2022), 'Future-oriented positive mental imagery reduces anxiety for exposure to public speaking', *Behavior Therapy*, 53 (1): 80–91.
The literature review in this article summarizes scientific studies on mental imagery in accessible language. The study reported in the article focuses on exposure therapy, which is used to treat anxiety disorders. While foreign language speaking anxiety is not a disorder, the literature on mental imagery within exposure therapy lends indirect empirical support for the usefulness of the technique in foreign language speaking.

## References

Cameron, L. D. and N. C. Overall (2018), 'Supplemental Material for Suppression and Expression as Distinct Emotion-Regulation Processes in Daily Interactions: Longitudinal and Meta-analyses', *Emotion*, 18 (4): 465–80.
Dörnyei, Z. and L. Chan (2013), 'Motivation and Vision: An Analysis of Future L2 Self-Images, Sensory Styles, and Imagery Capacity across Two Target Languages', *Language Learning*, 63 (3): 437–62.
English, T. and John, O. P. (2013), 'Understanding the Social Effects of Emotion Regulation: The Mediating Role of Authenticity for Individual Differences in Suppression', *Emotion*, 13 (2): 314–29. http://doi.org/10.1037/a0029847.

Hyland, P. K., R. A. Lee and M. J. Mills (2015), 'Mindfulness at Work: A New Approach to Improving Individual and Organizational Performance', *Industrial and Organizational Psychology*, 8 (4): 576–602.

Kabat-Zinn, J. (1994), *Wherever You Go There You Are: Mindfulness Meditation in Everyday Life*, Westport: Hyperion.

Lacey, S. and R. Lawson (2015), *Multisensory Imagery*, New York: Springer.

Landkroon, E., E. A. Van Dis, K. Meyerbröker, E. Salemink, M. A. Hagenaars and I. M. Engelhard (2022), 'Future-oriented Positive Mental Imagery Reduces Anxiety for Exposure to Public Speaking', *Behavior Therapy*, 53 (1): 80–91.

Lee, S., T. Parthasarathi and J. W. Kable, (2021), 'The Dorsal and Ventral Default Mode Networks Are Dissociably Modulated by the Valence and Vividness of Imagined Events', *Journal of Neuroscience*, 41 (24): 5243–50.

Lee, W. and K. Y. S. Ng (2010), 'Reducing Student Reticence through Teacher Interaction Strategy', *ELT Journal*, 64 (3): 302–13.

McConville, J., R. McAleer and A. Hahne (2017), 'Mindfulness Training for Health Profession Students – The Effect of Mindfulness Training on Psychological Well-being, Learning and Clinical Performance of Health Professional Students: A Systematic Review of Randomized and Non-randomized Controlled Trials', *Explore*, 13 (1): 26–45.

Ng, K. Y. S. (2023), 'Emotion Regulation and Foreign Language Anxiety: A Mixed-Methods Study of Chinese Learners of English as a Foreign Language (EFL) in Hong Kong', PhD diss., School of Education, University of Leicester, Leicester.

Papi, M. (2010), 'The L2 Motivational Self-System, L2 Anxiety, and Motivated Behavior: A Structural Equation Modelling Approach', *System*, 38: 467–79.

Reddan, M. C., T. D. Wager and D. Schiller (2018), 'Attenuating Neural Threat Expression with Imagination', *Neuron*, 100 (4): 994–1005.

Rossman, M. L. (2018), 'Guided Imagery and Interactive Guided Imagery', in D. Rakel (ed), *Integrative Medicine*, 4th edn, 930–6, New York: Elsevier.

# CHAPTER FIFTEEN

# Rewrite your inner script: Make friends with oral presentation

## Zsuzsa Tóth

Are you one of those language teachers who believe that oral presentations are useful in the foreign language classroom? Have you noticed that many of your students experience anxiety when delivering their speeches and thereby fail to achieve their full potential? Have you ever wondered how you could help them overcome their fear of speaking before an audience, what is more, in a foreign language? If your answer to these questions is *yes*, this is an activity for you!

Originally *Rewrite your inner script* was designed for students in university EFL classes, a setting where oral presentations are a commonly used speaking task, more than in other contexts. The activity is simple to implement and requires minimum preparation for the teacher. It is designed for groups in regular language classes and is planned for a whole class session prior to setting a presentation task. *Rewrite your inner script* is conceptualized as a series of short activities with different sub-goals, and its purpose is to provide psychological and mental preparation for the upcoming public speaking task.

How can learners benefit from this activity? Going through the following stages, like imaginary stepping stones – including phases of silent individual reflection, mingling, full class and small group discussions – learners will have a chance to:

1. Explore and discuss their own and others' feelings and attitudes concerning oral presentations
2. Identify and verbalize their fears and worries and pair them with potential coping strategies
3. Learn a practical, cognitive technique for dealing with public speaking anxiety: positive visualization, which they can subsequently use independently.

The activity will sensitize students regarding the workings and different manifestations of anxiety related to speaking a foreign language before an audience. It will also help them understand the basic causes of this anxiety and realize that it is not an individual or personal problem but one affecting most people. Promoting a 'you are not alone' 'we are in the same boat' mentality, *Rewrite your inner script* can also function as a group bonding exercise, creating a relaxed and accepting classroom environment, with students more sympathetic and supportive of each other when it comes to listening to each other's talks. Applying the method of collaboration all the way through, the session will also equip participants with useful strategies and practical tips for both aiding efficient speech preparation and delivery and reducing anxiety.

## Background to the approach

What prompted me to develop *Rewrite your inner script* in the first place was seeing my own students' uneasiness and discomfort whenever it came to oral presentations in my university EFL classes. To get a better understanding of the nature of this anxiety and my students' emotional experiences, I conducted two studies to explore their perspectives of this speaking activity (Tóth, 2019, 2021). These investigations confirmed that presenting in the target language is perceived as an overly anxiety-provoking task even by advanced-level learners (B2+/C1 on the *Common European Framework of Reference for Languages* scale), with an unexpectedly high percentage of them experiencing considerable or even extreme anxiety (≥8 on a scale of 10) in response to having to speak in front of their classmates.

Based on information gleaned from my participants' accounts, what lies at the root of this anxiety is learners' mental images or inner scripts of giving a speech in the language classroom, namely, their attitudes, thoughts, perceptions and concerns related to four salient features of this task: (1) *the asymmetrical communication situation* (which makes them feel different, spotlighted and exposed – in one of my students' words: 'as if under a magnifying glass'), (2) *themselves* (they worry about their abilities to perform well and how they come across, e.g. they fear coming across as uninteresting or boring), (3) *the speech* (on one hand they worry about delivery issues like forgetting what they want to say, losing their train of thought, etc., on the other hand about potential language problems like making mistakes, not finding the right words, mispronouncing or stumbling over words, bad pronunciation, etc.) and (4) *the audience* (they feel self-conscious and worry about what their classmates will think about them – as one of my students put, they see the audience as 'strict judges' – and fear being viewed negatively and losing face). Added to all this is awareness of potential bodily reactions like shaking, blushing, a quivering voice, etc., which only adds fuel to the fire and increases anxiety, as students fear nothing more than looking visibly anxious before their peers. Finally, inappropriate, or insufficient speech preparation (e.g. trying to memorize talk verbatim, not practising speech) also contribute to feelings of insecurity and nervousness.

The development of *Rewrite your inner script* was informed by the above findings. Given the complexity of the anxiety reaction – comprising elements of *public speaking* and *foreign language anxiety* – I wanted to create an activity that addresses the multifaceted aspects and all potential dimensions of this anxiety, including learners' *negative cognitions* (worries, preoccupations, concerns, beliefs), *emotional arousal* (physical responsiveness), as well as *behaviours* (e.g. talking fast/rushing through speech, repeating of oneself, poor concentration, dysfluency). As psychology-based interventions, including cognitive, affective and behavioural approaches, and a combination of these – cognitive-behavioural therapy – have proven helpful for treating social anxiety, communication apprehension and public speaking anxiety (Bodie, 2010), I adapted some of the methods and techniques employed in these interventions for the purposes of targeting oral presentation anxiety in the language classroom.

The different stages of *Rewrite your inner script* are conceptualized as imaginary stepping stones, taking students closer to 'making friends' with oral presentations. The journey starts with individual self-reflection. Students examine their first reactions/automatic responses to the prospect of having to make a classroom presentation and explore (1) what feelings/emotions and (2) what thoughts/fears/worries they associate with this activity. This method of introspection helps bring to light and verbalize emotional and cognitive responses, awareness of which is an important first step in understanding and confronting anxiety.

The following two steps allow participants to look at the same phenomenon from an outside perspective. By discussing others' experiences of public speaking with the help of cartoons and studying classmates' responses to the same reflection questions, students can realize that others are having very similar reactions, which can help them see their own fears and worries as normal. This realization itself can ease anxiety. Furthermore, shared experiences help students bond and feel comfortable with each other.

Once a climate of trust and openness is established, students are ready to take the next step together, breaking up into small groups. For each fear/worry/negative thought previously identified by the class collectively, they must come up with potential coping strategies. The benefits of this procedure are manifold. Most importantly, students realize that they *can* and *must* take an active role in addressing their fears and worries – systematically, one after the other. They can also discover that different anxiety triggers require different remedies. For instance, negative thoughts, unhelpful beliefs or dysfunctional attitudes need to be challenged and reframed, that is, require cognitive modification of some sort, whereas fears and worries regarding delivery and language use can be reduced by effective preparation strategies and plenty of rehearsal; that is, they require behavioural actions. The small group arrangement is ideal for sharing personal coping strategies, what is more, thinking together can bring about moments of revelation, whereby students can realize the absurdity of some of their fears. A good example is being afraid of the audience. As students discuss their worries related to the audience, it can suddenly dawn on them that the feared audience, in fact, will be themselves (except when giving their own talk).

On examining, articulating and rationalizing their fears and worries attached to oral presentations, as the last step, students are invited to take part in an exciting experiment: a positive visualization task. This involves the deliberate creation of a mental image or scenario according to a script or a series of instructions dictated by the teacher (Hadfield and Dörnyei, 2013). After a short and simple breathing exercise – helping students to empty their minds and putting them in a relaxed frame of mind conducive to visualization – they listen to a detailed script of an ideal presentation day. Following the teacher's instructions, they envision themselves as confident and successful speakers. As vividly as possible, they picture themselves actually delivering their talks before their classmates effectively, in a positive state of mind. This cognitive technique – successfully used for treating public speaking anxiety (Ayres and Hopf, 1993, 1989, Ayres et al., 1997) – allows students to realize that giving a talk in a foreign language does not necessarily need to be an anxiety-filled, negative experience. They can experience firsthand how replacing a negative script of the feared oral presentation task with a positive one can change their feelings about the situation as well as themselves for the better, due to the fact that our feelings and behaviours are affected by our thoughts (Kendall, 1991, Stallard, 2002). What is more, imagining positive rather than negative outcomes can, in fact, result in actual beneficial experiences, which is best demonstrated by the successful use of this technique by sportsmen to improve self-confidence and enhance performance (Dörnyei, 2014). Visualization functions as a mental simulation or rehearsal, and the reason why it can work is that the brain cannot tell the difference between a real, physical experience and the vivid mental imagery of the same experience (Cox, 2012). Regular practice with a personalized script written by the students themselves can help to break the negative involuntary association between speaking the target language in public and anxiety, as the positive images counteract the negative ones (Ayres and Hopf, 1985, Ayres et al., 1997), and the relaxed state of mind in which the visualization is practised gradually becomes associated with the feared communication situation (MacIntyre and Gregersen, 2012). Furthermore, this positive vision can give students a glimpse of their ideal future L2 self, i.e. what they could ideally become as speakers of the foreign language – a goal to be achieved and work for (Dörnyei, 2014, Hadfield and Dörnyei, 2013). This, in turn, might guide them towards actions helping them actually accomplish this goal, which is becoming a confident speaker, at ease and at peace with oral presentations.

## The activity

### *Aims*

*Rewrite your inner script – Make friends with oral presentation* can be useful for learners in three ways: as a tool helping them lower their anxiety about giving a speech in a foreign language, as a group bonding exercise and – if conducted in the target language – as an authentic communication activity. Working together all the way through, students express, catalogue and discuss their fears and negative thoughts related to oral presentations; brainstorm positive counter thoughts and strategies; and participate in a positive visualization experience introduced by a simple relaxation exercise. Guided through these steps, they can gain better awareness and understanding of their own feelings and learn practical techniques for reducing their anxiety.

- **Level:** Advanced (B2 and above). For lower levels the activity can be conducted in their L1.
- **Materials:** Slides, worksheets.
- **Time:** Ninety minutes.

### *Procedure*

**Step 1:** Individual and whole class

1. Announce oral presentation task and project *Oral Presentation* in a speech bubble. Ask students to write down their first reactions/emotional responses.

*Potential prompts: Happy about it? Looking forward to it? Like such tasks? Why/why not? What feelings and emotions do you associate with this speaking task?*

2. Project a set of cartoons illustrating oral presentation/public speaking anxiety, showing images of anxious speakers (you can easily find such

images online at Google Images or istock). Invite learners to describe how they think the people in the pictures are feeling about giving a presentation, what thoughts they might have on their minds, what problems they might experience etc. Elicit as many responses as possible.

*Establish that many people share these feelings/emotions; fear of public speaking is one of people's most common fears.*

3. Ask learners to consider to what extent they can identify with the pictures (i.e. to what extent they are personally affected) and make two lists: (1) what feelings/emotions they usually experience before/during oral presentations (affective/physiological domain) and (2) what is it specifically they tend to be afraid of/worry about/what thoughts they have on their mind (cognitive domain).

**Step 2**: Mingle and whole class

Students walk around the classroom and compare their answers to Q1 (first reactions to the task) and their two lists (feelings; fears/worries/thoughts). Whenever they find similarities (similar reactions, feeling, fear/worry/thought), they put a tick next to the item. Students are invited to put items with the highest number of ticks on the board under the categories: (1) first reactions, (2) feelings and (3) fears/worries/thoughts.

**Step 3**: Group work and whole class

Project an image of an anxious versus a happy presenter. Students work in small groups (of 3 or 4), and for each fear/worry/negative thought, they must come up with strategies/positive thoughts that could alleviate their fears/reduce their anxiety.

*Examples collected from my students and suggested strategies:*

- *Audience won't like my talk* → Make it interesting! Find a really good topic: talk about something you feel strongly or passionate about! If you like it, they are more likely to like it, too. Anyway, does everybody need to like it?

- *Audience will laugh at me* → Why would they? They're in the same boat: they'll be presenting too – will you laugh at them? They have the same fear as you. Don't look upon them as the enemy; you're one of them!

- *What will they think about me?/They will think I'm a stupid loser, etc.* → It's not about you but the talk! They will be listening, not thinking about you! Don't focus on yourself; focus on getting your message across! Don't be afraid of your audience: involve them!

- *I'll forget what I want to say/I'll leave out parts of my speech* → Put outline and main points on slides/note cards. Concentrate on key points rather than trying to memorize presentation material verbatim. Rehearse talk with slides/note cards! The more you practise, the less likely it is that you forget the contents of your speech.

- *My heart will be racing; I'll tremble like jelly* → Do some simple relaxation exercises before the talk: e.g., tighten your muscles for a few seconds, then release them; take some deep breaths. Wait until you're ready to start.
- *I'm not good at oral presentation; I don't have enough self-confidence* → Don't look upon giving a speech as an artistic performance requiring special abilities. Look upon it as a normal everyday communication encounter. Focus on your message and how it is understood by your audience. Preparation and practice are potential coping techniques: they can give you self-confidence and a positive attitude!
- *I'll make mistakes* → Nobody, even experienced speakers, aims at perfection! *But!* Many mistakes can be prevented. Prepare thoroughly: check vocabulary, grammar and pronunciation you're not certain about! Rehearse your speech several times! Practice enables you to identify and address problems with your speech prior to performing it; this will make you more confident during the presentation.
- *They will notice my anxiety* → Practise your speech aloud so that you get used to hearing your voice. You might want to practise in front of a mirror. Rehearse your talk with one classmate, then before two, three or four. Practising in front of an audience can help you get used to speaking to more than one person and reduce your anxiety. Ask them to give feedback to you. Before the talk, take some deep breaths and wait until you're ready to start.

Groups report the strategies they came up with to the rest of the class, and together they compile a class strategy pool. This can be complemented by the teacher with ideas, useful tips students did not mention. The final version could be turned into a handout and distributed to students to help them during the preparation.

Conclude class discussion: *You can do a lot to reduce your anxiety: you're not helpless! Don't let anxiety control you; control your anxiety using the discussed strategies (i.e. replacing negative and unhelpful thoughts with positive and helpful ones + careful preparation & plenty of rehearsal).*

**Step 4:** Guided positive visualization (read out by teacher)
1. Project an image of an anxious versus a confident presenter and invite learners to try another strategy for reducing their anxiety.

Read out the following visualization script slowly, pausing between instructions to give learners time to visualize the scene and actions.

*Begin to visualize the morning of the day on which you are going to give your oral presentation. See yourself getting up in the morning full of energy, full of confidence, looking forward to the day's challenges. As you're walking to the university, note how relaxed and confident you feel. You walk tall, almost fly. You're looking forward to delivering your talk. You're happy with your topic, it's interesting and thought-provoking and you feel your classmates will like it. You feel prepared and easy.*

*See yourself walking into the building and then entering the classroom. You say hello to your classmates, they appear friendly. See yourself sitting at your seat in the classroom, talking very comfortably with those around you. It is now approaching your time to speak. As you wait, you see yourself taking some slow deep breaths. It's your turn now, and the professor calls your name. See yourself moving to the front of the classroom. You are feeling very good about your presentation. You walk to the computer with confident steps, stick your USB stick in and project your title page. Everything works fine. You feel calm and confident. You stand straight and smile pleasantly at the audience. And they smile pleasantly back! It feels good.*

*Now see yourself delivering your talk. You begin to speak; you're really quite good. Your voice sounds confident, and you're speaking clearly. Your classmates are giving you head nods and smiles, you feel they are interested and it gives you wings! You deliver all your main points. You speak fluently, the words come easily as in everyday conversation and you're happy with your English. When your final words are concluded, you have the feeling that it could not have gone better. The applause is loud and appreciative!*

*You now see yourself answering audience questions. You feel competent and answer confidently. Now you walk back to your seat. You see yourself as relaxed, pleased with your talk. See yourself receiving the congratulations of your classmates. Hear them whisper:* 'It was good', 'Very interesting' and 'Really liked it'. *Congratulate yourself on a job well done!*

Source. Adapted from the script developed by Ayres, J. & Hopf T. S. (1989).

**Follow-up:** Students discuss how they felt during the guided visualization and whether it worked for them or not. Elicit how this technique can help: *your thoughts affect your feelings and behaviours; imagining positive rather than negative outcomes, you're more likely to have a positive rather than a negative experience; imagining delivering your speech in a relaxed state of mind can help you feel less anxious during the real presentation. But! This can only help you if you're well-prepared and practise your talk! Feeling insufficiently prepared is likely to result in anxiety and unpleasant experiences.*

**Homework:** For this technique to work, it needs to be practised by students outside class, on their own. Therefore, students are asked to write their *personalized* script of an ideal, successful presentation in first-person singular, which they can use any time independently. They can use the script above as a template. They're encouraged to include all the good things they would like to experience in as many details as possible (e.g. how they feel, how they speak, how they sound, their English, meeting their objectives, classmates' reactions and feelings of success). Encourage them to practise positive visualization using their script as often as possible while preparing for their presentations. Once they have put their talk together, it is also a good idea to practise this technique together with practising their speech until they feel that their actual experience comes as close as possible to the imagined one.

**Potential follow-on activities:** Students can be asked to keep a *presentation preparation diary* in which they reflect on their experiences of positive visualization and rehearsing their speech, which they can share with the teacher and ask for help if needed. Also, after giving their presentations, they can write about their experiences of preparing, practising and presenting their speech, reflecting on which of the strategies/techniques learnt they found efficient in helping them cope with their anxiety and gain confidence in giving their speech.

## Recommended reading

Bodie, G. D. (2010), 'A racing heart, rattling knees, and ruminative thoughts: Defining, explaining, and treating public speaking anxiety', *Communication Education*, 59 (1): 70–105.
This study provides a comprehensive but approachable review of the literature on public speaking anxiety. It discusses different theoretical approaches to understanding the sources of this anxiety and helps the reader understand how these theories resulted in corresponding treatment techniques to reduce public speaking anxiety and its negative effects, many of which can be adapted and completed in the classroom.

Tóth, Zs. (2019), 'Under the magnifying glass: Students' perspectives on oral presentations and anxiety in the EFL classroom', *European Journal of Foreign Language Teaching*, 4 (2): 126–45.
This article reports the findings of my research into university students' perspectives of oral presentations. The unique feature of the study is that it explores participants' affective reactions to an actual classroom presentation they participated in. Students' post-presentation reflections allow unique insights into their subjective experience of a classroom presentation, enhancing language teachers' understanding of the complex psychological experience of giving a speech in a foreign language.

# References

Ayres, J. and T. S. Hopf (1985), 'Visualisation: A Means of Reducing Speech Anxiety', *Communication Education*, 34 (4): 318–23.

Ayres, J. and T. S. Hopf (1989), 'Visualisation: Is It More than Extra-Attention?', *Communication Education*, 38 (1): 1–5.

Ayres, J. and T. S. Hopf (1993), *Coping with Speech Anxiety*, Norwood, NJ: AblexPublishing.

Ayres, J., T. S. Hopf and D. M. Ayres (1997), 'Visualisation and Performance Visualisation: Applications, Evidence, and Speculation', in J. A. Daly, J. C. McCroskey, J. Ayres, T. S. Hopf and D. M. Ayres (eds), *Avoiding Communication: Shyness, Reticence, and Communication Apprehension*, 2nd edn, 401–22, Cresskill, NJ: Hampton.

Bodie, G. D. (2010), 'A Racing Heart, Rattling Knees, and Ruminative Thoughts: Defining, Explaining, and Treating Public Speaking Anxiety', *Communication Education*, 59 (1): 70–105.

Cox, R. H. (2012), *Sport Psychology: Concepts and Applications*, 7th edn, New-York: McGraw-Hill.

Dörnyei, Z. (2014), 'Future Self-Guides and Vision', in K. Csizér and M. Magid (eds), *The Impact of Self-Concept on Language Learning*, 7–18, Bristol: Multilingual Matters.

Hadfield, J. and Z. Dörnyei (2013), *Motivating Learners*, Harlow, England: Pearson.

Kendall, P. C. (1991), 'Guiding Theory for Treating Children and Adolescents', in P. C. Kendall (ed), *Child and Adolescent Therapy: Cognitive-Behavioural Procedures*, 3–24, New York: Guildford Press.

MacIntyre, P. and T. Gregersen (2012), 'Emotions that facilitate language learning: The positive-broadening power of the imagination', *Studies in Second Language Learning and Teaching*, 2 (2): 193–213.

Stallard, P. (2002), *Think Good – Feel Good: A Cognitive Behavioural Therapy Workbook for Children and Young People*, Chichester, UK: John Wiley & Sons.

Tóth, Zs. (2019), 'Under the Magnifying Glass: Students' Perspectives on Oral Presentations and Anxiety in the EFL Classroom', *European Journal of Foreign Language Teaching*, 4 (2): 126–45.

Tóth, Zs. (2021), 'Two Heads Better Than One? Pair Presentation in the EFL Classroom – A Panacea for Anxiety?', *European Journal of Foreign Language Teaching*, 5 (5): 103–27.

# CHAPTER SIXTEEN

# Focusing attention outwardly:

# A coping strategy for speaking tasks based on task concentration training

*Jonathan Rickard*

When anxiety strikes, people feel tense, worried or preoccupied. The purpose of this activity is to intervene in these anxious thoughts and feelings. Unlike mindfulness techniques, which are for becoming more present and reducing stress in a more general and less situational way, this coping strategy draws on Task Concentration Training (TCT) (Bögels, Sijbers and Voncken, 2006) and is designed for use in the moment, to counter anxiety while it is being experienced. It will help the individual to proceed with the speaking activity and engage more deeply, rather than withdrawing from it, when they feel anxious.

As teachers, we know that speaking activities can be anxiety-inducing for students. Some activities, such as speaking in front of the whole class, are nerve-racking even in your first language! But since it might not be possible to design a full programme of language activities that completely avoid causing anxiety, it seems a good idea to equip students with strategies to cope with anxiety when it arises. Also, since anxiety affects performance, it would be good if we can support students to do well in the emotional aspect of the activities, too, just as we support them with activities practising other areas of language and content.

This activity needs no preparation or materials except a board and students' notebooks. It is suited to course-length programmes because it needs follow-on practice over several weeks for best results. It can be used in a class or one-to-one, and is useful anywhere FLA occurs – for example, in groups with limited speaking proficiency, or where there are high personal, parental or institutional expectations. It is also useful for high pressure situations such as speaking-based assessments.

## Background to the approach

This activity originated with my own classes at universities in Hong Kong. Most of the time, I work with students in a whole-class setting, but I also work one-to-one with students who approach me for help outside class. I teach academic English and job interview preparation classes in which students have discussions, give presentations, role-play job interviews and record themselves speaking. These activities are known to be stressors (Woodrow, 2006). Students may have limited proficiency in English, making it challenging to understand and express ideas (Evans and Morrison, 2011a). They may experience social anxiety because of the threats of making mistakes, being evaluated negatively, being laughed at or appearing to show off before peers and teachers (Jackson, 2002; Evans and Morrison, 2011b). Also, some speaking activities are used for assessment, which might cause test or performance anxiety.

In my classes, I noticed that anxious students avoided participating in speaking activities or reduced their involvement, ending them prematurely. But by doing so, they missed out on the benefits of participation, which include getting more exposure to language, receiving feedback on their own conversational contributions, building social relationships with classmates, and gaining enjoyment and satisfaction from doing the activity. In the case of assessed speaking activities, this also meant students were sometimes dissatisfied with their own performance, and blamed their nerves for not being able to demonstrate what they were really capable of. Some students reported feeling that if only they could reduce anxiety, they could do much better and be more satisfied with their speaking.

But despite anxiety being so prominent in students' experiences and influential in how speaking activities unfolded, I found that it was rarely, if ever, acknowledged in the courses that required those activities. It was left to each individual student to deal with. So, as a teacher, I wanted to support students by designing an activity that I hoped would (1) recognize anxiety as a common aspect of speaking activities, and (2) equip students with a coping strategy. This would help them to participate to a greater extent, enjoy speaking activities more and perform better as well.

I based the activity on TCT (Bögels, Sijbers and Voncken, 2006). TCT is a form of cognitive behavioural therapy (CBT) which teaches individuals to consciously control their attention and direct it away from anxious thoughts and feelings. When people feel anxious, they tend to pay more attention to potential threats, whether external (e.g. people looking at you when you are speaking) or internal (e.g. negative automatic thoughts, worries, fears). Even when threats are actually absent, anxious people scan widely for potential threats (Eysenck et al., 2007), which consumes much of their attention. But the problem is that this leaves insufficient attention for other stimuli unrelated to threats, including the actual task at hand, and this insufficient task-directed attention means that the individual's actions will be less guided towards completing the task or achieving the overall goal. This explains why anxious students may appear to lose track of what they need to do to complete the speaking activity, and withdraw when the task is incomplete or only minimally completed. Essentially, their attention is being consumed by other anxiety-related stimuli. Ideally, there is a balance: the individual attends both to concrete situational stimuli in and around them (i.e. a bottom-up attention system) and also to the more abstract task and goal (i.e. a top-down system (Yantis 1998)). Balancing the two systems enables people to act both responsively and strategically, while anxiety upsets the balance in favour of the bottom-up system, leading to the undesired effects described above.

TCT aims to counter this unbalanced attention. It gives learners a coping strategy for anxiety by helping them to first take conscious control of their attention and then redirect it away from anxious inner thoughts and feelings and towards non-anxiety-related aspects of the task or environment instead. This flexible control of attention should reduce anxiety and its impact on speaking activities. Many students lack such strategies. Woodrow (2006) reports that the most commonly used strategy for FLA is simply to persevere, which does little to address the anxiety. The second most common strategy is to improve language and knowledge, which seems effective but must be done before speaking, rather than during it. Her study did find some use of coping strategies including positive self-talk, compensation for anxiety (e.g. by smiling) and relaxation techniques (e.g. deep breathing), but they were used by few students overall (Woodrow, 2006).

TCT is also a good complement to mindfulness training. Bögels, Sijbers and Voncken (2006) point out that, like mindfulness, TCT is concerned with making individuals more aware of their own attention processes and how they affect thoughts, feelings and behaviour. But a benefit particular to TCT is that it is designed to be a practical strategy, deployable in the moment to cope with anxiety while it is being experienced.

Success isn't guaranteed, however, which is the first of several challenges with this activity. Students can become too consumed with nerves to use it. If this happens but you think it may still be useful, fine-tune the difficulty. If the group is large, try again in smaller groups or even one to one. If instructions in English cause difficulty, use the L1. If students lack rapport, assign regular pair work before redoing the activity so that they build up positive relationships. Once the right initial difficulty level is found, you can gradually increase it in subsequent practice.

A second challenge is resistance. For students not prone to FLA or those who believe that classes should only be for hard-content learning, the activity may seem irrelevant. If you nonetheless consider it worthwhile, try to gain buy-in by explaining your reasons for choosing it. For instance, explain that it increases task focus, which can improve students' actual speaking performance.

Another challenge is finding the time for repeated practice over several weeks, without which uptake of the strategy may be low. However, after the forty-five minutes for the initial activity, in subsequent weeks the follow-on practice is only ten or fifteen minutes and can be appended to regular speaking activities.

Students might also doubt how the activity works. It asks students to focus more on the task and environment. However, these can also present threats. For example, focusing on one's partner is unhelpful if the partner is the cause of the anxiety. I try to address these concerns in Steps 3 and 4 of the activity by showing how the task and environment can be broken down into various aspects. Students should avoid anxiety-inducing ones and select safer ones to focus on.

From my experience with this activity, I would recommend three things. Firstly, when introducing it, I point out that this activity is a bit different from regular language course activities since its objective is related to controlling FLA, rather than language learning per se. If students approach this activity looking for vocabulary to learn or treat it primarily as listening and speaking practice, they'll find it less useful and miss its main benefit. I point out that we all feel anxious at times, and this strategy will help students to cope with it. Secondly, I point out that repeated practice is vital, in and outside class. As a one-off activity, it will have little lasting benefit, but if students can make attention control habitual, it should be very useful. Thirdly, it may work best if done in combination with other mindfulness activities (Bögels, Sijbers and Voncken, 2006).

Finally, here is a couple of stories to show how my students responded to the activity. One student, Sam, was notably anxious. He avoided eye contact, and his voice was shaky. He rarely initiated conversation with classmates, and ended discussions early. However, he seemed motivated to study English and often stayed to chat with me after class. It wasn't that he disliked learning a language or English – in fact, he studied various European languages by himself. One day, Sam told me that he wished he could speak more freely, so I introduced him to this activity and encouraged him to practise it. Some weeks later, as our class had finished and students were leaving, the next teacher came into the room to start her class – by chance, a French class. Sam did not speak, but he watched as I exchanged a few words in French with the teacher. The following week, the French teacher was there again, and this time Sam greeted her and introduced himself in

French. He told me afterwards that he'd tried to relax using the strategy that he'd practised. He still preferred to avoid direct eye contact, but instead he focused on the goal he'd set, which was to say something in French and have a little conversation. He felt pleased after achieving it.

Another student, Tom, joined my class mid-semester. By then, social groups had formed and Tom seemed left out. Tom was an international student, which added to the difficulty of integrating. When he spoke, I had the impression that he had rehearsed it, and he hesitated when I asked him something spontaneously. His nerves also prevented him from registering what I'd said when I spoke, as he didn't seem to respond to it. I tried to ease his anxiety by pairing him with a kind and patient classmate. Later that semester, we practised the coping strategy over several weeks. Tom said that when he did it, he focused more on his partner. I noticed that over time, they built a good relationship and Tom became more responsive in interaction, relying less on rehearsal.

# Activity

## *Aims*

The activity will help students to reduce anxiety by flexibly controlling the focus of their attention and avoiding anxiety-inducing stimuli.

- **Level:** Intermediate; also possible with lower levels if you use L1
- **Materials:** None
- **Time:** Forty-five minutes for the first session; ten to fifteen minutes for follow-on practice in subsequent weeks

## 1 Introduction

Start by saying:

- 'Speaking in English is an anxious experience for many people. Do you ever feel like that?'

Students usually agree enthusiastically! Ask what happens when they feel anxious – perhaps physical effects like shaky hands, or performance-related comments like 'I can't speak well'. This clarifies what anxiety looks and feels like.

Introduce the activity:

- 'It's good to find ways to reduce anxiety. Then, you can speak more freely and easily, and enjoy speaking more too. Today, you'll learn a way to do that.'

## 2 Speaking task

In pairs, students do a simple task for five to eight minutes that requires both partners to listen and speak. It could be a task from your course, or one of these sample tasks (write it on the board):

- Find out what food your partner likes and doesn't like. Then suggest a restaurant that you think he/she would like.
- Find out what free time activities your partner likes and doesn't like doing. Then suggest an activity that you think he/she would like.
- Imagine a new student is going to join the class. Together, decide on some tips that will help them to do well.
- Talk to your partner and make a list of things you have in common (the more interesting, the better!).

Students do the task. Afterwards, draw Table 16.1 on the board.

Briefly explain the three aspects: *Myself*, i.e. inner thoughts and feelings; the *task*; and the *environment*, i.e. the space, people and objects around. Students copy the table in their notebooks and fill it in for the task they just did. Then they compare their percentages with a partner – but point out that there's no 'right answer'. I find that some students, including the more anxious ones, have a 'Myself' focus of up to 40 per cent or 50 per cent, with the rest of their attention roughly equally distributed between the task and environment. Other more task-focused students have a higher rating there and a 'Myself' focus of 20 per cent to 30 per cent.

Then introduce the strategy:

- 'When anxious, people often focus on themselves a lot. So here's my tip – reduce attention to yourself, and increase your attention on the task and environment instead. What I mean is, move your focus from the *inside* of you, that is, your own thoughts and feelings, to something on the *outside* of you. We'll practise this next.'

To get the idea across, draw arrows from 'Myself' in the table to 'task' and 'environment'.

## 3 Focus on the task

Point to the instructions on the board for the task in Step 2. To break down the task, ask students what the keywords are and circle them. Then ask:

- 'What do you need to do to do this task well?'

Note their ideas on the board – this will be a useful reference. Here are suggestions from my students for a presentation task, for example:

**TABLE 16.1** Task table

| | % of my attention on ... | | |
|---|---|---|---|
| What was the task? | Myself | The task | The environment |
| | | | |

- Eye contact
- Control the speed (start & stop)
- Correct pronunciation
- Smile and be confident
- Keep the pace
- Keep calm
- Suitable body language
- Clear voice
- Keep it simple (focus on key messages)
- Good organization (people are easy to understand)
- Clear signalling words
- Hand gestures

Repeat the main idea: if you feel anxious, focus on one of these things instead. Ask students now to select one or two things to focus on, and mark them (e.g. with a star) so that they stand out. Say that it's fine to avoid anything that causes them anxiety in the list.

Explain that in a few minutes, they will try focusing on what they selected, so now ask them to plan how they will do that. For example, to focus on eye contact with a partner, they could plan which spot to look at (e.g. one eye, or the bridge of the nose), and decide how long to hold eye contact before looking away. To focus on body language, students could consider what gestures they can make, and when to use them (e.g. nodding while listening, or pointing to part of the PowerPoint slide when they explain it). For other aspects, writing a few key reminders down somewhere visible during the task might help. During this time, walk around and engage with individuals, assisting them if needed.

## 4 Focus on the environment

Say that we'll now become more aware of our environment. Take students through the three main senses in turn. I say something like this:

- 'First, focus on your *hearing*. Listen to the sounds around you. What can you hear? Are there any quiet sounds that you start to notice?' (Pause for ten to fifteen seconds between sentences so they have time to tune into their environment.)
- 'Now, *seeing*. Let your eyes look softly ahead and become aware of what's in front of you. What do you see? What colours, shapes, spaces?' (Pause.)
- 'Now, *touching and feeling*. Move your attention to that. Can you feel the chair touching your legs or body? Are your hands or feet touching anything? Is the air hot or cool on your skin?' (Pause.)

Wrap this part up by asking whether students felt anxious just now, when they focused on the environment. My students generally say no, and that they find it relaxing. Then give them a few minutes to select a sense or environmental aspect that they find helpful to focus on, and ask them to mark it clearly.

## 5 Repeat the task

First, ask students to note down their ideal percentages for attention distribution for the task in Step 2 (again, there's no right answer – it depends on the individual).

Then students repeat the task, but this time, if they feel anxious, they try shifting their attention onto the task (e.g. one of the suggestions in Step 3) or the environment. Encourage them to use the strategy even if they actually don't feel anxious, and fill in the table after the task.

Elicit any reactions or comments. Did students reduce their 'Myself' percentage? (I find most students do.) Did they use the strategy? If so, did they refocus on the task, environment or both – and did it work? Consider making this a more formal reflection activity by asking students to write down their experiences and reflections on the activity. This should help them to identify and remember what worked for them and in turn help uptake of the strategy in the future.

In my experience, responses are generally positive, but not everybody will have used the strategy. One reason for this might be if the class atmosphere is generally relaxed and low anxiety.

## 6 More challenging practice

Students repeat the task with a new partner, which may increase the challenge. Encourage them to use the strategy during the task and fill in the table afterwards.

## 7 Follow-on activities

Over the following weeks, students continue recording any speaking tasks they do on the table. Challenge them to try more anxiety-inducing tasks and use this strategy to manage the anxiety. Follow-on tasks could include:

- Speaking in front of the class
- Speaking about complicated subjects
- Being audio/video-recorded
- Speaking with a native or proficient speaker
- Speaking with little or no preparation

I find that it's easy for students to stop practising – perhaps because they don't feel too much FLA, or they have other ways of managing it. But this strategy should be useful for at least some, so it's worth encouraging them to keep it up.

By the time this activity is finished, learners should have strengthened their ability to cope with anxiety by shifting from self-focused attention to focusing on aspects of the task and environment.

# Recommended reading

Bögels, S. M., G. F. V. M. Sijbers and M. Voncken (2006), 'Mindfulness and task concentration training for social phobia: A pilot study', *Journal of Cognitive Psychotherapy*, 20 (1): 33–44.
A clinical study in which patients with social phobia were treated with a course of TCT and mindfulness training. It details the contents of each treatment session, as patients are taken through activities to train their attention control and gradually increase the difficulty of situations. Positive outcomes were found after the study and two months post-treatment. Although it is unclear to what extent TCT rather than mindfulness was responsible, the researchers had the impression that TCT was an essential part of the treatment. They also give a useful theoretical explanation of how TCT intervenes in maladaptive attention processes and interesting comments on how TCT complements mindfulness.

Mulkens, S., S. M. Bögels, P. J. de Jong and J. Louwers (2001), 'Fear of blushing: Effects of task concentration training versus exposure in vivo on fear and physiology', *Journal of Anxiety Disorders*, 15 (5): 413–32.
This experimental study compared the clinical effectiveness of TCT with that of simple exposure to the feared situation for patients with social phobia and fear of blushing. TCT appeared to be more effective. TCT also resulted in more positive cognitions about blushing than exposure did, which suggests that the increased awareness from TCT may disconfirm and change negative self-beliefs.

# References

Bögels, S. M., G. F. V. M. Sijbers and M. Voncken (2006), 'Mindfulness and Task Concentration Training for Social Phobia: A Pilot Study', *Journal of Cognitive Psychotherapy*, 20 (1): 33–44.

Evans, S. and B. Morrison (2011a), 'The First Term at University: Implications for EAP', *ELT Journal*, 65 (4): 387–97.

Evans, S. and B. Morrison (2011b), 'The Student Experience of English-Medium Higher Education in Hong Kong', *Language and Education*, 25 (2): 147–62.

Eysenck, M. W., N. Derakshan, R. Santos and M. G. Calvo (2007), 'Anxiety and Cognitive Performance: Attentional Control Theory', *Emotion*, 7 (2): 336–53.

Jackson, J. (2002), 'Reticence in Second Language Case Discussions: Anxiety and Aspirations', *System*, 30 (1): 65–84.

Woodrow, L. (2006), 'Anxiety and Speaking English as a Second Language', *RELC Journal*, 37 (3): 308–28.

Yantis, S. (1998), 'Control of Visual Attention', in H. Pashler (ed), *Attention*. Hove, UK: Psychology Press. 223–56.

**PART FIVE**

# Well-Being Techniques: Creating Mindful Foreign Language Speakers

# CHAPTER SEVENTEEN

# 'I see you, I hear you, I cheer for you!':

# How to overcome speaking-related anxiety through dialogue skits with positive communication in mind

Dorota Záborská

'I see you, I hear you, I cheer for you' is a speaking activity in which students construct and perform dialogue skits. The purpose is for students to (a) experience the joy of being seen and heard while satisfying their (hidden) creative needs, (b) practise positive communication with one another and thus (c) discover the relevance and applicability of positive communication in their everyday life. In combination, these experiences help them find speaking meaningful. And while there are various underlying linguistic, cognitive and affective factors of foreign language speaking anxiety, all intertwining in a complex way and fluctuating in their degree or presence, it is this meaningfulness that has a great impact on students' willingness to engage and encourages them to overcome their fears or reluctance to speak. The older the learners, the bigger the difference between what they can say in their first language and what they can express in their foreign language.

This gap is very frustrating and discouraging. A Turkish-British novelist Elif Shafak (2010), already a fluent English speaker and writer herself, eloquently expressed such a state of mind:

> For me, like millions of other people around the world today, English is an acquired language. When you're a latecomer to a language, what happens is you live there with a continuous and perpetual frustration. As latecomers, we always want to say more, you know, crack better jokes, say better things, but we end up saying less because there's a gap between the mind and the tongue. And that gap is very intimidating. But if we manage not to be frightened by it, it's also stimulating.
>
> (Shafak, 2010)

The desired effect of students engaging in the dialogue skits, in both their creation and performance, is actually to lessen the feelings of such intimidation and frustration. At the same time, when they can find their own and their classmates' dialogues stimulating, students will also experience little 'victories' over their speaking anxiety. Such victories or successes greatly contribute to their perseverance. Besides addressing foreign language speaking anxiety by shifting students' focus on the enjoyment of the creative process, there is one more intention disguised in 'I See You, I Hear You, I Cheer for You'. And that is to teach them about and let them consciously practise positive communication, which will have a positive impact on their interpersonal communication skills and enhance their overall well-being. The activity itself is anchored in Mirivel's Model of Positive Communication and its six core behaviours: (1) Greeting, (2) Asking, (3) Complimenting, (4) Disclosing, (5) Encouraging and (6) Listening (Mirivel, 2019).

## Background to the approach

This activity's approach has the aim of raising awareness of the power of positive interpersonal communication and enhancing the well-being of all participants in the language classroom. It is informed by a wide range of constructs within the field of positive psychology, all contributing to an increase of psychological literacy in both educators and learners. Educators do not need to be persuaded to see the benefits of understanding grit, resilience, perseverance, signature strengths, self-efficacy, optimism, compassion and other similar constructs on a deeper level. The focus on these constructs helps us not only to understand language learning processes better but also to develop more effective language learning activities. Plus, combining positive education with language education, as advocated by Mercer et al. (2018), allows us to educate learners holistically, both in academic subjects and in strategies promoting their well-being.

My initial incentive to introduce positive communication was to appeal to students who seemed more reluctant to speak in class, especially after more than a year of taking classes online during the Covid-19 pandemic. With very limited in-person interactions, the students did not have much chance to really befriend each other as they would have in the physical classroom. So, I wanted to combine building trust with language practice. Let me briefly explain the concept of positive communication, or more precisely, positive interpersonal communication.

Socha and Beck (2015, cited in Socha, 2019: 31) defined positive interpersonal communication as 'message processes that facilitate human needs-satisfaction' (188). Such needs include belongingness, love, esteem, self-actualization and more (31). Building on their ideas, Mirivel (2014) developed a seemingly simple yet very effective and easy-to-follow model of positive communication (see Figure 17.1). The model 'explores the small, but concrete, behaviours that seem to create happiness and joy for people' (50). The six components play the following roles: (1) *greeting* to create human contact and acknowledge other people's existence, (2) *asking* (open-questions) to discover and possibly to change the direction of interaction, (3) *complimenting* to highlight a person's strengths and so affect a person's

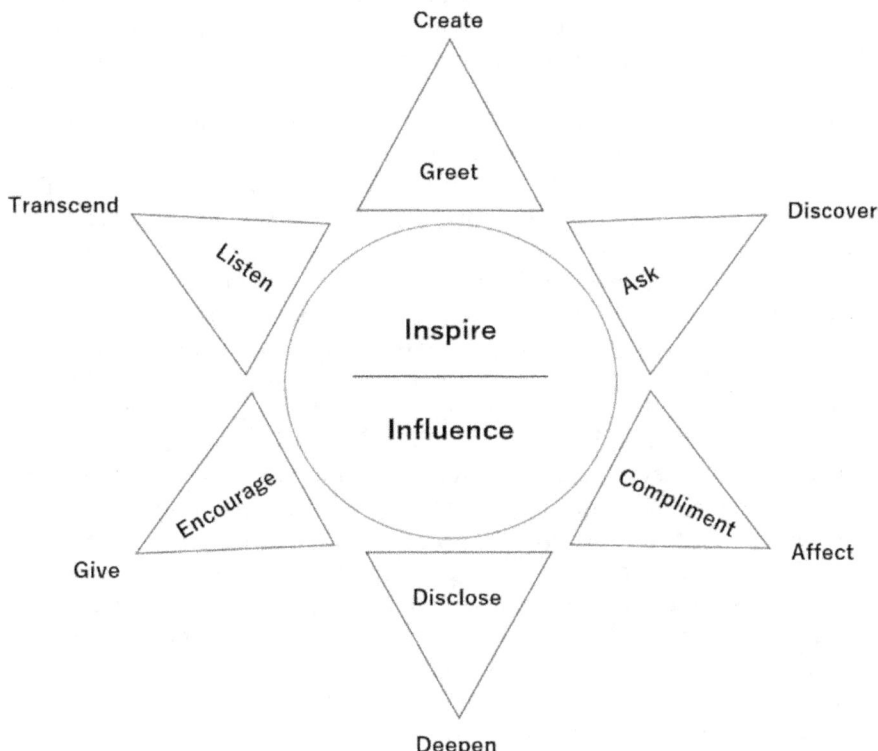

**FIGURE 17.1** *Model of positive communication (Mirivel, 2014).*

sense of self, (4) *disclosing* to deepen relationships, closeness and intimacy, (5) *encouraging* to give and provide support and (6) *listening* to transcend perceived differences (52).

Mirivel's model turned out to be a perfect fit for my students because it became a kind of formulaic framework for them, which eased the pressure of being asked to talk with each other in English on a prescribed topic. The simple instructions were only to include the model's six behaviours in their dialogue skit, and that allowed them to be creative and completely free. Students appreciated having this sort of agency, and their focus shifted to the joy of co-creating a dialogue and sharing it with their classmates from the initial pressure to express their opinions on something they might not be interested in or know enough about. In their reflections, students voiced their satisfaction, and the positive impact that following the positive communication model had on their interactions. Many mentioned that since they were not used to debating or expressing their opinions on unfamiliar topics even in their first language, being able to choose their own topic was very helpful. In general, English classes focused on practising communication skills, and the topics are very often 'far away' from the students' everyday life. While it is important to think about various and serious topics, this can be discouraging and/or triggering for anxious learners. The freedom in their choice of topic helped them to move from 'I don't know what to say about this in the first place!' to 'Hmm, I want to say …. How can I say that?' While our curricula demand covering particular content, fitting in this type of activity whenever possible will not only help more anxious students but also improve the overall classroom atmosphere.

Although in this chapter, I offer 'I See You, I Hear You, I Cheer for You' as a one-time speaking activity, from my personal experience in the classroom, I recommend you try doing it as a series over one whole semester, or at least for two or three rounds, that is in two or three class meetings. (In Round 2, students present their dialogue skit # 2, in Round 3, they present their dialogue # 3 and so on.) Meaningful activity requires sufficient time. If you choose to try this activity in two or three classes, you will find that students inspire and motivate each other to make their dialogue skits better with each subsequent try. You will also find the level of performance getting higher with each new attempt and the level of anxious learners' anxiety getting lower. What I was able to observe was that even the shyer students, those who would identify themselves as usually experiencing speaking anxiety, would start using prompts such as small objects or sound effects from their smartphones to make their skits more entertaining for their classmates as well as more satisfying for themselves. Very probably, not both of the students in one pair will have the same level of speaking anxiety. One is usually braver than the other and will lessen the pressure on the more anxious student.

Moreover, you can encourage your students to try to include greet-ask-compliment-disclose-encourage-listen behaviours in other communicative tasks. Practising positive communication will no doubt have a beneficial impact on your students' well-being, too. Many of my students have reported how often they found these positive communication strategies useful at home, in clubs and circles or classes, or at their part-time jobs. I would like to share a short (unedited) excerpt from a student's final reflection on positive communication dialogue skit classes.

> *All of my classmates were smiling when we were listening to positive communication. While I noticed it, I was able to feel the goodness of positive communication again. Also, this time, some elements of positive communication were decided by my teacher, but there are many other positive components, and I thought that they could be created naturally without being aware of them. Furthermore, I think that positive communication has the power to make both creators and listeners happy. I paired with one of my classmates three times in a row, but we always smiled when we did this assignment and forgot that it was part of the lesson or task. By thinking about positive conversations, I was able to find out what words make people happy and how to encourage them so that they don't get hurt. Everyone else in the class created great conversations. Some of them are realistic and others are unrealistic, and I feel that many of them were created as jokes. Also, there were many conversations that I could sympathize with, so it was interesting to listen to them. Also, most of the people spoke in fluent English, so it was very easy to hear, and at the same time as it became a listening practice, I wanted to be able to speak better like them. I have learned through this lesson that it is very important to talk positively when talking to someone, and what you should be careful about at that time is to think about things from the other person's point of view.*
> (KR, 18 years old, 1st-year student, Faculty of Global and Regional Studies, January 2022)

## Activity

### *Aims*

Students will learn about what makes our interactions meaningful and pleasant in a structured way. They will be guided to practise and consciously incorporate six basic behaviours of positive communication into their conversations. This activity facilitates an approach to more mindful interactions. Students' freedom to choose a topic for their dialogues allows them to focus on the creative process. Both performing the dialogue skits and watching classmates' performances contribute to greater enjoyment in a foreign language class and consequently alleviate foreign language speaking anxiety.

- **Level:** University students above CEFR A1.
- **Materials:** A handout with Mirivel's Model of Positive Communication (use Figure 17.1), worksheet of model skits (online materials).
- **Time:** One ninety-minute class (or preferably two classes: Class 1: explanation and instructions, Class 2: dialogue skit performances + reflections and comments). If you choose to try this activity only in one ninety-minute class meeting, I would suggest the following: brainstorming and initial discussion, explanation and instructions (thirty minutes), writing and practising their skits (thirty minutes), watching performances by as many groups as time allows (thirty minutes).

## Part 1. Brainstorming and initial discussion

1. Write the following questions on the board:

- What is the first thing you do when you meet your good friend? What do you do next?
- What makes you feel *positive*, *empowered* and *energized*?
- How can we make each other feel positive, empowered and energized?

Depending on the level of the students, write the questions one by one or all at once. Also, feel free to experiment with other opening sentences, such as: 'Think of a recent conversation that you enjoyed. What was it about the conversation that made you happy?' Explain difficult vocabulary as needed, e.g. empowered = feel like you have the/more power (freedom) to do something, energized = feel more motivated to do something.

2. Let the students brainstorm/discuss in small groups for a while, and then invite them to write their points on the board.

3. Add the title on the board: *I See You, I Hear You, I Cheer for You*. Ask the students to share with the class what this title means in their opinion.

## Part 2. Explanation and instructions

1. On the board, draw the 'Sun' diagram of the Art of Positive Communication (Figure 17.1), starting with a circle which will fit the words *inspire* and *influence* inside. Add six triangles around, filling them with *greet*, *ask*, *compliment*, *disclose*, *encourage* and *listen* while engaging with your students in a discussion. Ask the students to copy the diagram into their notebooks simultaneously with you. Handwriting will help them 'digest' and internalize the behaviours.

Explain briefly each of the six behaviours and the functions they serve while keeping discussing everything with your students and writing the keywords down above the triangles. For example, ask your students: 'Why do we greet?' 'When do we greet?' 'How do you feel when someone you know does not say "Hi!" to you even though they saw you?' You want to make your students think about the meaning of each component on their own first. Let them talk in small groups for a while. Listen to them, and pick up on the points that will lead them to the realization of the functions each component has.

Offer synonyms for the difficult vocabulary, e.g. compliment = say something nice, disclose = share something personal, transcend = bridge (various differences we might think there are) and so on. Identify some of the behaviours in the notes that students wrote on the board. Invite them to add any ideas they might have about positive communication.

2. Instruct the students on how to create positive communication dialogue skits. In the box are example instructions when creating the skits as a homework assignment, but points A to D can be used when students work on their dialogue skits only in that one particular classroom. The time of the dialogue can be shortened.

> A. Create a dialogue with the six components of positive communication in pairs or small groups of three.
> B. Because you will be talking in front of everyone, it'll be slightly artificial and not completely genuine (e.g. the 'disclose/ deepen' part – you can make this part up) but the whole dialogue should be believable and realistic.
> C. At the beginning of your dialogue, tell us who you are (e.g. we're friends from high school/we're classmates in XYZ class/we're colleagues at our part-time job/we're siblings etc.)
> D. Remember that out of the six components, only the 'greeting' part comes at the beginning and at the end. All other parts will appear in a different order and can be repeated several times.
> E. The easiest way to approach this assignment is to have a free conversation first for a while, then look at it and check which parts you've covered and which parts are missing or aren't sufficient. Then you can think together about what you can add.
> F. Your dialogue should last more than five minutes (and less than ten).
> G. You can read your lines from your notebook, but practise reading it until it's really smooth and the dialogue flows seamlessly.
> H. I'll ask you to submit your dialogue after our class next week.

## Part 3. Performing and reflecting

1. Let the students perform their dialogue skits in front of the whole class.

2. Encourage students to reflect on their feelings triggered by conversations with the greet-ask-compliment-disclose-encourage-listen components. Let them record their thoughts and feelings in short, simple written reflections. Allow some time for sharing their reflections at the beginning of the following class.

# Follow-up tasks and suggestions

- If you decide to use this activity more than once, i.e. Round 2, Round 3, students can (i) create a sequel to their first dialogue skit or create a completely new one, and (ii) stay with the same partner or work with someone else.

- Final Project: Ask students to reflect on their overall experience of positive communication in your class (or outside as well), and share an inspirational and/or influential conversation in the form of a presentation. Have them make use of both their reflection and notes taken in class.

FIGURE 17.2 *Students engaged in PC dialogue skits.*

- After this activity, students should have acquired some practical knowledge and awareness about some of the most important components of positive communication and mindful dialogues. For example, they learn about the importance of asking open questions, complimenting not only on appearance but also on actions. They realize that encouraging and offering a piece of advice are two different things, and so on. Through this experience, they should be equipped with and aware of the existence of some useful communication tools which they can apply in their interactions in English (and in their first language). Although the ultimate and ideal goal is to cover all six components of positive communication in a dialogue, some are easier to incorporate, and some are more difficult. Constantly remind your students of this and of the fact that only practice makes perfect. Remind also yourself to listen to your students' dialogue skits with kindness rather than with a checklist to tick off what they got right and what they did not.

## Recommended reading

Záborská, D. (2022), 'Learning from positive psychology: Soft-CLIL approach in communicative English class', *Language and Culture Collaborative Research Project (Gengo Bunka Kyodo Kenkyu Project)*, 43–52.
This short article describes a series of communicative English classes in which the author implemented tailored, soft-CLIL approaches with the aim of (1) teaching learners about interpersonal communication using Mirivel's Model of Positive Communication, (2) addressing foreign language speaking anxiety by shifting students' focus towards enjoying the creative process and (3) enhancing overall well-being in both online and face-to-face classroom settings.

## References

Duckworth, A. (2016), *Grit: The Power of Passion and Perseverance*, New York: Scribner/ Simon and Schuster.
Mercer, S., P. MacIntyre, T. Gregersen and K. Talbot (2018), 'Positive Language Education: Combining Positive Education and Language Education', *Theory and Practice of Second Language Acquisition*, 4 (2): 11–31.
Mirivel, J. C. (2014), *The Art of Positive Communication: Theory and Practice*, New York: Peter Lang Publishing.
Mirivel, J. C. (2019), 'On the Nature of Peak Communication: Communication Behaviors That Make a Difference on Well-Being and Happiness', in J.A. Muñiz-Velázquez and C.M. Pulido (eds), *The Routledge Handbook of Positive Communication: Contributions of an Emerging Communication of Research on Communication for Happiness and Social Change*, 50–9, New York: Routledge.

Shafak, E. (2010), 'The Politics of Fiction', *TED Conferences*, (July, 2010), Available online: https://www.ted.com/talks/elif_shafak_the_revolutionary_power_of_diverse_thought (Accessed 20 March 2023).

Socha, T. J. (2019), 'The Future of Positive Interpersonal Communication Research', in J. A. Muñiz-Velázquez and C. M. Pulido (eds), *The Routledge Handbook of Positive Communication: Contributions of an Emerging Communication of Research on Communication for Happiness and Social Change*, 31–40, New York: Routledge.

Socha, T. J. and Beck, G. A. (2015), 'Positive Communication and Human Needs: A Review and Proposed Organizing Conceptual Framework', *Review of Communication*, 15 (3): 173–99. DOI: 10.1080/15358593.2015.1080290.

Záborská, D. (2022), 'Learning from Positive Psychology: Soft-CLIL Approach in Communicative English Class', *Language and Culture Collaborative Research Project* (Gengo Bunka Kyodo Kenkyu Project): 43–52.

# CHAPTER EIGHTEEN

# Three good things about their English:

# A positive psychology-inspired evaluation, building confidence and encouraging learners to speak

*Katarzyna Budzińska*

As a foreign language teacher, you must have experienced learners who appear unprepared or indifferent and who are highly motivated to avoid engaging in those classroom activities which they are afraid of the most. They tend to give short responses, cut class, crouch in the back row and avoid speaking (Young, 1992). Teachers might often put students' poor performance down to their lack of ability or motivation. However, they should always bear in mind the possibility that it is language anxiety that may be responsible. Learners affected by this apprehension are often afraid of being evaluated by others, avoid evaluative situations and expect that others will evaluate them negatively (Horwitz, Horwitz and Cope, 1986).

To address language learners' fear of negative evaluation, I propose an alternative assessment method that looks at strengths rather than weaknesses. In this approach, instead of the teacher correcting errors, students evaluate each other by pointing out positive aspects of each other's speech, which can reduce their anxiety, boost their self-confidence, encourage engagement and increase general well-being. Most importantly, in line with positive psychology, instead of healing the negative, positive evaluation allows learners to expand the positive. This approach raises students' awareness of their strengths and lets them capitalize on them. Used regularly, positive evaluation can help learners build resilience, which can empower them to cope with challenges, such as overcoming foreign language anxiety.

The main advantage of positive evaluation lies in its universality. The Three Good Things activity is suitable for learners of all languages, levels, contexts and ages. The second advantage is that the exercise is very simple to use, which can encourage new teachers to implement it. It requires no preparation apart from photocopying an optional chart. The activity is also highly versatile – it can be repeated regularly with any speaking task. It is very easy to adapt – categories can be changed, added to and adjusted to the level and purpose. Evaluation can focus on language as well as skills. Other aspects, such as cohesion and tone of voice, can also be included for advanced learners. Primarily meant for peer evaluation, the activity could be used by teachers in addition to usual error correction techniques. Positive evaluation is suitable both for the classroom and for online education. Learners could also use it on their own as a reflection activity.

## Background to the approach

Many foreign language learners experience foreign language classroom anxiety, defined as 'the worry and negative emotional reaction aroused when learning or using a second language' (MacIntyre, 1999). Fear of negative evaluation is a fundamental part of this apprehension affecting about a third of language learners (Horwitz, Horwitz and Cope, 1986; Budzińska, 2015). Even though language anxiety was identified over thirty years ago, and scholars then urged for student-centred instruction and sensitive error correction (Young, 1991), some teachers today still place themselves at the centre, believing that their role is to correct every single mistake and that a little intimidation is necessary. Negative evaluation, frequently occurring in front of other learners, may lead to further confidence loss, learners' unwillingness to practice speaking skills, and consequently hindered progress. To stop this vicious cycle, learners need positive evaluation.

This activity is grounded in positive psychology, which, unlike traditional psychology that looks at disorders, focuses on positive aspects, such as happiness, success or fulfilment. According to Fredrickson's broaden-and-build theory (2001, 2013), positive emotions broaden one's thinking and build strengths that can be utilized for overcoming anxiety and summoning the courage to speak. In addition, as Gregersen (2016: 71) observes,

Learners who replace negative-narrowing thoughts and experiences with positive-broadening ones, not only generate more enjoyment in the process but also generate greater stamina for the long haul.

This activity addresses Gregersen and MacIntyre's (2014) call for teachers to praise the good and not wait for the perfect. Since errors are natural in language learning, students are more likely to benefit from positive feedback, which gives them a sense of achievement. The activity is based on a classic positive psychology intervention called 'Three good things in life', in which, originally, participants were expected to describe three good things that happened to them and to explain why they happened.

Regularly performed, this intervention was empirically proven by Seligman et al. (2005) to increase happiness and decrease depressive symptoms for six months. The idea to use interventions in positive psychology originated from Seligman et al.'s (2005: 883) dissatisfaction with traditional psychology and psychiatry which concentrates on how to reduce suffering and make people 'less depressed and less anxious and less angry'. Seligman et al. (2005) sought to find ways to achieve lasting happiness and found the answer in building strengths and increasing awareness of what is most positive about oneself, rather than talking about troubles and weaknesses.

More recently, MacIntyre, Gregersen and Mercer (2019) have found an application for positive psychology interventions in the foreign language classroom and demonstrated that they are a strong basis for building other interventions specially designed for the purpose of language learning. Such interventions contribute to positive language education (PLE), which is positive psychology in language education. Answering MacIntyre, Gregersen and Mercer's (2019) call, this is a novel version of the *three good things* intervention, which is specially adapted to help anxious foreign language speakers build strengths to overcome their fear of negative evaluation and encourage them to speak.

The idea for this activity originated from my own personal experience as an anxious foreign language learner. In fact, I had not been an anxious language learner until high school when I had the most terrifying English teacher. She constantly criticized everything I said, often using ridicule and humiliation, which made me feel so anxious that I was afraid to open my mouth. Consequently, when I came to study English at university, my self-esteem was very low. I compared myself with confident speakers, which made me feel even more anxious and less willing to speak for fear of being negatively judged by my peers as well as professors. Therefore, I decided to stay silent, which enlarged the gap between myself and others, even if the gap was only imaginary to start with. Many years later, when I was choosing the topic for my doctoral dissertation, language anxiety was an obvious choice. Reading excerpts from anxious language learners on the opening page of Horwitz, Horwitz and Cope's (1986) seminal paper, my heart jumped since I saw myself in their words. I instantly recognized a 'Martian death ray' (p. 125) in my high school teacher of English.

Thus, knowing how anxious foreign language learners feel, I decided to do something to help them overcome their insecurities, build on their strengths and encourage them to speak. In order to address language learners' fears of negative evaluation, I decided to tap into my research on positive institutions and positive institutional policies. Both of these studies showed that positive evaluation was a feature contributing to learner well-being. Trying to think of a suitable, empowering method of positive evaluation, Three Good Things emerged as a way of using positive psychology to alleviate language anxiety. I envisaged that receiving positive feedback from peers about one's speaking performance would be the complete opposite of what anxious learners dread the most. Hearing favourable comments about their speaking could enable apprehensive students and make them believe that their peers are not necessarily their enemies but perhaps supportive friends who could help them build lasting confidence.

# Activity

## *Aims*

This activity helps learners to gain confidence by listening to their classmates' positive comments about their performance. This is an alternative to commonly used evaluation methods that concentrate on mistakes.

- **Level:** Any
- **Materials:** Optional chart, pieces of paper or sticky notes
- **Time:** Ten to twenty minutes

1. The activity can be included in any free-speaking, communicative practice in pairs or groups during a language class. Each learner writes down three good things about their partner's performance. When the activity is used for the first time, each learner could use a handout with a table that has categories to comment on (see Table 18.1). Categories can be adapted by the teacher (see the start of the chapter).

2. Learners listen to each other and write three positive things about their partner's speech. They either use the chart distributed by the teacher or write their comments on a piece of paper. No negative comments are allowed.

3. At the end, students verbally exchange positive comments about their partner's speaking either in pairs or groups. Volunteers could report three positive things about their partners' speaking in front of everybody as a form of public praise. At this stage, completed charts or pieces of paper with positive comments can be exchanged as permanent reminders of learners' strengths. Table 18.2 shows some example responses from one of my classes. Here are some students' reactions to the Three Good Things activity:

### TABLE 18.1 Three Good Things chart (optional)

| Positive aspect – Choose 3 | My comments |
|---|---|
| **Content:**<br>Was the speech interesting, original?<br>How did it make me feel? | |
| **Clarity:**<br>Was the speech easy to understand? | |
| **Vocabulary:**<br>Did the partner use any interesting/<br>newly learnt vocabulary? Give examples. | |
| **Grammar:**<br>Examples of correctly used (challenging)<br>grammar. | |
| **Pronunciation:**<br>Examples of challenging words, correctly<br>pronounced. | |
| **Exclusive use of L2**<br>Did the partner manage to speak<br>without using their mother tongue? | |
| **Fluency** | |
| **Other positive comments** | |

### TABLE 18.2 Example responses of Three Good Things chart

| Positive aspect – choose 3 | My comments |
|---|---|
| **Content:**<br>Was the speech interesting, original?<br>How did it make me feel? | Very interesting speech. You were very creative and gave me lots of good ideas.<br>   Informative, original and straight to the point.<br>   Advice was interesting and original. It motivated to improve the company.<br>   The ideas were clear to understand and easy to adapt in the company.<br>   The ideas were good, which gave CEO fulfilment and the understanding that the disruptor is in fact positive for the company.<br>   The disruptor was really interesting, and original; it gave me a lot of room to give some advice.<br>   The speech was interesting; it answered the problem perfectly. |

| Positive aspect – choose 3 | My comments |
|---|---|
| **Clarity:** Was the speech easy to understand? | The speech was clear and easy to understand.<br>    Really fluent answers that were easy to understand, provided you understand some complex business vocabulary.<br>    Speech was perfectly understandable.<br>    No problem with understanding, very clear.<br>    After a brief discussion, it became highly understandable. |
| **Vocabulary:** Did the partner use any impressive, newly learnt vocabulary? | Well learnt plus used correctly new words.<br>    You used newly learnt vocabulary like 'complacent', 'plough into'.<br>    There were several challenging words used and also correctly pronounced. Examples are: fleeting success, complacent.<br>    You use newly learned vocabulary without a problem.<br>    Yes: disruptors, subscribe to, software, abandon, attached to, agile. |
| **Grammar:** An example of correctly used (challenging) grammar. | Really great grammar.<br>Correctly used grammar.<br>'If I were you'. |
| **Pronunciation:** An example of a challenging word, correctly pronounced. | Very good, easy to understand pronunciation.<br>    Proper pronunciation, easy to understand. |
| **Fluency** | It was quick pace, very fluent speech.<br>    It was fluent; there weren't any silent moments or stops in the conversation.<br>    You didn't stutter at all. |

*I think it's great and it gives people more motivation to keep learning, because it focuses on positive things rather than negative ones.*

*Yes, I enjoyed Three Good Things activity. It's worth to know what you are good at, and as a result of that you also know what you should improve without criticism. It's helping to gain more confidence as well. I think listing good points and bad points are equally useful but I personally prefer Three Good Things exercise.*

*I like the idea of focusing on positives because it's a great way for getting to know what we can already do well.*

> Yes, I did enjoy it. It is nice to find out some good things about your speech and not just the mistakes. It really boosts your confidence and makes you more eager to participate in future conversations.
>
> It was a great activity, because it focuses on someone's positive sides and by that we can gain more confidence.
>
> Yes, I enjoyed it as it focused on searching for positive things instead of mistakes. It keeps me motivated to improve.
>
> I enjoyed the Three Good Things activity, because I think it's good to know what you are good at. I liked the idea of focusing only on positives.

## Follow-up tasks and suggestions

- Students could think of three good things about their own successes in language learning at the end of each class. They should be encouraged to celebrate small successes; e.g. very anxious learners could write: 'I volunteered to speak today for the first time', 'I spoke without preparing my sentence in advance' and 'I managed to speak using L2 only'.
- Those studying in the L2 environment could do the activity on their own at home about English (or another L2) they use outside their language classroom.

## Recommended reading

Budzińska, K. (2021), 'Positive institutional policies in language education contexts: A case study', in K. Budzińska and O. Majchrzak (eds), *Positive Psychology in Second and Foreign Language Education*, 141–87, Cham: Springer.
I propose that enacting positive language education (PLE) only through teachers incorporating positive interventions into their classes may not be sufficient. If a school wishes to introduce PLE, it is not enough to just do this at the level of teaching, as this may result in a mismatch with the implicit message about well-being being conveyed by the institution as a whole. It is vital that the institution also embodies and communicates the principles of PLE in its structures, policies and organizational culture. The chapter has outlined what factors contribute positively to learner and teacher well-being from Seligman's (2011) PERMA (Positive Emotion, Engagement, Relationships, Meaning and Accomplishment) perspective. Eleven features of the institution's policy reflecting PERMA transpire from the study. Positive evaluation, the topic of the present chapter, is one of them. The positive policies presented in the paper could serve as

guidelines for other schools that care about learners' progress as well as well-being.

Budzińska, K. and O. Majchrzak (eds) (2021), *Positive Psychology in Second and Foreign Language Education*. Cham: Springer.
This is my first edited volume and the third edited volume on positive psychology in (F)SLA in the world. The book is close to my heart since most of the contributing authors, some of which are pioneers in the field of positive psychology in SLA, are my friends. What brought us together is our common interest in language learner and instructor well-being. The volume demonstrates how resources taken from positive psychology can benefit both teachers and learners. It explores a range of topics, such as affectivity and positive emotions, engagement, enjoyment, empathy, positive institutions, a positive L2 self-system as well as newly added positive language education. Some papers in this collection introduce new topics, such as the role of positive psychology in international higher education, a framework for understanding language teacher well-being from an ecological perspective and positive institutional policies in language education contexts.

Budzińska, K. (2018), 'Positive institutions: A case study', *Theory and Practice of Second Language Acquisition*, 4 (2): 33–54.
Positive psychology was founded on three main pillars: positive emotions, positive character traits associated with good living and positive institutions that create conditions for students to flourish (Seligman and Csikszentmihalyi, 2000). Nevertheless, the research in psychology so far has been concentrating on positive emotions and character strengths. Positive institutions have been the least well-studied of the three pillars. A salient additional perspective, as MacIntyre and Mercer (2014) propound, would be to concentrate on the context in which students can experience enjoyment and flourish in foreign language learning. I fill the niche by analysing a private language school in Poland which seems to be a positive institution. I base my study around two criteria: enabling success and promoting positive language learning environments or student well-being. This is the pioneering paper investigating positive institutions in the (F)SLA context.

# References

Budzińska, K. (2015), *Foreign Language Classroom Anxiety in a Further Education Context*. An unpublished PhD thesis, University of Lodz.
Budzińska, K. (2018), 'Positive Institutions: A Case Study', *Theory and Practice of Second Language Acquisition*, 4 (2): 33–54.
Budzińska, K. (2021), 'Positive Institutional Policies in Language Education Contexts: A Case Study', in K. Budzińska and O. Majchrzak (eds), *Positive Psychology in Second and Foreign Language Education*, 141–87, Cham: Springer.

Fredrickson, B. L. (2001), 'The Role of Positive Emotions in Positive Psychology: The Broaden and Build Theory of Positive Emotions', *American Psychologist*, 56 (3): 218–26.

Fredrickson, B. L. (2013), 'Positive Emotions Broaden and Build', *Advances in Experimental Social Psychology*, 47: 1–53.

Gregersen, T. (2016), 'The Positive Broadening Power of a Focus on Well-Being in the Language Classroom', in D. Gabryś-Barker and D. Gałajda (eds), *Positive Psychology Perspectives on Foreign Language Learning and Teaching*, 59–73, Cham: Springer.

Gregersen, T. and P. D. MacIntyre (2014), *Capitalizing on Language Learners' Individuality*, Bristol: Multilingual Matters.

Horwitz, E. K., M. Horwitz and J. Cope (1986), 'Foreign Language Classroom Anxiety', *Modern Language Journal*, 70: 125–32.

MacIntyre, P. D. (1999), 'Language Anxiety: A Review of the Research for Language Teachers', in D. J. Young (ed), *Affect in Foreign Language and Second Language Learning: A Practical Guide to Creating a Low-Anxiety Classroom Atmosphere*, 24–45, Boston, MA: McGraw-Hill.

MacIntyre, P. D and S. Mercer (2014), 'Introducing Positive Psychology to SLA', *Studies in Second Language Learning and Teaching*, 4 (2): 153–72.

MacIntyre, P. D., T. Gregersen and S. Mercer (2019), 'Setting an Agenda for Positive Psychology in SLA: Theory, Practice, and Research', *The Modern Language Journal*, 1: 262–74.

Seligman, M. E. P. (2011), *Flourish*, New York, NY: Free Press.

Seligman, M. E. P. and M. Csikszentmihalyi (2000), 'Positive Psychology: An Introduction', *American Psychologist*, 55 (1): 5–14.

Seligman, M. E. P., T. A. Steen, N. Park and C. Peterson (2005), 'Positive Psychology Progress: Empirical Validation of Interventions', *American Psychologist*, 60: 410–21.

Young, D. J. (1991), 'Creating a Low-Anxiety Classroom Environment: What Does Language Anxiety Research Suggest?', *The Modern Language Journal*, 75: 426–37.

Young, D. J. (1992), 'Language Anxiety from the Foreign Language Specialist's Perspective: Interviews with Krashen, Omaggio Hadley, Terrell, and Rardin', *Foreign Language Annals*, 25: 157–72.

# CHAPTER NINETEEN

# Being positive in the present moment:

# Mindfulness meditation for reducing anxiety in foreign language classes

*Nihan Erdemir and Sabahattin Yeşilçinar*

This chapter introduces activities that are based on mindfulness meditation (MM) techniques used in positive psychology (PP) theory. Internalizing these mindfulness practices may enable students to be aware of their own concerns, judgements and fears in EFL classes, particularly in a speaking activity. Also, students learn to accept their present feelings non-judgementally. In contrast to external approaches, such as instruction, suggestions and feedback, the approach in this chapter is based on an inner source, where the students are empowered by the autonomy they gain to regulate their own emotional state. In this way, with its positive returns for language anxiety, motivation and self-efficacy, mindful classrooms have been recently found to facilitate language learning (Koçali and Aşık, 2022).

Instead of leading the students to suppress or ignore their negative emotions during speaking activities, mindfulness meditation practices help to recognize their negative feelings, and appreciate that they are people who might sometimes have these feelings, and it's OK. Preceded by group discussions where students with similar concerns can share their feelings, volitionally paced breathing practices stimulate the parasympathetic nervous system and relax the brain stem. Then, students are asked to be aware of their bodies and surrounding environment to experience the present moment with all the negative or positive feelings they have. For a better evaluation of their own feelings, students journal and listen to their inner voice. Lastly, they are expected to appreciate their anxiety by being kind and accepting of their feelings. As a result, this intervention is mainly aimed at helping students to meet the present moment with openness, acceptance and kindness, and thus free themselves from past experiences and also future anxieties.

## Background to the approach

In recent years teachers, rather than focusing on negative emotions which have been extensively investigated, have started to look at the deliberate training of positive emotions, such as 'well-being and satisfaction (past); flow, joy, sensual pleasures and happiness (present); and constructive cognitions about the future – optimism, hope and faith' (Seligman 2002: 3). Among positive psychology interventions (PPIs), mindfulness meditation (MM) has arisen as one of the most popular techniques, having been practised in the East for years (see Brown and Ryan, 2003; Morgan and Katz, 2021). MM is defined as 'the awareness that emerges through paying attention on purpose, in the present moment, and nonjudgmentally to the unfolding of experience moment by moment' (Kabat-Zinn, 2003: 145). Based on their findings, the practitioners reported improved regulation of emotions (Zhang et al., 2019) and attention control (Basso et al., 2019). To reduce students' anxiety, teachers can use various mindfulness practices (or relaxation exercises), such as knowing oneself, sharing feelings, being in the present moment, raising perceptions of the body, raising awareness of the environment, journaling and being mindful. These practices in language classrooms have been observed to provide positive outcomes for language learning. For example, Wang and Liu (2016) indicated that MM practices increased learners' awareness towards their own language learning processes, and led to learning from each other and thinking critically and reflectively.

Mindfulness has been associated with alleviating speaking anxiety, as it contributes to student performance in oral presentations in English (Charoensukmongkol, 2016). Previous research has shown that individuals performed better in stressful situations through MM practices (See Witek-Janusek et al., 2008; Hofmann et al., 2010), and the results showed that students in language classrooms might also lessen their public speaking anxiety through these practices and have a better presentation performance. As various researchers advocate (e.g. Brown and Ryan, 2003, Hofmann et al., 2010), mindfulness provides several benefits: such as helping individuals enhance their focus and lower their levels of stress and anxiety, as well as promote mental clarity and creative thinking.

Our activity is based on techniques used in MM, focusing on evoking positive emotions (e.g. Tasan et al., 2021). Regular training has been proven to pave the way for students in the foreign language classroom to have better emotional regulation, longer attention control and decreased stress levels (Fallah, 2017, Morgan and Katz, 2021). Teachers can use mindfulness practices in their foreign language classes while teaching most ages because mindfulness has become more commonly practised from childhood to adolescence, along with the development of self-regulation and executive functioning skills (e.g. working memory, flexible thinking and self-control) (Blakemore and Choudhury, 2006). Using mindfulness-based techniques can also develop and strengthen schoolchildren's social and emotional resilience, which helps them cope with adverse situations. Students feel self-confident and learn better as their affective state is focused (Gül-Peker and Erdemir, 2021).

In addition to creating a positive and supportive atmosphere, the use of these techniques can promote learning. For example, students might start to use their knowledge in creative and flexible ways. Langer (2016) advocates that mindfulness creates more meaningful and long-lasting effects because it enables students to reinterpret a particular activity from their own experiences and insights by means of making a deeper connection between content and process. For example, if a student is anxious about speaking tasks in a language classroom, they may not challenge their speaking anxiety to overcome it. However, through mindful meditation, anxious students reinterpret speaking activities from their own experiences and insights, encouraging them to accept and appreciate their speaking anxiety. Based on Langer's suggestions, once students adopt a mindful approach, they become more ready to identify their goals, create solutions and critically reflect on their outcomes. Moreover, teachers can also benefit from mindfulness-based techniques to effectively combat their own stress because these practices aim to strengthen the emotion-focused coping skills of both teachers and students.

Given that students encounter various challenges during the process of learning a foreign language, they should be supported to overcome these problems and develop their oral communication in English. We believe that teachers may benefit from MM because being mindful can reduce students' anxiety (Brown and Ryan, 2003). An example of this is the study carried out by Charoensukmongkol (2016) in which the influence of mindfulness on students' level of anxiety in English as a second language (ESL) classes and their speaking skills during classroom presentations was investigated. He found that students with higher levels of mindfulness while speaking English tended to experience less anxiety during their presentations. In addition, those with low anxiety also obtained higher scores on their presentations than those who reported high levels of anxiety. These findings indicate that 'lower ESL public speaking anxiety is related indirectly to the contribution of mindfulness to the level of performance that the students achieved' (2016: 423).

Mindfulness is not an immutable phenomenon but can be developed through training. Research (e.g. Kabat-Zinn, 2003) introduces MM as a technique that helps individuals develop the quality of mindfulness. Schools in Germany (e.g. Fritz-Schubert, 2011) and Turkey (e.g. Bahçeşehir Colleges) have started to benefit from these techniques in recent years. The theoretical approach we have adopted in this activity is based on and highly influenced by the studies of Fallah (2017) and Morgan and Katz (2021) in using MM with EFL students coping with anxiety, and we highly recommend reading their robust work suggesting that mindfulness practices are associated with decreasing levels of FLCA so you will get a better picture of the positive returns of this technique.

Our intention to integrate MM techniques into foreign language classrooms was derived from the positive outcomes of the first author's personal experience and Gul-Peker and Erdemir's research (2021), suggesting 'affective factors, if not addressed, can hinder learners' effective use of compensation strategies' in speaking activities (2021:351). This action research was conducted to teach compensation (communication) strategies in order to help the students enhance their speaking skills and reduce their L1 use. Though most of the students became successful, a group of students could use these compensation strategies effectively only after affective strategies were also practised. Therefore, this raised a question in our minds about whether we should care for our students' affective issues as well as their cognitive issues in the classroom, and we wanted to use these practices in class with students who undergo differing levels of anxiety. In our classes we observed that students were very concerned about the possibility of making speaking mistakes but kept speaking by suppressing their feelings of stress and anxiety. Therefore, they were very surprised when we asked them to face the feelings they tried to avoid by sharing them with their peers, and then accepting their own negative feelings. In order to convince them, we presented them with the evidence-based benefits of the approach. In addition, it was hard to get the students to understand the new concepts and terms; therefore, we switched to the students' L1 and practised all the MM activities in their L1. Lastly, it might be better to have students work in groups at differing levels because first we observed that they learn by interaction in groups, and second it is difficult to match the students with others at the same levels of anxiety because you would need to measure their levels of anxiety. We would like to emphasize that it is important for students to regularly do these practices in order to achieve behavioural changes. However, teachers might face challenges, such as time constraints and, most importantly, fitting activities in with curriculum requirements. Therefore, the teacher might need to be flexible in order to allocate time for MM practices as well.

# Activity

## *Aims*

This activity is particularly useful for foreign language classroom anxiety by using awareness, breathing and meditation to develop a more positive mindset. Students are also able to see that they are not necessarily alone with their fears, and also the more they realize their feelings, the less these feelings will bother them in the present moment. There are a great number of scripts for MM practices; however, teachers can write their own scripts in accordance with their students' needs in language classes like the script in this practice. For example, according to research by Fallah (2017), after students in the foreign language classroom regularly followed MM practices, they were found to have better emotional regulation, extended attention control and decreased stress levels.

- **Level:** Any level from young to adult learners.
- **Materials:** Sticky notes, audio player, diary notebook.
- **Time:** Twenty-five to thirty minutes for five weeks minimum. (It might take longer with young learners, so the duration can be extended to forty-five minutes a week. In addition, the first practice should be allocated to familiarizing the students with the terms and approach, so, the remaining four is to get them into the habit of meditation.)

You should have your students practise the MM activity at least four times a semester. Observe your students, and if they feel anxious, keep practising. You will see how it helps them over time. Students may tend to be unfamiliar with meditation and breathing practices, so you should be ready for half-convinced or unconvinced students. If so, you can present some evidence-based benefits of MM (e.g. from Charoensukmongkol, 2016; Fallah, 2017; Morgan and Katz, 2021).

Procedure:

*1. Knowing themselves*
Ask students to write on a sticky note what feelings and concerns they have when they are speaking English in class and give some examples from your own feelings. For example, '*I feel afraid of making mistakes in front of my peers.*' It is important to start with this step so that they gain awareness of themselves. The aim is to make the students first face their feelings. At this point, there might be a resistance to face any negative feeling, which is sometimes difficult.

*2. Sharing feelings*
Ask them to move around the classroom with the sticky note in their hand, find students with similar feelings to each other and become a pair or group

and ask them to share their feelings with their classmates. They discuss the reasons for their feelings to understand others. Creating these types of support groups in class can improve their empathic skills. There might be a few students who avoid sharing their feelings; however, they should feel comfortable after a while.

*3. Being in the present*
Before starting the MM, play meditation music at 432 Hz frequency, which can easily be found online at platforms such as YouTube. It has been found to relax the body and mind and significantly reduce anxiety (Aravena et al., 2020).

Ask them to sit within their groups, close their eyes and pay attention to inhaling and exhaling. This is called *anulom vilom pranayama*, which is a type of controlled breathing in yogic breathing exercises. First, they need to close the right nostril with their right thumb and inhale deeply through the left nostril. Then, ask them to exhale slowly from the right nostril by removing the right thumb and at the same time closing their left nostril with the middle finger. This is one cycle. They are expected to perform this for two to five minutes, and finish by exhaling through the left nostril. This step helps in calming the energy in the body and lowering levels of stress and anxiety. After this practice, some students might experience dizziness, and this is a very normal reaction of the body because the right and left lobes of the brain are activated at once through this breathing technique. However, it is important to ensure all students are sitting down for safety reasons.

*4. Raising perceptions of the body*
Have them sit up straight, eyes closed and their shoulders dropped. While taking a few deep breaths, students calm their bodies and minds. Then, ask them to focus their perception on a body part which feels tense or painful, and try to relax this part. This step is practised to have them experience the present moment for two to five minutes.

*5. Raising perceptions of the environment:*
Now, it is time to cast their perception from their body to the environment. Give directions for them to follow:

> *Now you hear clear sounds around and then other sounds as well. You let these sounds enter your brain and leave gently. If you get distracted, you focus on your breathing cycle again. You allow your ideas to pass by like clouds run in the sky. By being an observer of your ideas, you put away all your opinions regarding how this moment should be. You think of how you feel in language class. This could be about your anxiety, tension and any uncomfortable feeling, and then you allow all these ideas in English language class to go by non-judgmentally while you exhale deeply.*

After two to three minutes, ask them to take normal breaths: *'Now you can start to take breaths in the normal way.'* They open their eyes when they are done with the experience and become ready to end the activity. You may need to use the students' L1 when doing this part of the activity, or adjust the script to the level of your students.

*6. Journaling*
This writing activity is one of the techniques in MM for self-expression of the subconscious mind. Ask them to write how they feel now by identifying negative and positive thoughts, and have some space for self-talk regarding their fears and concerns, or for pleasure and fun. It is explained that this activity is private, and their ideas are not shared. If some students wish to share their notes, allow them to. In this activity, students are given some questions to awaken their 'blind spots' and reflect:
   *'How do you feel when you are asked to speak in front of your classmates?'*
   *'How do you feel when your teacher asks you a question?'*
   *'How do you feel when asked to make a presentation in English language class?'*

*7. Follow-on activity: Being mindful*
This activity allows students to better communicate with themselves by talking to their subconscious minds, so it is important for students to feel the emotion(s) in their subconscious mind deeply.
   Ask them to repeat aloud:
   *'I know speaking English can be difficult for me, and I feel that I am anxious.'*
   Ask them to hold their hand on their heart and to repeat aloud:
   *'The difficulties are parts of a learning process, and I accept them as they are.'*
   Request them to be kind to themselves and remind themselves of their humanity. They should repeat silently:
   *'I allow myself to be kind at this moment.'*
   *'I allow myself to be merciful at this moment.'*
   *'I allow myself to be mindful at this moment.'*

## Suggestions

As stated above, it's a good idea to practice the activity at least four times during the semester, and continue if they still apear to have anxiety. Sometime later you become sure of their understanding and focus on the practice. All in all, the students were into trying out something new, and especially communicating to their inner self was of interest to them. They were finally glad to understand themselves and be kind to themselves, and their peers.

## Recommended reading

Brown, K. W., D. J. Creswell and R. M. Ryan eds, (2015), *Handbook of Mindfulness: Theory, Research and Practice, New York*. The Guilford Press. This book offers a timely and inclusive snapshot of the current state of mindfulness and how it might work. Besides, it describes mindfulness-based interventions for specific populations. The book makes an exceptional contribution as it informs readers about how mindfulness can be used to improve well-being and reduce suffering. Moreover, the book makes suggestions for further studies and facilitates more effective interventions.

Morgan, W. J. and J. Katz (2021), 'Mindfulness meditation and foreign language classroom anxiety: Findings from a randomised control trial', *Foreign Language Annals*, 54 (2): 389–409. This research investigates the possible results of mindfulness-based interventions on FLCA. In a time-restricted learning environment, their findings cannot indicate a clear effect of MM on language anxiety. However, in accordance with the detailed interviews with the university students having MM experience, the study demonstrates positive outcomes for their language learning anxiety and well-being. In addition, this study might lead researchers to reliable instruments such as the *Freiburg Mindfulness Inventory, Foreign Language Classroom Anxiety Scale* and *Mindfulness Experience Questionnaire* if they need data collection tools.

## References

Aravena, P. C., C. Almonacid and M. Ignacio Mancilla (2020), 'Effect of Music at 432 Hz and 440 Hz on Delta Anxiety And Salivary Cortisol levels In Patients Undergoing Tooth Extraction: A Randomised Clinical Trial', *Journal of Applied Oral Science: Revista FOB*, 28: 1–8.

Basso, J. C., A. McHale, V. Ende, D. J. Oberlin and W. A. Suzuki (2019), 'Brief, Daily Meditation Enhances Attention, Memory, Mood, And Emotional Regulation In Non-experienced Meditators', *Behavioural Brain Research*, 356: 208–20.

Blakemore, S.J. and S. Choudhury (2006), 'Development of the Adolescent Brain: Implications for Executive Function and Social Cognition', *Journal of Child Psychology and Psychiatry*, 47: 296–312.

Brown, K. W. and R. M. Ryan (2003), 'The Benefits of Being Present: Mindfulness and its Role in Psychological Well-being', *Journal of Personality and Social Psychology*, 84 (4): 822–48.

Charoensukmongkol, P. (2016), 'The Role of Mindfulness in Reducing English Language Anxiety among Thai College Students', *International Journal of Bilingual Education and Bilingualism*, 22 (4): 414–27.

Fallah, N. (2017), 'Mindfulness, Coping Self-Efficacy and Foreign Language Anxiety: A Mediation Analysis', *Educational Psychology*, 37 (6): 745–56.

Fritz-Schubert, E. (2011), *Glück Kann Man Lernen. Was Kinder Stark fürs Leben Macht, 1. Auflage*, Berlin: Ullstein Verlag.

Gul Peker, B. and N. Erdemir (2021), 'Does Compensation Strategy Instruction Work? An Action Research Study', *ELT Journal*, 75 (3): 351–61.

Hofmann, S. G., A. T. Sawyer, A. A. Witt and D. Oh (2010), 'The Effect of Mindfulness-Based Therapy on Anxiety and Depression: A Meta-Analytic Review', *Journal of Consulting and Clinical Psychology*, 78 (2): 169–83.

Horwitz, E. K., M. B. Horwitz and J. Cope (1986), 'Foreign Language Classroom Anxiety', *The Modern Language Journal*, 70 (2): 125–32.

Kabat-Zinn, J. (2003), 'Mindfulness-Based Interventions in Context: Past, Present, and Future', *Clinical Psychology: Science and Practice*, 10 (2): 144–56.

Koçali, Z. and A. Aşık (2022), 'A Systematic Review of Mindfulness Studies in ESL and EFL Contexts', *I-manager's Journal on Educational Psychology*, 15 (3): 47–61.

Langer, E. J. (2016), *The Power of Mindful Learning*, London: Hachette UK.

Morgan, W. J. and J. Katz (2021), 'Mindfulness Meditation and Foreign Language Classroom Anxiety: Findings from a Randomised Control Trial', *Foreign Language Annals* 54 (2): 389–409.

Seligman, M. E. P. (2002), 'Positive Psychology, Positive Prevention, and Positive Therapy', in C. R. Snyder and S. J. Lopez (eds.), *Handbook of Positive Psychology*, Oxford University Press, 3–9.

Tasan, M., E. Mede and K. Sadeghi (2021), 'The Effect of Pranayamic Breathing as a Positive Psychology Exercise on Foreign Language Learning Anxiety and Test Anxiety Among Language Learners at Tertiary Level', *Frontiers in Psychology*, 12: 1–12.

Wang, Y. and C. Liu (2016), 'Cultivate Mindfulness: A Case Study of Mindful Learning in an English as a Foreign Language Classroom', *IAFOR Journal of Education*, 4 (2): 141–55.

Witek-Janusek, L., K. Albuquerque, K. R. Chroniak, C. Chroniak, R. Durazo-Arvizu and H. L. Mathews (2008), 'Effect of Mindfulness-Based Stress Reduction on Immune Function, Quality of Life and Coping in Women Newly Diagnosed with Early Stage Breast Cancer', *Brain, Behavior, and Immunity*, 22 (6): 969–81.

Zhang, Q., Z. Wang, X. Wang, L. Liu, J. Zhang and R. Zhou (2019), 'The Effects of Different Stages of Mindfulness Meditation Training on Emotion Regulation', *Frontiers in Human Neuroscience*, 13: 1–8.

# INDEX

*anulom vilom pranayama* 202
archer (Cicero) 78–9
attributional retraining 6, 109, 112–14
attribution theory 110–12, 115
Aurelius, M. 73–4, 76
autotelic experience 53–4

Beck, A. T. 74, 120
behavioural factors 131
behavioural theory (BT) 120
body scanning 146, 148
Bögels, S. M. 167

challenge-skill balance 62–3
Challenge your Beliefs activity 124–7
Charoensukmongkol, P. 199
Cheng, Y. 109
Cicero 78–9
cognitive behaviour therapy (CBT) 14, 74, 119–22, 124, 130–2, 134–6, 139, 166–7
cognitive distancing 5, 73–6
cognitive factors 131
cognitive therapy (CT) 120
confidence 6–7, 132
    defined 86
    lack of 124
    questionnaire 93
Confidence Building Diary (CBD) 5, 83–90, 94–6
controllability 111
Cope, J. 2, 14, 51, 57
Covid-19 pandemic 76, 100, 178
critical thinking 79–80, 121–2
Csikszentmihalyi, M. 52–3, 62

Curry, N. 1–7, 13–19, 119–127
Czimmermann, E. 53

Deci, E. L. 86
Dewaele, J. M. 85–6
digital format procedure 47
Dubois, P. 74–5
dysfunctional assumptions (DAs) 121

Ellis, A. 74
emotional vocabulary 104
emotions
    negative 1–2, 14–15, 17, 38, 54, 85, 100, 111, 119–20, 149, 153, 188, 197–8
    positive 1, 7, 22, 63, 83–6, 120, 153, 188, 198–9
*Enchiridion* (Epictetus) 74, 80
English as a foreign language (EFL) 38–9, 61, 64, 86, 109, 155–6, 197, 200
English as a second language (ESL) 44, 199
environment 202–3
Epictetus 73–8, 80
experience-centred 99

Fallah, N. 200–1
fear of ridicule 105
The First Steps Module 84
flow theory 51–7, 61–8. *See also* task design
foreign language anxiety reduction (FLAR) 2
Foreign Language Class Anxiety Scale (FLCAS) 2, 14

Foss, K. A. 122
Fredrickson, B. L. 188

Gkonou, C. 13
goal-setting 121
Gregersen, T. 188–9

Hegel, G. 73
higher order thinking skills (HOTS) 55
Horwitz, E. K. 2, 14, 51, 57, 109
Horwitz, M. B. 2, 14, 51, 57

Ideal Classmates (IC) 43–6, 48
individual differences 130

Jin, Y. X. 86
journaling 203

Katz, J. 200
Kennerley, H. 121
King, J. 22, 132
Kirk, J. 121
Klippel, F. 66
knowing self 201

Langer, E. J. 199
language proficiency 61, 130
learning advisor (LA) 97–8, 123
Liu, C. 198
locus dimension 110
Lou, N. M. 112
lower order thinking skills (LOTS) 55
lyre player 77–8

MacIntyre, P. 54, 189
Maher, K. 1–7, 13–19, 22, 129–139
Managing Your Emotions (MYE) 13
McLoughlin, D. 122
mental imagery 145–6, 148, 158
Mercer, S. 178, 189
mindfulness 6, 145–6
mindfulness meditation (MM) techniques 7, 197–203
Mirivel, J. C. 178–81

Morgan, W. J. 200
Murphey, T. 20, 44

near-peer role models 17
Nervousness Metric (NM) 21–5, 29
Noels, K. A. 112

Oxford, R. L. 13

PC dialogue skits 184
peer-collaboration 99–100
personal identity 36, 40
physiological factors 131
Piniel, K. 53
positive communication 7, 177–85
positive language education (PLE) 189
positive psychology intervention (PPI) 85–6, 189, 198
positive psychology (PP) theory 197
psycho-education 122
psychological discomfort 105
psychology of language learning (PLL) 3

rational approach 6, 75
Rational-Emotive approach 122
Rational Emotive Behavioral Thinking (REBT) 74
Reitzel, A. C. 122
Rewrite your inner script 6, 155–63
Robertson, D. 75
Rubio-Alcalá, F. D. 52, 54, 57
Ryan, R. M. 86

Sampson, R. J. 14
Saudi EFL 61–2, 64, 68
Schallert, D. 109
self-access learning centre (SALC) 84
self-awareness 99, 101
self-confidence 39, 158, 161, 187
self-consciousness 53–4, 56
self-determination theory (SDT) 98–100
self-esteem 35–8, 111, 189
self-verification 37–8
Seligman, M. E. P. 189
Shafak, E. 177
sharing feelings 201–2
Sijbers, G. F. V. M. 167

situated learning 37
situational factors 131
Socratic 74–5, 122–3
solidary preferences 105
Sparling, H. 54
stability dimension 110–11
Stallard, P. 122, 126
Stoicism 73–80
Stoic/Stoicism
    maxims 75–6, 79–80
    philosophy 73, 75, 78
    principles 75–6
structured prompts 98–9

Tamayo-Rodríguez, L. 57
Task Concentration Training (TCT) 165–7
task design 61–8

testing strategies 103–4
*Think Good, Feel Good* (Stallard) 122
Three Good Things activity 7, 188–93
Toyama, M. 1

visualization functions 158
Voncken, M. 167

Wang, Y. 198
Wenger, E. 37
Westbrook, D. 121
Wilding, C. 120
Woodrow, L. 167

Yamazaki, Y. 1
Young, D. J. 1–2

Zhang, X. 112

www.ingramcontent.com/pod-product-compliance
Lightning Source LLC
Chambersburg PA
CBHW062224300426
44115CB00012BA/2203